# The teaching of history
# in secondary schools

*Scène d'école*, the school master, 1780

# The teaching of history in secondary schools

**Issued by the Incorporated Association of Assistant Masters in Secondary Schools**

**FOURTH EDITION**

**CAMBRIDGE UNIVERSITY PRESS**
Cambridge
London . New York . Melbourne

Published by the Syndics of the Cambridge University Press
The Pitt Building, Trumpington Street, Cambridge CB2 1RP
Bentley House, 200 Euston Road, London NW1 2DB
32 East 57th Street, New York, NY 10022, USA
296 Beaconsfield Parade, Middle Park, Melbourne 3206, Australia

© Cambridge University Press 1975

Library of Congress Catalogue Card Number: 74-19519

ISBN 0 521 20568 9

First published 1950
Reprinted 1952
Second edition 1956
Reprinted 1958, 1961
Third edition 1965
Fourth edition 1975

Composition by Linocomp Ltd., Marcham, Oxon
Printed in Great Britain
at the University Printing House, Cambridge
(Euan Phillips, University Printer)

# Contents

# Illustrations

# Members of the committee

A. J. Holland (*Chairman*)
King Edward VI School, Southampton

N. H. Brasher (*Vice-Chairman*)
Bexley Grammar School, Welling, Kent

P. J. Bamford
Richard Taunton Sixth Form College, Southampton; later Sixth
Form College, Long Road, Cambridge

R. L. Bowley
Bancroft's School, Woodford Green, Essex

A. Collis
West Hatch Technical High School, Essex

A. F. R. Johnson
Hartridge High School, Newport, Monmouthshire

D. G. Kirby
Graham Balfour High School, Stafford

N. H. Ricketts
The United World College of the Atlantic, St Donat's,
Glamorganshire; later Wolverhampton Grammar School

P. D. Wenham
Thornes House School, Wakefield; later Schools Council
Project History 13–6, University of Leeds

B. Williams
Gillingham School, Dorset; later Sherborne School for Girls,
Dorset

J. Williamson
Preston Manor High School, Wembley, Middlesex

I. D. Cleland (*Secretary*)
Crewe County Grammar School for Boys, Cheshire

# Acknowledgements

The Committee is greatly indebted to the following correspondents, most of them members of the Association, working in a variety of schools, colleges and universities, whose help and continuous generosity has been of great value in the preparation of this book: P. Anderton, G. H. Bennett, H. A. Bodey, P. Brice, H. G. Cartlidge, B. L. Cottee, C. Cox, M. H. Crosby, J. H. Fox, W. R. Griffiths, P. F. Hand, G. N. Harby, J. Higham, J. Hunter, R. A. Lewis, F. J. Martin, S. J. Parker, H. Rockliffe, F. R. Smart, H. E. Smith, M. R. B. Symons, F. H. Terry, Dr P. Thompson, J. Whyman, R. Whyman, R. G. Whyman.

Thanks are due to the following for permission to reproduce photographs: the Orbilian Society for Fig. 13(a), R. A. Smith for Fig. 13(b); Radio Times Hulton Picture Library for Fig. 17(a) and (b); Frank Rodgers for Figs. 21 and 29; Heinemann Educational Books Ltd for Fig. 22 from *Germany 1919–39*, edited by T. Edwards in their Heinemann History Broadsheets series; the University of London for Fig. 24; Ironbridge Gorge Museum Trust for Fig. 25; the Buckler's Hard Maritime Museum, Pitkin Pictorials Ltd and Sydney W. Newbery for Fig. 27(a); Castle Museum, York, and G. Bernard Wood for Fig. 27(b).

The frontispiece is a detail from an engraving by J. J. de Boissieu, *c.* 1780.

# Foreword

This fourth edition of a book which was first published in 1950 is effectively a new book which attempts to set down the best practices current in the teaching of history and to offer advice to both young and experienced teachers of the subject. There can be no doubt that the approaches adopted by teachers of the subjects in the secondary school curriculum have undergone many changes in recent years and that teachers of history have played a full part in the development of courses which are relevant and appropriate to the needs of secondary school pupils. History teachers are in a very strong position in this respect since their subject covers such a wide field of interests, and this book reflects this and offers encouragement to teachers to make the most of it.

The Association is yet again fortunate in having a group of members who have been willing to devote so much of their own time to the preparation of a book and have brought to bear upon this task a wealth of experience in the teaching of history at all levels in secondary schools. We are particularly indebted to the Chairman, Mr A. J. Holland, who was the Secretary of the Committee which prepared the third edition of the book and who has been able to achieve a balance between the traditional and the modern leanings of the members of the Committee. To all of them, and to those members who assisted by completing questionnaires and providing material, the Association is very grateful. Acknowledgement is also made of the very good service given to the Committee by the Publishers.

It is my earnest hope that this book prepared by a group of practising teachers will be of considerable interest and assistance to all teachers of the subject, both in this country and overseas, and to students in training and to the teachers of those students.

A. W. S. HUTCHINGS
*Secretary, Assistant Masters Association*

# Preface

The Committee was convened by the Association's Executive Committee early in 1972 to consider a revision of the 1965 edition, and, like its predecessor, agreed that an almost new book was required. Developments in the teaching of history which a decade ago could legitimately be largely neglected now need greater emphasis. The reorganisation of secondary education since 1965 has affected history as it has all other studies; the growth of C.S.E. and more varied techniques in the examining of history; the increased use of documentary source material; enquiry-based learning with mixed-ability classes; the slow but developing use of various media are all more obtrusive than they were ten years ago. Further, the greater communication between teachers of history, engendered in part by the publication of *Teaching History* by the Historical Association, by local associations of history teachers, and by some teachers' centres, has led to some common ground in various types of school.

The book has similarities with its two predecessors. It contains passages from the previous volumes; it is written by practising teachers with wide and varied experience; it is intended to help history teachers, both experienced and inexperienced, of boys and girls in all types of secondary school and in the upper reaches of middle schools.

The Committee has tried to keep a level course between the often unattainable ideal and the humanly possible. It has tried to keep a balance between fanaticism and reality.

The Committee has benefited from the enterprise and efficiency of its secretary, I. D. Cleland, who has cheerfully and intelligently directed its labours. I am greatly indebted to him, and indeed to all members of the Committee, for their time, wisdom, and endeavour.

*January 1974*                                                                 A.J.H.

# History and the teacher

## The subject – aims and objectives

The academic historian, by nature of his craft, is self-inquisitory. He is trained to question the validity of reasons, to be sceptical of panacea, and to be balanced in the appraisal of values. He may even give some countenance to Augustine Birrell's description of his subject – 'that great dust-heap called "history" ' – yet be scornful of Henry Ford's succinct but much too simple 'History is bunk'! But history in schools is a far, far different matter from the history of the universities, and the question 'Why history in schools?' is far removed from the realms of the academic debate.

Every young teacher feels that history in schools is being challenged by reformists and this has meant a need for increasing attention to the formulation of aims and objectives. The current challenge in some quarters to the continued inclusion of history in the curriculum and the trend towards integration have stimulated teachers to clarify the contribution of their discipline to the intellectual and social development of secondary school pupils.

Moreover, each generation rightly feels that history teaching in the past was imperfect. Too much memorisation; too great an emphasis on facts; too little cognisance of skills – such criticisms are both valid and trite. Emphases have changed with the more advanced techniques and the availability of cheaper materials used by the modern teacher. Yet the study of history by the young, through whatever methods, new or old, has benefited the pupil as much as that of any other accepted 'subject'. The wise teacher of history would claim no more, and certainly no less, for his own special study.

If history is the study of all that is known of the past, of men's actions, thoughts, joys and sorrows, it will contain much that is beyond the intellectual capacities of school children. But the same is true of any other study, be it fine art, literature, or mathematics. History in schools should not delve deeply into realms outside the comprehension of the juvenile; but there is a constant danger that it will do so. The teacher of mathematics will not attempt to teach calculus to the very young. The teacher of history may not avoid so easily concepts and situations which are beyond the understanding of his pupils. He will, however, be more likely to do so if he realises that he is not training historians, but helping the young to develop through the study of history. History in schools can make a unique contribution to the education of pupils but the problems inherent in the nature of the discipline must be recognised. For instance, history is mostly about the doings of adults; pupils cannot experience the past directly and the language of history is frequently at a high level of abstraction. The concepts of time and change present difficulties and because history is based on evidence it is often of a propositional, deductive and inferential nature.

Of even greater significance is our increasing awareness of the intellectual development of pupils. In general, recent research has tended to confirm that the intellectual development of most pupils up to the age of sixteen does not advance beyond what has been termed the concrete operational stage. This stage is characterised by the ability to give answers to problems but these are usually limited to what is immediately apparent. Moreover, pupils find it difficult to cope with vocabulary which includes abstractions and accounts which present too many variables. It is only with the transition to the formal operational stage that the abilities to deal with abstract concepts, to make hypotheses and to realise the multiplicity of possible links develop. This stage is not reached until most pupils are aged at least sixteen.

The teacher of history should provide his pupils with some introduction to the achievements of their ancestors and to the contributions of past ages. Children have a natural curiosity about the past, they love 'a good story', and it is therefore these aspects of historical study which provide much of the inspirational, enjoyable and enriching elements in the classroom. History provides an opportunity to stimulate imagination and to widen the sense of experience. The pupil may gain from history some insight into ways of life different from his own. He can experience, though vicariously, the thrill of sailing with Drake or Chancellor in uncharted seas, or explore the unknown with Livingstone. He may match such endeavours with those of modern astronauts. He can campaign with Wilberforce or Shaftesbury against social evils. He may measure their successes in terms of the conditions of living in his own society. An examination of the ideals, weaknesses, actions and motives of real people of another time and place can contribute greatly to the personal development of adolescents who are preoccupied with establishing their own identities. In schools, despite the caveats of the sociologists, history can be 'about chaps'; for the young can comprehend human feelings and human failings.

School history will, and should, frequently overlap the boundaries of knowledge which are the concern of subjects such as science, divinity, geography, literature and art: history is the ideal link subject, and has a strategic place in the curriculum. Here the pupils may find a key to the deeper understanding of many arts and skills. The craft of navigation, the artistic merit of Raphael, the skill of Torrigiano, the architecture of medieval cathedrals, the mechanics of steam power, can all be surveyed under the general heading of history. In this context, then, a significant aim, in view of the increasing time for leisure, is to open up a variety of interests and hobbies. The popularity of archaeology, local history societies and historical books amongst adults is well established. It is important that pupils are made aware of the rich potential in history for various leisure pursuits.

Because the teacher of history is concerned with a humane study he must constantly and consciously train his pupils to assess values and to form judgements. The long-term consequences of what he does will not be the facts that linger, but the attitudes of mind that are formed. Here he is confronted with the 'moral' role of history, and he has an important function to fulfil. Historical topics frequently have certain implicit moral issues and to exclude them from the classroom is impossible. The teacher is entitled to take a standpoint – if he considers the execution of Charles I to have been morally right, he should say so. But he will increasingly show his pupils that there are shades between black and white. This will not necessarily be easy. The younger his pupils and the less able they may be, the harder it will be to establish such graduated differences. Ultimately, he must hope that his pupils are helped towards an interpretation which he himself would value on religious and moral grounds. At the same time, he must recognise that the teaching of history should never be a vehicle of propaganda, that an authoritarian standpoint may well produce a reverse effect, and that the influence of psychology has made us less willing to praise or to condemn men's actions without qualification.

We would stress the teacher's obligation to present some coherent picture of contemporary events. There are those who would have no part in the teaching of current affairs, on the grounds that such courses are unscholarly and cannot properly be designated as an academic study. Teachers less concerned with the hallowed production of historians may give current affairs a warmer welcome. Nevertheless, at all levels of teaching, a strong compulsion to instruct the young in the contemporary institutions of their own society should be recognised. To show how the contemporary world has been shaped by the past is of paramount importance. For example, tension over the Middle East can be identified as an issue of universal concern. An enquiry into the historical origins and development of the problem can provide an essential and illuminating perspective. Moreover in history pupils can study change and continuity in the perspective of time, and develop understanding of the complexity of causation in human affairs. Historical study can also introduce a pupil to his cultural heritage, and if this awareness is extended to other cultures, it can lead to a more open and balanced attitude. The wise history teacher will realise that it is his responsibility to ensure that his pupils do not leave school uninformed about contemporary problems in the society in which they will live their lives.

One of the prime concerns of history in schools is to help pupils to develop their critical faculties by the practice of certain skills and habits of thought. The investigation of a historical topic by a pupil will require him to draw up a plan, and to select works of reference. He will need to collect and examine relevant evidence: to distinguish between primary and secondary sources: to use an index: to exploit the resources of a library. He will need to understand and to interpret the evidence of pictures, maps, charts, and diagrams. He will need to become conversant with specific terminology, such as 'franchise', 'monarch', 'coup d'état', 'revolution'; and he will have to use chronological conventions correctly, e.g. 'decade' and 'century'.

The comprehension and analysis of evidence – the primary and secondary sources which constitute the raw material of history – though a skill fully attainable only by the mature student, can and should be done in schools. The child can be made aware of similarities and differences in two or more pieces of evidence. He can be trained to detect bias, to separate fact from opinion, to uncover hidden assumptions and to recognise gaps in evidence. He will gradually realise, too, that explanations in history are compound rather than simple.

At the end of his school history course, the pupil should be able to synthesise, to argue a conclusion from given facts, and to differentiate between values of the present day and those of an earlier period. Perhaps some pupils will be able to use honest caution and to admit some doubt in the interpretation of evidence, without descending into cynicism, or the ultra-caution of the student who wrote 'The battle of Hastings probably took place in 1066.'

Besides fostering certain skills the history teacher will aim to develop judgement in pupils. This is a form of thinking which human beings need when they are in a situation for which there is no single ready-made answer but rather a series of responses satisfying various criteria. History in schools can give pupils the experience of, re-thinking some of the problems which people in the past encountered and the decisions they made. In this way pupils can develop their own judgement skills in a subject which provides a wealth of opportunity for exercising the imagination; but also one in which imaginative reconstruction is at once stimulated and disciplined by the evidence and the context in respect of time and place.

No history course in schools can be regarded as satisfactory if it does not require pupils to present their findings. Such presentation should be done in a variety of ways, dependent on the topic and the ability of the students. They can be made to make a coherent report according to some organising principle; to construct a credible and fluent narrative; to describe the condition of life in a particular era; to make diagrams and pictures to emphasise important features; to present their findings in dramatic form, or by oral discussion. It is true that some of these skills are more difficult and complex than others but many can be carried out at the concrete operational level of thought.

Once the teacher has clarified the characteristic level of his pupils' thinking he can use it as a basis for encouraging more advanced understanding. A recent study, for example, has confirmed what many teachers have long believed, that the development of thinking is to a large extent a matter of learning. It is essential that the materials on which the pupils learn to exercise these skills should be appropriate to their present understanding. If the teacher can help the pupil to exploit the subject matter to acquire an armoury of skills, as time passes, and with systematic teaching and learning, the skills will be exercised at a higher level of difficulty and proficiency. In this way the thinking abilities of pupils in history may be accelerated.

If history in schools is regarded as an approach to knowledge rather than as a body of knowledge, then it will be of great value. It can, and generally does, make a significant contribution to the education of the young not only by virtue of its potential for satisfying many of the needs of pupils, but through the special insights and durable skills which lie at the heart of history teaching.

## The teacher

The teaching of so valuable and so complex a subject as history needs to be in the hands of those who have specialist history qualifications, obtained by degree through university, polytechnic, or college of education. Unless the teacher is aware of the ever-shifting, often disputed, and tentative character of historical 'truth', he is likely to become an unwitting propagandist at the very moment he thinks he is most objective. Although, for example, classics teachers may illumine aspects of Greek and Roman history, language teachers some features of European civilisation, religious education specialists much Christian background, and art teachers the development of architecture, sculpture, and painting, they are not usually well-equipped to teach a full history course. Their help, when appropriate, is welcome, but will almost certainly be occasional. The sociologist, with his own skills, let loose on teaching history, is potentially harmful. Many aspects of British, French, and American history have been explored with success by historians with sociological skills, but the total range of their work is small, and certainly insufficient to qualify a teacher for a general history course in schools. Enthusiasm has to be joined with trained perception, and the non-specialist is much more likely to fall into the traps of over-simplification, bias, and dogmatic assertion which even the specialist sometimes fails to avoid.

The main quality a history teacher must learn early in his career is flexibility. The content of his degree course should not lead a young teacher to be unwilling to teach topics outside it. Those with research degrees, or whose studies have been mainly confined to economic history, or history after 1700, may well find the wide range of the school course initially even more taxing than will those who have followed a more traditional degree course. If the history staff are trained historians, there is a greater likelihood of their working together as a team, for, in some indefinable way, historians have some common denominators in outlook and approach. Anyone who has worked on a committee comprising historians can sense that this is so. The historian questions the validity of his task, but having questioned it, believes that the subject is more than worthwhile.

The demands of everyday teaching are such that a deliberate effort has to be made to keep one's knowledge up to date. Periods of leave are needed for this purpose, and one sabbatical term in seven years, rare enough, is insufficient. That term, for most, would be best devoted mainly to history, for it would not give enough time to look in depth at the wider aspects of education as well. The fortunate few may gain a sabbatical leave by means of a School-master Fellowship. To keep up to date between sabbaticals, if they occur, revision courses in the holidays are useful, if incomplete. Membership of the Historical Association is helpful, and one can claim tax relief on its subscription. Its library has a good collection of history text-books which can be borrowed, as well as other books. Its A.G.M., besides providing some good history, is a useful place for making and developing contacts. Most L.E.A.s, which ought to pay the full cost of attendance at all professional courses, at present give substantial grants towards the cost. Local associations of history teachers can also keep one in touch with colleagues and with new developments.

The history teacher will always read much, and he will build up his own library. He will also belong to a good outside library, by post if necessary. Books bought for sixth form work may qualify for tax relief; specialist periodicals certainly do. A full list of them is given in the Historical Association's *A Guide to Historical Periodicals in the English Language*, Helps for Students of History No. 80 (London 1970). The historian will keep as much formal and informal contact as he can with his old college, university, or department, and will try to form links with his nearest institution of higher learning engaged in historical studies. A certain amount of personal research, combined with some writing, is helpful and salutary. To contribute something to the fund of scholarship is refreshing. To write, whether thesis, book, or article, is to experience a self-discipline which not only reminds the author of the difficulties of the historian's craft, but invigorates his historical awareness, and gives him a vivid understanding of what he demands from his students when he sets and marks essays.

Teachers of history have to find employment, but some jobs are more worth having than others. When seeking a post applicants should have as much information at their disposal as possible, so that they can make a reasoned decision about acceptance, if offered the job. For a first post the historian might be asked to teach another subject, and help with out-of-school activities. The applicant should see the school in action first. He should meet the head of department, and have a clear idea of the syllabus followed. If either of these desiderata is omitted his suspicions should be aroused. A few boards of governors hold interviews out of hours as the only means of trapping greenhorns. Some authorities do not even appoint to particular schools but only to the general service. This will appeal to those with a sense of mystery and adventure, but the beginner should think carefully before accepting challenges he is not equipped to face.

During his first year, the young teacher will need all his energies. He has to concentrate on getting to know his students, adapting to their needs, and to preparing his work. He has also to learn about the school, and to learn to work with his colleagues in the department, and in the staff room. He will have little time to do much else. Once he has built up a stock of historical knowledge and teaching experience, the pressures change and he can begin to look around and consider teaching-strategy as well as teaching-tactics.

After three or four years it is probably a good thing to move, though one would rarely turn down internal promotion, if available, for the sake of this principle. The second post should give a wider and different experience from the first. It would be reasonable to expect to teach only history, though any special strengths should be offered and used. In this post the possibility must be given of covering the full range of history teaching available, and of trying a different syllabus. One has to work with the head of department, and should seek to be compatible with him. This is probably the time to consider such things as exchange teaching in other countries, or secondment for a period. Marking for public examinations, while not richly paid, can be useful experience for those prepared to undertake it, and by this stage one is qualified to seek it.

In seeking a post as head of department one may well be choosing a job that will last for the rest of one's career. It would be undignified and wrong to approach the position as a humble supplicant, gratefully accepting charity from a board of governors or a head. The job has to be negotiated, and one should try to obtain clear terms of reference, and a realistic understanding of future possibilities. There are questions to be asked. Why is the post vacant? What is the existing position with regard to colleagues, syllabus, allocation of money, facilities, stock? What is the position and strength of history in the school, and what are the possibilities of change? What promises affecting the future of the department can be negotiated? The applicant should, at his interview, make clear his own views and aims concerning the subject, for if these are unwelcome the time to find out is before taking a particular job.

The head of department has much to do, and in his first year must not accept too heavy a burden of extraneous duties. The number of teachers in his department may vary between one and more than ten, a variation which will clearly affect the way the department is run, but in all cases the head of department should see himself more as a team-leader than as a paterfamilias. He must, ultimately, make some important decisions, which are likely to be better ones if he consults his colleagues first. This may be done by informal conversation, or by more formal and regular departmental meetings. With this approach his colleagues are much more likely to accept, and perform, delegated functions which have been agreed after rational discussion.

The organisation of departmental resources is an important part of his work. Much of this work can be shared and delegated, but the head of department must make sure that the system works. Increasingly, with the widespread use of individual and group study methods, the amount and range of books, papers, materials, equip-

ment, artefacts, records, tapes, slides, and files, requires considerable time and energy to administer. The days have passed when
stock control consisted largely of issuing a few sets of text-books at
the beginning of the year, and counting them again at the end. The
manufacture and filing of work- and topic-sheets require a good
level of clerical assistance. The constant issuing and collection of
small sets of books, individual copies, materials, and work-sheets is
tedious, time-consuming, and necessary. Things inevitably go astray,
and a certain proportion of loss is acceptable, but the amount can,
and must, be diminished by careful recording. Ancillary help is
necessary here, too, if the teacher is to teach properly. There are
still far too many schools where teachers are expected to do these
things unaided.

Just keeping track of resources is, however, not enough. All
members of the department must know what is available, and be
able to use it with the minimum of fuss. This needs careful planning.
Access to tape-recorders, slide-projectors, and other items of
equipment, together with the appropriate accompanying software,
must be convenient and easy, otherwise they will be under-used.
The use of television sets and video-tape recorders is likely to be
under the control of someone else. The head of department will try
to influence the system of use so that that too facilitates accessibility
and convenience. When films are to be shown, maximum use should
be made of them. Careful planning will ensure that they arrive at the
right time of year to fit in with the topic being covered. Arrangements for someone to preview the film, and suggest ways of using it,
should, ideally, be made.

An important resource for all history teachers should be the
school library. The responsibility of the head of department here is
to see that the purchase of history books is both adequate in amount,
and suitable in content, range, and balance.

The spending of the annual capitation allowance requires many
difficult decisions. Too often the amount of money available is
hopelessly inadequate. We have found, for example, a department
given ninety pounds to spend on twenty-five classes. Another school,
only slightly larger, may give five hundred pounds. The head of
department will ask his colleagues' advice about needs and priorities. He must balance the claims of different year groups, and decide
priorities between the need for books, equipment, and materials.
He should try to keep a small reserve for unexpected contingencies,
but will probably try to spend most of the money early, for two
reasons. The speed of price rises in recent times has been such that
delay has reduced the amount that can be bought. There are,
secondly, some schools where delay in spending means that other

departments get the money – a most regrettable and unfortunate occurrence.

The head of department should be consulted on all appointments of new staff to the department. We have been surprised to learn that there are schools which make such appointments without consultation. The practice is reprehensible, and we condemn it. The teacher in his first post will need considerable help from the head of department who will have to give advice about the amount of work to be set, and about techniques of marking. He is a good source of information about the telling anecdote and vivid example which can enliven a topic, and about the type of material available at the students' level. He will give guidance about the level of approach, and the standards expected. Especially in the first few weeks he should go into the newcomer's lessons so that his help can be constructive and informed. If his approach, manner, and attitude are right, this help will be welcomed, and not resented as interference. He will have an important role in helping the newcomer to find his feet in the staff room, and quite often in the local community as well.

Students in their years of training have to be helped. It is the head of department who draws up their timetable, and maintains contact with the tutor at the institute or college of education. He must give good, detailed guidance as to what should be taught in each lesson. He will discuss the methods to be used, help smooth the way with materials, and make constructive criticisms of the lessons he observes. He will make sure that the student takes classes for colleagues who will be equally helpful. He must insist that the student arrives early enough in the morning, and stays late enough in the evening, for both to have useful discussions of the student's work. He should try to let the student teach something at every level in the school at some time during teaching practice, but the particular needs of the examination classes may prevent this.

Within the department he, like Bagehot's monarch, has the right to advise, the right to encourage, and the right to warn. He is also more than a figurehead. He draws up the syllabus, and supervises its implementation. He arranges the setting and marking of internal examinations, and organises the groupings which are decided on for public examinations. He requisitions supplies. Wherever possible he should ensure that he, or a colleague, attends meetings of the local C.S.E. History panel. He may have to fight for his department, on the one hand to increase the allocation of money to be spent, and to improve facilities and equipment, and on the other to prevent a policy of allowing history to become merely an option at too early a stage of a student's career. In allocating teaching time, he should aim to keep in touch, himself, with the full age and ability range of the school, and not hog the 'best' groups, but he should also make sure that he has enough free time to do his own job.

The history teacher does not remain cloistered within the confines of his own subject or department. For him all human life is relevant, and much of it is for him to experience. It is this that so often makes him one of the most widely-informed members of staff to whom his colleagues often turn for answers to questions needing information. In his purely scholastic concerns he cooperates with colleagues in other departments, both to use their skills to illuminate history, and to give his skills to benefit them. Equally helpful are history advisers, where the local authority employs them. They expect to be asked for help, and welcome the approach. The well-run Teachers' Centre is also there to be used by those with initiative. It can provide valuable supplementary help with aids, as can the audio-visual aids services of the authorities, where they provide them. The centre provides a meeting place for working parties to develop resources for classroom use. Meeting people, making contacts, and noting new sources of information and help, all enrich the history teacher's contribution.

Who, then, is the ideal history teacher? He is the essence of the temperate man. His enthusiasm is tempered with realism, his beliefs with doubt. He distrusts emotional and emotive thinking without discarding warmth and understanding. He has high principles, but knows the frailty of humanity. His convictions are firm, but he eschews dogmatism. Obsessions, fanaticism, superstition, and prejudice, he abhors. His judgement is sure because it is based on knowledge. He is not swept away by novelty for he can distinguish between what is recent and what is new, between the ephemeral and the lasting. He combines commitment with objectivity, high standards with compassion. He uncovers feet of clay, and is the first to see that the emperor is naked. He loves the young, and is mature among adults. He is the epitome of wisdom. To those who ask for more than this he answers with James I and VI, 'The greatest fool can ask more than the wisest man can answer.'

# 2 Syllabus

A syllabus is a summary of the content of study, and the best history syllabus enables the aims and objectives of history teaching to be converted into practice effectively and successfully. This is easily said, but the simple question, 'What shall we teach?' at once raises a host of problems and a many-sided conflict of differing opinion. The young teacher should not think of this as a disease to be cured at once by searching for some agreed formula. Professor Asa Briggs has remarked that history has always invoked debate and has always advanced understanding through controversy and argument. Thus, diversity of approach and continual reappraisal should be healthy features of the subject as practised in secondary schools today.

Moderate reform of syllabuses in general is a continuing process, and despite the lack of familiar phrases like 'Nuffield Science' and 'New Maths', changes in history have been less spectacular but almost as important. Even young parents have remarked, 'History was never like this when I was at school.' This attitude stems in part from the wealth of new materials available, but also from changes in syllabuses which are now less Eurocentric, wider in scope, yet with provision for study in depth of selected themes.

Every history department should work from a carefully constructed syllabus, whose most important qualities are: that it facilitates the fulfilment of the aims of teaching history; that it should be an orderly, coherent and helpful statement of the content of study; that it should be subject to periodic revision and reasonable change; and that it should meet any particular teaching problem of the individual school concerned. Because of these variable circumstances, in which both the interest of the pupils and the special enthusiasms of teachers must play a decisive part, it is impracticable to lay down a model syllabus. Instead this chapter will point out the factors which influence the framing of a syllabus; will discuss the general structure and particular subject matter of its content; and finally will present a selection of varying syllabuses.

## First considerations

The idealist might hanker after *carte blanche*, but the classroom history teacher is only too aware of his complex environment which exerts pressure in many ways on a proposed syllabus.

First, the nature of the school has to be considered, with the variation of age and ability in its pupils. The term secondary education today includes a greater variety of school than ever before: there are the independent and state-maintained grammar schools which retain the mainly academic approach; there are the comprehensive schools, a term itself that covers a considerable variety of educational organisation, ranging from a 2,000-strong, purpose-built unit to the smaller hybrid of 700 pupils formed by merging an existing secondary grammar and modern school; and there are the middle schools, and the junior and senior high schools which completely alter the traditional age-structure of the secondary school. As many heads of department now need to plan for a twelve-form entry and the widest possible ability range, does this demand one syllabus or several? Several of our correspondents wrote, 'Yes if the ability range is wide', but one comprehensive school teacher wrote, 'It is intended that there shall be a common syllabus for all children . . . Methods must vary more than syllabuses.' In principle this is a more sensible approach. To speak of a common heritage and then arbitrarily to teach one part of it to some children and another part to the rest is wrong and possibly dangerous. Another correspondent wrote, 'It is bad enough with new and old text books; with different syllabuses in the same year you are causing jealousy amongst forms.'

Nevertheless in practice the idea of the same syllabus must be reconciled with the fact that some children will be able to study more topics than others and will be able to appreciate them in greater depth. The point (which will be developed later) is that the syllabus should be common to all in its general theme, but in detail it should be flexible enough to cater for different pupils. If this applies within a particular school situation, it is also clear that where movement takes place of children between schools during the secondary stage, close consultation is necessary between local history teachers to seek a sensible pattern of study.

Secondly, the number of periods per week allotted to history and the possibility of history being one option amongst others at a certain level are important variables. In the educational traffic jam which results from too many subjects chasing too few periods in the weekly timetable, the teacher in the lower school can consider himself fortunate if he secures more than two lessons a week per class. Closely associated with this situation are two developments over which the historian may have little control, yet may deprecate. Within the same age band, classes of less able children are given, say, four periods, not because of the merits of the subject but as a timetable filler for children not able enough to take a foreign language or specialist science. The historian thus has to adapt his syllabuses considerably as well as cope with the 'soft option' image that can result. With the more able children, he may find a 'Modern Studies' label given to a combination of history and geography with possibly only three periods a week. Such organisational devices adopted merely to facilitate timetable construction should be condemned. The second development occurs usually at the fourth form level, when as one correspondent states: 'My syllabus is determined by the fact that at the end of the third year the pupils choose Chemistry or History.' It is rarely possible to forecast which choice children will make. The historian may wilt at the problem of constructing a satisfactory course to cater for the needs of a class, some members of which will pursue the course for three and some for five years. If, despite representation to the headmaster, the internal organisation of the school does not permit history to remain a core subject, the head of department should consider seriously the implication of this on the syllabus, especially when a five-year course has been developed on a chronological basis. It is difficult to defend a system whereby many of our young citizens, turned by their own aptitudes or by external pressures towards chemistry or geography, go out into the world with an impression of the things that happened between Palaeolithic man and the Fire of London, but with no formal teaching of the events of the last three centuries. Teachers in this position would do well to consider the merits of 'patch' studies discussed later in this chapter.

A third consideration in syllabus construction is the availability of materials – audio-visual as well as books. Whilst it is true that to exclude a topic merely because it is not in the currently used text-book may be the sign of an unimaginative teacher, there are wider problems. Except in a new school, materials are mainly an inheritance of a department: one teacher coming to a post deplored its concentration on a particular century, but commented, 'It is impossible to change when faced with the financial problems.' Another says we must not be 'too airily dismissive about this point; it supports the dangerous illusion that enthusiasm is enough.' To include a series of lessons on the growth of the U.S.A. may be educationally very desirable, but is unwise if the class cannot be provided with at least some printed information or illustrative material to supplement verbal instruction by the teacher. However, should any history teacher find himself, as did a member of the committee, with some forty-year-old text-books, and an annual department grant of £90 for 700 comprehensive school children, temporary

*THEN AND THERE*

respite can be gained by investing in a variety of cheap 'patch' studies such as the Longman's 'Then and There' series, and considerably modifying the syllabus to meet such a contingency.

Whilst acknowledging the importance of teaching aids, the conscientious teacher should not permit them to dictate the syllabus. Teachers who are slaves to a particular text-book, following a dull routine of a chapter a fortnight, with the occasional omission of an unpopular topic, or who use the age-old model of a medieval castle merely because it is to hand, should reconsider their approach. Material equipment must be the tool, and not the master.

Fourthly, many teachers still feel that external examinations dominate the syllabus, but many of the evils attributed to such examinations are the result of attitudes and policies for which the teachers within the schools are themselves responsible. G.C.E. and C.S.E. boards offer a wide range of periods and themes, whilst teachers may design their own syllabus for either if they wish. The frustrations of the teacher and the boredom of the pupil are caused not so much by the content of the syllabus as by the approach towards it. As one teacher states, 'The syllabus does not have to consist of an indigestible stodge of terms of acts and treaties.'

One more factor in the school which is of great importance in the construction of a syllabus is the personality of the teacher; for it is on him and his departmental colleagues that the value of the course absolutely depends. For this reason it is generally desirable for a new head of department to revise the syllabus of his predecessor, although radical changes hurriedly instituted will confuse rather than help the pupils. Moreover the head of department would be ill-advised to imprint his own special enthusiasms too rigidly on his course, without due allowance for the preferences of his colleagues, and for the traditions of his school and social background of its pupils. In areas of high staff turnover it helps continuity if the syllabus is presented in detailed form.

Finally, there are some sections of the British community for whom a history syllabus must be constructed with an exceptional degree of care, sensitivity and imagination. Wales, Scotland and Northern Ireland offer an obvious challenge. Then there are the schools in the deprived, inner-city areas, which contain a much higher than average proportion of pupils indifferent or hostile to school. No panaceas are offered, but it is worth remembering that the syllabus must not be so far from the experience of the young as to be meaningless. (Should one, for example, teach about agricultural strips to someone who has never seen a field, open or enclosed?) The search for meaning should not however become so mundane as to deprive the pupil of the opportunity of the imaginative response to distant places and epochs that history can give. Immigrant communities, too, can be bound in the cycle of deprivation, but this is not a universal truth. Such communities are from a variety of backgrounds, and the majority of their children are born in Britain. The history teacher has to identify in his own area what are the dominant attitudes. Is there a desire to know about national and cultural origins, or is there a prevailing search for assimilation? Once he has the knowledge the teacher can decide whether he is going to include the slave trade, the decline of Byzantium, Moslem dominance of India, the medieval Italian city-states, or the history of Bedford, Bradford or Birmingham.

### Content: the general framework

When considering the actual content of a syllabus, two problems must be solved. What should be the overall pattern and balance of work? Should, for instance the third-year course be British history or American history or a mixture? Then the detail must be settled: for example in a fourth-year course on nineteenth-century Britain, is there time to consider Palmerston as well as poverty?

For the general framework, it would not be unfair to describe the traditional syllabus as a five-year course of British history, with some glances at Western civilisation especially in the ancient and modern periods. A typical scheme may range from the early civilisations to the second world war. This has represented a well-tried formula, which, in the hands of the best teachers, has instilled into many generations of pupils a sound knowledge of history, a love of history and an introduction to the understanding of history. However, teachers must be prepared to answer accusations of inertia, and this type of syllabus has been heavily criticised in recent years. For example, it over-emphasises national history, sometimes to the exclusion of important developments in Africa, Asia and America; and local history is left to the whim of individual teachers. Several trends in the last twenty years have considerably modified the general framework of the traditional syllabus.

In view of the enormous space and time span involved, some teachers have asked themselves whether there was not something of Rome they could leave to the Latin specialists, something of Europe to the modern linguists, something of the Industrial Revolution to the geographers, something of Christianity to the divinity specialists, something of man's conquest of nature to the scientists, thus leaving more time for dealing with themes in depth. Others have stressed the importance of family and local history as a useful corrective to the national scene. Considerable insight into the nature and difficulties of history can be provided by giving children an opportunity to investigate their own families; mental time scales, the value of artefacts, the distortion of memories – and even skeletons in the cupboard – introduce pupils to important concepts in history preliminary to studies on larger canvas. Local history, too, has found growing support, especially with the increased use of locally-based evidence, whether written from the archives or through visits to the museum, record office, stately home, disused canal, factory, farm and archaeological site. Some teachers see local history as a springboard into the wider waters of national history, but others justify the study of the local community in its own right as an educationally desirable proposition. The parish pump was not an unimportant institution to those whose livelihoods depended on it, and there can be great value in seeing history through this dimension.

A third trend is to balance British and overseas history. National bias starts with the compilation of the syllabus and is accentuated by the kind of selection that tends to overstress national heroes and national triumphs and to play down the villains and the disasters. The first introduction many children have to the history of non-British peoples is contained in the form of British foreign policy, which by its very nature may lend itself to a narrow and subjective approach. Teachers no longer have the confidence that it is British history that matters. The answer to this is not to eliminate or disregard patriotic feeling, but to place it in a wider setting. D. C. Watt of the University of London has added a timely caution: 'To know a little of the history of China, India, Byzantium, the Kingdoms of the African Savannah and the seagoing exploits of the Polynesian colonists is no doubt a valuable widening of a pupil's knowledge – but not if it is achieved by the forfeiture of the pupil's understanding of his own society.'[1]

Different solutions to the problem have been tried. An early one was the recognition that British history is only one part of the history of Western civilisation, and it can be fairly claimed that today thousands of schoolboys and girls know as much at least about Bismarck as they do about Gladstone, as much about Calvin as about Cranmer, and as much about Henry Ford as about George Stephenson. The move across the Atlantic has been one of the most successful efforts, many schools allotting a half or even a full year to a study of American history. The Commonwealth has been a theme that has lost its stigma of being an even more biased form of

---

[1] D. C. Watt in *The World and the School* (May 1971), p. 61.

national history; but, despite new approaches which highlight the emergence of a unique form of partnership of self-governing states, evidence from publishers and examination boards suggests that it has lost its appeal as well.

It appears that world history is thought to be a more admirable alternative. The present century, with its revolution in communications, its two world wars, and its evidence of the increasing interdependence of peoples in all quarters of the globe, has given a new significance and a new urgency to the idea. In the past, what has been called 'world history' in the syllabus has really been a survey of extra-European events, in which Britain or the other European Powers have played some part. It has been well argued that peoples that were highly civilised when all our fathers worshipped sticks and stones are usually mentioned in European books only when they happen to have a quarrel with emissaries of some European country. The history teacher today is successfully facing the challenge of bringing into the classroom not only the India of the Raj but the India of Akbar and of Nehru, not only the China of the opium wars, but the China of Taoism and of Mao Tse-tung. Recent events, to be intelligible, demand both a universal outlook and a deep sense of history.

The choice of course then is large. *All* is manifestly impossible but the head of department should aim for a balance of the options. Ten years ago the progressive history teacher might have found his ideas thwarted by a dearth of books at classroom level on such topics: a glance at current publishers' catalogues will show that this is certainly not so today, though the quality of such books is variable.

### Content: selection of subject matter

Whatever broad framework is chosen, detailed guidance on subject matter must be given in the syllabus. Here again a balance must be sought. The strict division of history into such watertight compartments as political, social, economic or ecclesiastical need not be condoned. There is no point in arguing the virtues of one particular approach as opposed to another, for it is as misguided to overstress military history as to omit it altogether. Somewhere in the course, room should be made for wars, for the art and practice of government, for economic and scientific change, for the world of ideas and culture, and for the world of religious belief. Much criticism has in the past resulted from a concentration on one or two of these aspects to the almost total exclusion of the others.

In choosing a balance of topics two issues arise. How much

background information should be included? This depends on the level of ability of the class, though even with the high flyers it is wrongly passed over as of only peripheral importance. But some knowledge of political structures, economic concepts, social relationships, technical data and artistic standards ought to be imparted. One has only to reflect how many generations of girls must have 'learned' about Newcomen and Watt without having any idea of the function of piston and cylinder to see the desirability of this. Again, there is little point in asking pupils to write a paragraph on the Great Leonardo unless they have some simple notions of artistic excellence. In the senior school the importance of political and economic matters has long been recognised: A level Boards offer to examine courses on the structure and working of British government, and on English social and economic history. However, a strong case can be made for building some basic information on government and economics into the middle school syllabus. The need to combat ignorance of political responsibility, for instance, seems a clear duty of the history teacher; also, an understanding of the procedure whereby a bill moves through parliament is vital at some points in history. Words like 'power' and 'government', 'investment' and 'capitalism' present such difficulties to the average pupil's mind that the teacher ought to consider a properly structured course in elementary politics and economics,[2] before beginning topics like 'Tariff Reform' and 'Liberal Government 1906–14'.

The other issue is central to the whole problem of the syllabus, namely, the selection of topics. The head of department must decide how much advice on choice and treatment to give. One teacher has emphasised that 'considerable latitude must be left to the staff'. Yet the younger teacher and non-specialist would perhaps welcome a note such as 'Canal Transport – start from local examples' or 'Frederick the Great – begin with a discussion on the function of Monarchy' and even welcome a syllabus which contains outlines of lessons.

Clearly a mere overall summary will not answer the question: if the time factor is important, is Darwin's *The Origin of Species* more important than Cardwell's army reforms? What is really important: the character of Marie Antoinette and the career of Walpole *or* the price of bread in France in July 1789 and the English pig-iron statistics around 1780 *or* Pasteur and Bleriot? Selection is inevitable and must be ruthless. There is a danger that certain topics remain in the syllabus simply because they are traditional. Does the repeti-

2 See A.M.A., *The Teaching of Economics* (1973).

tion of the details of Magna Carta or the events of the South Sea Bubble merit the considerable emphasis placed upon them in many textbooks? The significance of many topics speaks for itself, but the syllabus should help secure both variety and suitability in the history that is taught. For the conflict is not between the useful and useless, but between the more important and the less important. To help resolve this, three questions may be asked.

'Is this subject within the grasp of the pupils?' This is often overlooked by the teacher recently down from university, laden with notebooks of history that are intellectually attractive only to the more mature mind. School history should never be a watered down degree course.

'Can I make this interesting?' There is obviously a link with the first question, but also so much depends on the ability of the teacher and on the choice of method and material. There are few other subjects in the school curriculum that can offer so varied and attractive a fare for the young mind as can history. The thrill of discovery, of physical and mental conflict, the adventure derived from a life of action, the humanity of the saints and the failings of the sinners – these are some of the things that need never produce the complaint that history is dull.

'Is this subject significant?' Some history teachers have reacted defensively to complaints that history is 'useless and boring' by drawing the wrong conclusion. Instead of reviewing their methods and materials, they have argued that significant history must be relevant by which they mean topical; hence the proliferation of contemporary history syllabuses and integrated studies. The importance of such history cannot be denied but the career of Alexander the Great is no less worthy of study than the career of John Kennedy, merely because it happened over two thousand years ago. Again, teaching history 'backwards', as it were, may seem to appeal to young people who wonder how issues in the news came about. But such syllabuses easily slip into something akin to Butterfield's Whig interpretation or that all that is past is merely preparation for the present. If the impression is given that the present represents man's efforts through history, then it is an easily formed notion in young minds that, through the idolisation of 'progress', the present must be better than the past. It is but a short step to select and praise only those things which have directly contributed to the present. So, whilst supporting a recently argued plea to replace the hectic quest for relevance with a rediscovery of significance, it must be added that room should be found in a syllabus for topics which demonstrate failure as well as success, weakness as well as virtues, retrogression as well as progress.

## Arrangement

The task of setting down on paper the final version of the school history syllabus is one that may well daunt newly appointed heads of departments, so a summary may be useful.

(1) Include in the headings the name of the school, the date when the syllabus was drawn up and the name of the head of department.

(2) Give a brief statement of aims and approach.

(3) Include a concise summary of the main themes of work for each year, showing any variations between the work of different forms in the same age group.

(4) On separate sheets (to facilitate periodic revision) provide a more detailed exposition of each year's work. Include lists of topics, with some flexible indication of the time allocation expected for each. Also add books and aids which are available. Note also the teaching and homework time allotted.

(5) Provide sufficient copies to supply one to the head of the school and one to all members of the department, with a few spare copies for students on teaching practice, and other teachers interested in correlating their work with what is being done in history.

Out of the efforts of teachers in the past to find a satisfactory way of arranging the syllabus, two ideas have survived the test of time, and most schools try to combine the virtues of each. These are the 'chronological' approach and the 'patch' or brief theme approach.

The chronological approach relies on a course that begins in the first forms with prehistoric, classical and medieval times, and teaches the present day four or five years later. It has been criticised not so much for what it is, but because of attempts to cram too much in, which has involved a scamper through the centuries that has destroyed so many people's interest in history. Phrases like 'the history of the world from Plato to Nato' and a 'wild rush to the present in five instalments' imply criticism, and teachers could well ask themselves if a nodding acquaintance with all the great names and events of the past is what they are really wanting. Yet it is only right to add that many teachers are convinced that the chronological approach is the best way to teach history and the only way to convey to pupils a true sense of time and a logical impression of the course of human development. One teacher has written that since history is concerned with change, this syllabus 'presents a rational and logical structure'. Set against this approach are three arguments: its inexorable trend to become just one damned thing after another; its faith in pupils having a sense of time when psychological research suggests that the young have little sense of time; and the fact that early themes, such as ancient Greece, always get a very simplified treatment because they are studied by the most immature. Nevertheless the chronological syllabus has survived the reaction against it because its virtues were easily adapted to meet the challenge of the 'patch' approach.

The 'patch' method permits a study in depth to be undertaken either of a special theme (the Jacobite Rebellion) or a short period (1640–60) or a single year (1914). It obviates the superficiality of the general historical sweep. Such selections are, by definition, not continuous and need not be studied in chronological order; and it is clear that there is no room for working at trends unless change takes place within the short space of time studied. Yet the method has been enthusiastically taken up by many history teachers who believe that the greater the depth of study, the more historical it is, for it demands an immersion in the past which calls up important powers of historical imagination. The enormous success of publications in the 'patch' field lend support to this conclusion: there are few schools today that do not have sets of such series as 'Then and There' on their history shelves, and, as will be shown later, many resources packs combine the patch method with a documentary approach. W. H. Burston of the University of London has written: 'The process of imagining oneself in a past age can in the end be the greatest and most distinctive intellectual challenge entailed by the study of history, and the "patch" syllabus is unique in stressing this, for it not only assumes such powers, it may justly claim to foster them.'[3]

Few teachers today adopt one approach to the exclusion of the other, and most hold that the chronological should be used as a framework, but only as a framework, for certain patches. Other experiments have been tried, but found too restrictive. The 'lines of development' method, where the course is planned by reference to themes stretching over long periods of time, gained some support in the 1950s. Those like 'The Story of the House' and 'Medicine' give an opportunity for project work, help develop a chronological sense, and give a specific structure to the pupil's work in that he knows what he is looking for. But many teachers believe the 'lines of development' approach to be a dead duck. It has been vigorously challenged because of its tendency to concentrate on the history of things in society rather than on the history of man in society, and also because a subject is dealt with in isolation.

[3] W. H. Burston and C. W. Green (eds.), *Handbook for History Teachers*, (Methuen, 2nd edition, 1972), p. 68.

## A la carte

The argument developed so far would point to a syllabus based on diversity within a broad framework, with balance as the main criterion in selection. There is no purpose in defining a body of knowledge which all should acquire; nor in attempting to find a hotch-potch compromise and call it a model syllabus. Yet a charge of 'mere entertainment' could well be levelled at a syllabus based on 'teach anything that's interesting'. So, an à la carte approach within a structure tight enough for appreciation to become cumulative seems the best. Teachers wishing to pursue the theoretical side of syllabus formation and to find some practical examples, should consult Burston, *Handbook for History Teachers*, already cited; M. B. Booth, *History Betrayed?* (Longmans: 1969); R. Ben Jones in *History* (October 1970); and four articles in *Teaching History* by D. Heater, G. Preston, P. G. Boldero, M. C. Atkinson in the issues of May 1969, November 1969, May 1970 and November 1970 respectively.

The following suggestions should enable teachers to make a start on mapping out their own programmes.

(A) 1st Year
Britain before the Romans
The Roman World, and the Conquest and Settlement of Britain
The Barbarian Invasions of Europe and the English Invasions and Settlement
The Growth of Christianity
The Vikings
King Alfred and Anglo-Saxon England
The Normans, the Conquest and its consequences
Henry II and the quarrel with the Church
Islam, the Crusades and Richard I
King John and Magna Carta
Simon de Montfort and the Growth of Parliament
Edward I and Wales and Scotland
Medieval methods of justice
Life in a medieval village, a medieval town and a monastery
Castles
The Hundred Years War
The Black Death and the Peasants' Revolt

2nd Year
The Renaissance and the end of the Middle Ages
The Discoveries
Henry VII and Henry VIII
The Reformation
Mary Tudor
Mary Stuart and the Counter Reformation
Drake and the Sea Dogs, the Spanish War and the Armada, 1588
Social Discontent of Tudor Times
Quarrels with Parliament, Elizabeth to 1642

1st Civil War 1642–6, and the execution of Charles I, 1649
The Interregnum (and Cromwell), 1649–60
The Restoration 1660
The Plague, the Fire, the Dutch
The Exclusion Bill Controversy and aftermath, 1678–85
James II, the English Revolution 1688 and the reign of William III
The War of the Spanish Succession 1702–13

3rd Year

Walpole and Peace. Jacobitism. Chatham and war in (1) America, (2) Europe, (3) India
George III and Wilkes. The Loss of the American Colonies
The Church and Methodism. Eighteenth-century life
Cook's voyages. The Agricultural Revolution
The Industrial Revolution (Coal, iron, engineering: textiles and factory development effects; science; canals and roads)
The French Revolution (causes and course: effects on Britain)
Pitt and the Revolutionary War
Napoleonic War (Invasion scheme and Trafalgar: Continental system and Peninsular War: Moscow and Waterloo campaigns: sea power 1793–1815)
The Arts in the eighteenth and nineteenth centuries. Repression 1815–22
The Liberal Tories 1822–30. The Whig Reforms in the 1830s
Railways and Steamships. Corn Laws. Chartism and Peel.
Foreign Affairs 1815–30. The Growth of Empire to 1850 (Canada, Australia, South Africa, India)
Working conditions in the first half of the nineteenth century

(B) Years 1 and 2

Egypt, Greece, Rome
Aztecs, Incas, Arabs and Vikings
India, China: study of life and achievements

Years 3, 4 and 5
*Either*
Features of medieval and modern world:
  Feudalism, Reformation, English Civil War, American Civil War, Industrial and French Revolutions, 1914–18 and 1939–45, Russian and Chinese Revolutions and Japanese Imperialism
*Or*
Themes of British history:
  National expansion, industrial change, social reform, development of modern institutions of government – to be covered in two years followed by twentieth-century world history.

(C) Entry from Middle School where no formal history has been studied.

Year 3

Medieval English and Tudor History

Years 4 and 5

English society and Civil War
Colonial society and War of Independence
French society and the Revolution

American society and Civil War
English society and Industrial Revolution
African society south of Sahara before 1870

(D) A year's 'patch' approach studying themes and periods in American history:
Pilgrim Fathers and Roger Williams, Jamestown and tobacco; Anglo-French struggle for Canada, American War of Independence; westward pioneers, America 1850–65 – a term on each of these sections

(E) **Term 1**
Introduction to Anglo-Saxon England – 1 week
Vikings – depth study with final emphasis on Alfred – 4 weeks
1066 – depth study of a single year – 3 weeks
Feudalism and castles – 3 weeks

**Term 2**
English warfare, reference to Crecy, Agincourt and Crusades
The Black Death and Peasants' Revolt *or* patch study 1346–99
*Either* Church and monastery *or* Village and town

**Term 3**
Tudor society: half term on Richard III, princes and Bosworth, Henry VIII and 'divorce', England 1547–58, Mary Queen of Scots, trade; half a term on country life, London life, court life, fashion, theatre and education

(F) A history course correlated with geography
Year 2 (A term or half a year's work)
African history – Olduvai and origin of man; Ancient Egypt, Nile, Pharaohs, science
Medieval kingdoms of Ghana, Mali, Monomatapa and Zimbabwe; Partition, Boers and Rhodesia, industrial development and apartheid
African geography – Nile, Egypt and Sudan; Sahara and its peoples; farming and copper in central Africa; West African peoples; farming and mining in South Africa

(G) The 'Wild West': one year's course of special, though not exclusive, interest to less able children (a course greatly dependent on teacher enthusiasm, materials and method of approach)
An investigation into location and climate of Great Plains; sparse settlement of white people pre-1865; culture of Plains Indians; pioneers and mountain men; miners, cowboys and farmers; 'How the West was won', 1865–90 – human energy and technology, weapons, the Winchester, canned foods, railways, Little Big Horn
Materials from comics, television series, cinema and books to inquire into 'real West'; Custer, Jesse James, Geronimo
Work on songs, drawings, role-playing, woodcraft and following a trail; the frontier idea

(H) A one-year course for the very bright pupils, not taking 'O' level, but intending to enter the sixth form to study history
Pre-sixth-form work on, for example, Southampton
Historical skills, including primary and secondary sources, historical concepts and jargon

Practical work in regional and local history
Visits to medieval walls, dockland, commons, museums, with some archaeological practice

The following syllabus developed by the Schools Council Project
History 13 – 16 is being tried out, together with classroom materials,
in schools throughout the country. The syllabus framework is based
on the uses of history for pupils as identified by the Project:

(1) It provides material for the understanding of human development and change in the perspective of time.
(2) It helps pupils to understand people of a different time and
place.
(3) It helps to explain their present.
(4) It can stimulate leisure pursuits.

The syllabus is designed to show pupils a variety of approaches
to history. Moreover, in the last years of a general education, it
offers the opportunity of studying a variety of historical content
rather than specialising in one period of the past.

## SCHOOLS COUNCIL PROJECT HISTORY 13–16*

### SYLLABUS FOR A TWO-YEAR COURSE AND EXAMINATION IN HISTORY AT G.C.E./C.S.E.

| FRAMEWORK OF SYLLABUS | EXAMPLE OF CONTENT FOR TRIAL SCHOOLS | POSSIBLE FUTURE OPTIONS | SUGGESTED TEACHING TIME 2½ HOURS A WEEK – 4–5 PERIODS |
|---|---|---|---|
| *Study in development* | | | |
| A study of the factors affecting the development of a topic through time. | Medicine | The story of flight<br>Women in society<br>Education<br>History of science | 1 term |
| *Enquiry in depth* | | | |
| Study of aspects of a period of the past involving imaginative reconstruction and contrast with the present, and also a biographical study showing the interrelation of a person and his times. | One of the following:<br>Renaissance Italy 1450–1500<br>Elizabethan England 1558–1603<br>Britain 1815–51<br>The American West 1846–90 | Fifth-century Greece<br>Chaucer's England 1340–1400<br>The Spanish conquest of South America 1500–50<br>England 1640–60<br>Russia 1905–24 | 1½ terms |
| *Studies in modern world history* | | | |
| Three studies on modern issues viewed historically. | Three of the following:<br>The rise of Communist China<br>The move to European unity<br>Arab–Israeli conflict<br>The Irish question | India–Pakistan<br>America as a World Power<br>Wind of Change in Africa<br>Origins of the cold war<br>Pollution | 1½ terms |

| FRAMEWORK OF SYLLABUS | EXAMPLE OF CONTENT FOR TRIAL SCHOOLS | POSSIBLE FUTURE OPTIONS | SUGGESTED TEACHING TIME $2\frac{1}{2}$ HOURS A WEEK – 4–5 PERIODS |
|---|---|---|---|
| *History around us*<br><br>A study of the history around us using the visible evidence as the starting point. This will involve visits to sites. | One of the following:<br>Prehistoric Britain<br>Roman Britain<br>Castles and fortified houses 1066–1550<br>Country houses 1550–1800<br>Church buildings and furnishing 1066–1900<br>Studies in the making of the rural landscape<br>Town development and domestic architecture 1700 to the present<br>Industrial archaeology<br>Aspects of the historical development of the locality | | 1 term |

*Reprinted by permission of Schools Council

# Accommodation 3

The purposes which the history teacher is trying to fulfil, and the method which he uses to fulfil them must, and do, make demands on the accommodation which he needs. If his teaching is to be effective he must be able to create, in conditions suited to his purpose, his own distinctive atmosphere of learning. The equipment which he uses is frequently expensive and cumbersome. It has to be immediately and easily accessible to him, and, at the same time, it must be protected from misuse and vandalism, as, indeed, must his books, displays and models. Considerations such as these have led teachers of history to agree that, if they are to do their work efficiently, they need accommodation which has been designed for their purposes and which is under their own control. History teachers must have their own specialist rooms. Yet it remains true that, at a time when specialist rooms are being provided for the teaching of languages, or careers guidance, many education authorities and headmasters are unwilling to accept that history teaching has any requirement other than a classroom full of desks. Others, accepting in theory the case for specialist accommodation, take no active steps to provide it. Teachers themselves need, therefore, to take the initiative in making their legitimate demands heard.

## The suite

What, then, ought history teachers to expect by way of accommodation? Clearly the number and size of the rooms will depend upon the size of the school, the age of the pupils, and the number of pupils in the teaching groups, but, whatever else it may or may not be possible to have, each teacher of history should have his own teaching room and other subjects should not be taught there. Where a department has two or more rooms it is equally important that they should be close to each other and adjacent to their storage facilities. Unless they are, departmental cooperation will be difficult and teaching efficiency will be reduced.

Similar factors operate in respect of the school library. If the library and the history rooms are at opposite ends of the school buildings the problems of supervision and time-wasting become so pressing as to discourage the library's free use. Yet it is an essential resource centre for pupil use and if it is at all possible the history rooms and the library should be close together. On the same grounds an additional advantage would be proximity to the school's hall and/or drama facilities.

Some L.E.A.s, the more enlightened ones, do already take these factors into account in providing history rooms. The plan of the accommodation prepared by a city architect as part of a comprehensive school complex shown in Fig. 1, goes a long way toward meeting our needs.

However, just as the planning and disposition of the history rooms in their relation to one another and to their key facilities does affect teaching methods, so methods will be partly determined by the size of the classrooms. Some L.E.A.s have recognised this and have taken a more helpful view of an appropriate size. The plan of an L.E.A. proposal for a history room, shown in Fig. 2, illustrates what can and ought to be done.

If it is assumed, as unfortunately it has to be, that groups of pupils in the age range 11–14 will be 30 or more strong, then a classroom should have an area of 800 sq. ft. (75 square metres). If it is smaller than that clear access to equipment becomes difficult and displays of work or drama cannot be mounted effectively. Thus a room of less than 800 sq. ft. will restrict teaching methods, and teachers of history should accept such a room only with great reluctance.

History teaching is not limited to younger pupils and accommodation is needed for groups of older pupils who may be following an examination course. G.C.E. O Level candidates will not need as active a view of history as younger ones, but they will need access to a variety of books, pictures, tapes and films, a factor which underlines the need for the teaching rooms to be close to the department's storage and resource facilities. Equally the sixth form will have its own specialist needs,[1] most significantly easy access to the departmental and school libraries, while the sixth formers themselves ought, doubtless, to appreciate comfort, quiet and informality.

Another factor that has to be borne in mind, when accommodation is being planned, is that teachers are becoming involved in interdisciplinary schemes of work, and are taking part in team teaching. Where such teaching arrangements are practised it is

[1] See pp. 185–8.

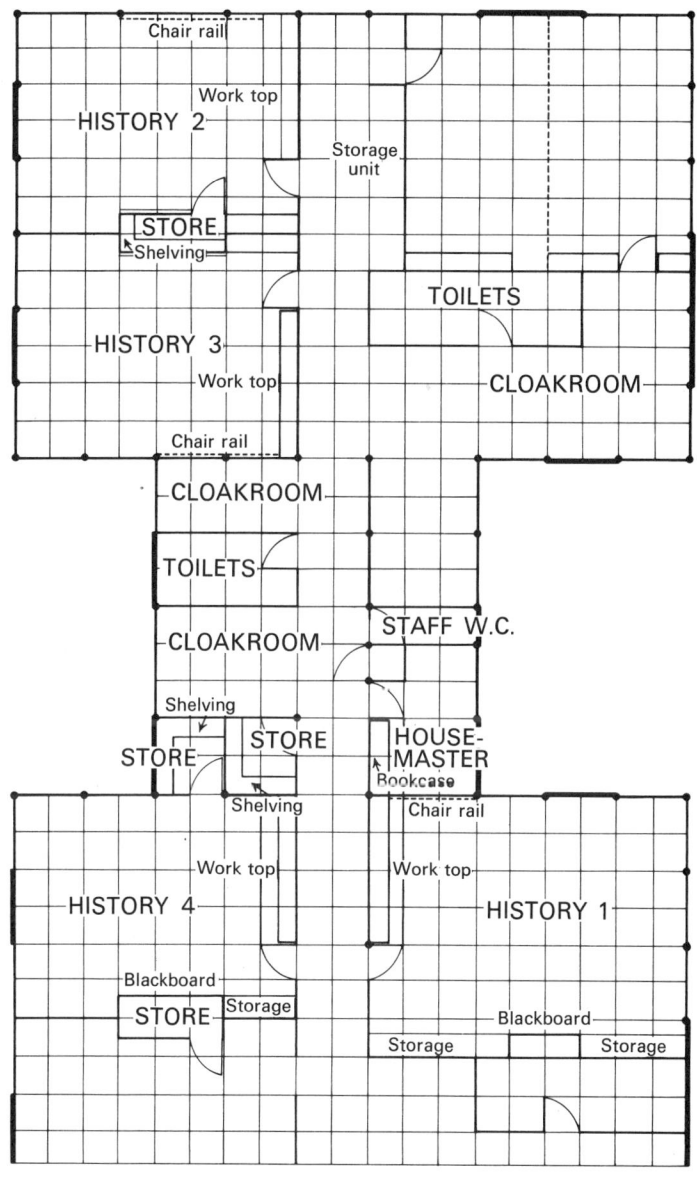

FIG. 1. *A suite of history rooms*

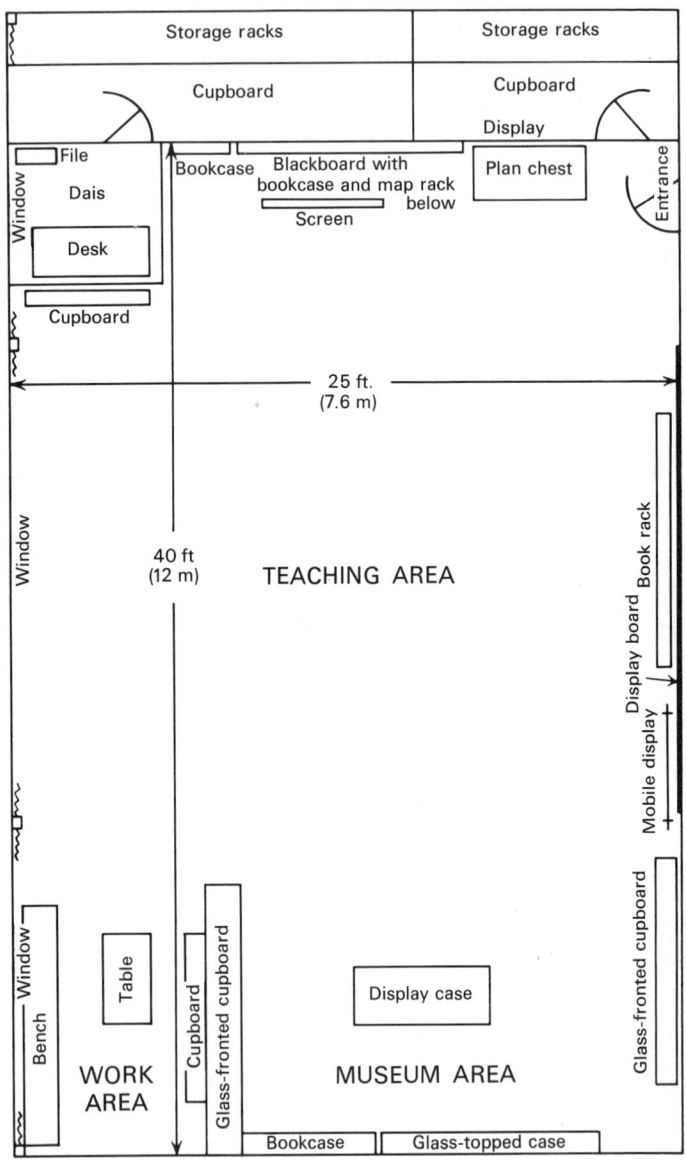

Fig. 2. *A history room*

common for all the pupils of an age or ability group to be brought together for their lead lesson. In these cases rooms should be planned so that pupils may sit in comfort, and may see and hear what is going on. When the group breaks up into smaller classes for the follow-up work there will need to be adjacent classrooms. The practice of dividing up the large teaching area into normal class-room size by means of partitions should be examined very critically. Experience suggests that 'sound-proof' partitions are not proof against films or tape recorders, or even loud-voiced colleagues, let alone rowdy classes. Team teaching can only be made to work if adequate facilities are provided from the outset.

Thus it is vitally important in planning the history teaching ac-commodation to provide for the needs of pupils who, at various stages in their development, have their own particular requirements. It is not good enough to reduce them all to an overcrowded box containing 40 desks.

Nor is it good enough to expect books and equipment to be carted about at every lesson change. Teaching methods should determine not only the arrangement of rooms but also the sort of storage facilities which the department will need. History teaching requires the use of so many different sorts of equipment and materials that even a small department cannot be expected to exist on a couple of cupboards along the corridor. A history room needs a lockable storeroom of at least 50 sq. ft. (between 5 and 6 square metres), though a group of rooms could share a proportionately larger store. Whatever the arrangements *the stores should be close to the teaching rooms.* Experience shows that, where they are not, books will be lost and equipment is very likely to be damaged. Ex-perience also shows that slides, films, strips and television pro-grammes will not be used at all when they cannot be used con-veniently.

In addition, organising for teaching is made immeasurably easier when the store opens into the classroom and when it has independent access from outside. It would be extremely helpful if there could be one store large enough to be used as a staff preparation room.

In short it must be made clear that, if history is to be taught dur-ing the 1970s and 80s in accord with the best practices, teachers must have accommodation designed for or adapted to their special needs. Where proper facilities do not exist the history department must take the initiative in demanding them, and they must speak out persistently against conditions which make their task more difficult than it ought to be. They should enlist the support of the County Adviser and the H.M.I.; they should not take 'no' or 'perhaps' for an answer.

## Furniture

The choice of furniture will be a matter for individual needs and tastes. However, assuming that use of textbook, topic and reference books, audio-visual equipment, model-making, map drawing and play-acting will form a normal part of lesson technique, a room full of desks and chairs will be inconvenient. It would, therefore, seem reasonable that history teachers should be able to request, and should expect to be supplied with, laminate-topped tables. They permit far greater flexibility even within an inadequately small room. They can be butted together, provided that they are of the correct proportions, to form larger working surfaces. They can be more quickly stacked to clear the classroom and give space for the active lesson. They can be used for making models on, and can be improvised into display surfaces.

Another reasonable expectation is that the history room should have stacking chairs, which will again allow the room to be cleared for action. Preferably they ought to be the metal and moulded-plastic ones which are very durable and are much more comfortable and more cheerful than traditional furniture.

It must be accepted that only the L.E.A. will be able to ensure that the basic classroom furniture is provided and is of the standard required. However, over and above this, teachers have what some-times seems an insatiable need for additional pieces of furniture which are not so easy to wring from an impecunious authority. Colleagues have suggested other sources which it may be possible to tap for new or secondhand pieces.

If the school has a Parents' Association a direct approach with a carefully prepared case may well prove successful. Most L.E.A.s have a store of abandoned or neglected furniture, accumulated from schools that have closed or have been refurnished. An approach to the man in charge has proved fruitful. Pupils, too, can be used in the hunt. They may know of tables and cupboards that no-one else wants, in or out of school. Should they be in school it ought to be possible for the silver-tongued historian to negotiate their removal to his own domain. Pupils may, too, be able to bring in news of shops that are refitting, where a variety of furniture and display materials are being thrown out. Negotiations by staff could well result in handsome acquisitions free of charge. Once obtained, such secondhand furniture can be adapted to suit an infinite variety of needs, a few of which are considered below. But, whatever the degree of improvisation, the fundamental responsibility for ensuring that teaching rooms are properly equipped is the Local Authority's and they should not be allowed to shirk it.

**Storing resources**

One of the history teacher's most pressing and basic problems is storing his resources – books, maps, leaflets, magazines, newspapers, slides, strips and tapes. It cannot be emphasised too strongly that such things should be housed in a storeroom adjacent to the classroom in which they will be used. Not many schools, however, will be able to meet this demand; in those which cannot, cupboards, drawers and filing systems are essential. It should be possible, in adapting a room for teaching history, to provide some such storage facilities along the length of one classroom wall at a low level. They could then have a surface across the top which could be used for display.

Our correspondents, no doubt reflecting the lack of planned facilities at their own disposal, were not short of suggestions for improvising storage space for loose-leaf materials, magazines and maps. Pieces up to foolscap or A4 size are easily kept in large envelopes which are cheap to buy and easy to store. Cardboard boxes, such as those marketed by Lawtons of Liverpool, are more expensive (about 25p each at the time this book was written) but are better. They are large enough to take 500 sheets, are stoutly made, have drop fronts and can, therefore, be stacked. If the situation should be so desperate that there is absolutely no money available, an eloquent appeal for shirt or shoe boxes, or polythene shirt bags might produce sufficient for immediate needs, but they will be inconvenient as they will not be in standard sizes and are unlikely to last very long.

For storing the large envelopes, files, or shirt bags an empty desk could be pressed into use. Should the school be unable to produce even an empty desk or two one might in desperation beg large cardboard cartons from shop or supermarket.

Larger sheet materials such as maps and charts may be kept in large envelope files such as those marketed by E. J. Arnold of Leeds (about 20p each at the time this book was written). If these are not suitable then two large sheets of stiff card or hardboard and four bulldog clips may be used. They will certainly be kept clean and flat and they can be suspended by the clips.

One of the recurrent and niggling problems facing teachers is the storage of small items of equipment such as film strips and tapes. There are, of course, pieces of furniture designed for the job but most teachers will probably prefer to make do with something cheaper. Two suggestions are offered for making a film strip or slide rack.

To make a rack, hardboard lengths 80mm deep will be needed

to form both the shelves and their supports. The lengths will be determined by the length of shelf and the number of shelves wanted.

1.   80mm from the end of each shelf saw a slot 40mm long, i.e. half the depth of the shelf. (See Fig. 3.)

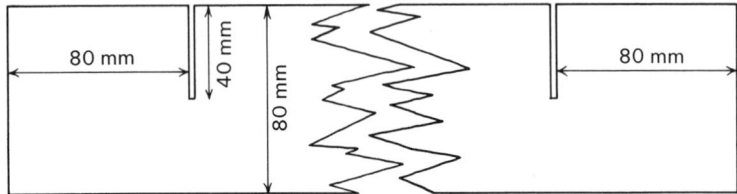

FIG. 3. *Making shelves for film strips: the shelves*

2.   The supports for the shelf are made in the same way. At 40mm intervals along each support cut slots 40mm long. There will be at least two supports, perhaps more, depending upon the length of the shelves. (See Fig. 4.)

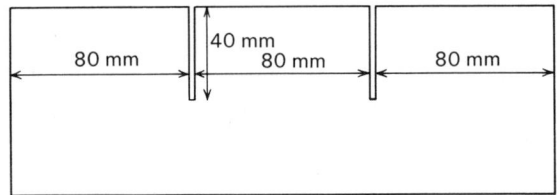

FIG. 4. *Making shelves for film strips: the supports*

3.   Assemble the supports and the shelves by sliding them into the slotted positions. (See Figs. 5 and 6.)

The consequent rack will be quite substantial enough to hold film strips, boxes of slides, and small tapes, and be light enough to be easily mounted on a wall.

The second suggestion is simpler. The only materials needed are a number of expanded polystyrene tiles and some adhesive. Three layers of tiles can be mounted on a wall and holes can be cut into the tiles to make nests for filmstrip cans or small slide boxes (see Fig. 7 on p. 38). This rack might, however, constitute a fire hazard.

The storage of books is a perennial problem. The cheapest shelving is deal planking fixed to the wall by angle brackets and supported by props on the outer edge. It is comparatively cheap and easy to erect, but even the possession of adequate shelving does not solve all the problems that are likely to arise.

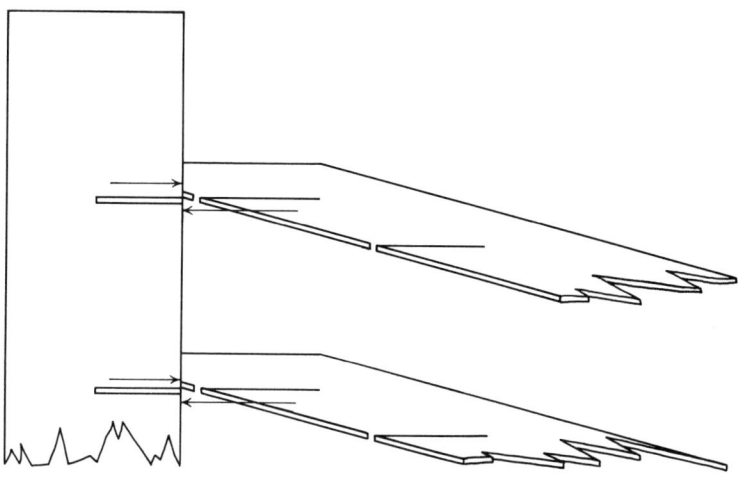

FIG. 5. *Making shelves for film strips: assembling shelves and supports*

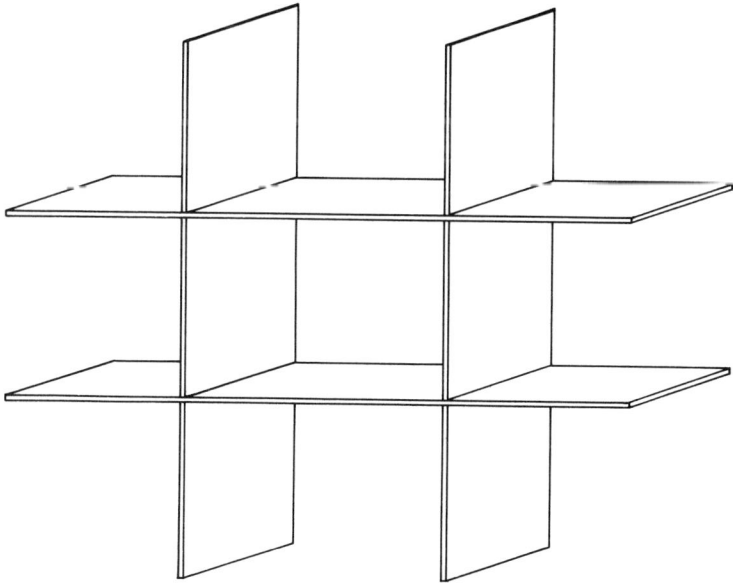

FIG. 6. *Making shelves for film strips: the assembled shelves*

The provision of a number of different books to enable topic work to be done poses some particular problems. The books must be accessible yet, if they are left on open shelves in the classroom, they will be easily lost, damaged or stolen. If they are kept locked up they cease to be accessible to pupils and are, therefore, less useful. Perhaps the simplest compromise is to use a book trolley. Provided that the department has a lockable store of more than cubicle size, a trolley may be loaded beforehand, produced when needed, taken away when finished with and unloaded when convenient.[2]

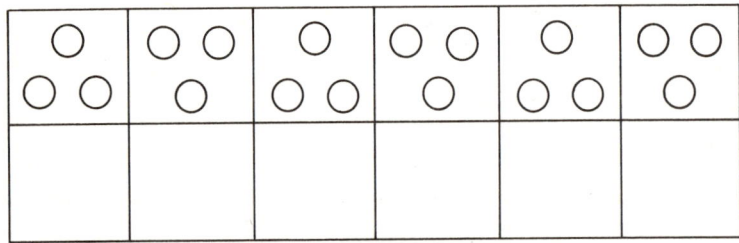

Fɪɢ. 7. *Film strip nests*

If the history rooms are close to the school library, as they should be, then it may be possible to dispense with the departmental library. Pupils would have to be trained in the use of the library, and the librarian would have to be consulted before this could happen. Nonetheless, such instruction will ease the history teacher's burden and may foster a more independent spirit among the pupils. A disadvantage of such a system is that it makes it rather more difficult for the teacher to know who is making regular use of the books.

### Equipment

While the choice of teaching equipment must be personal and subjective, whatever is chosen must be as simple to use and as effective in use as is possible.

Despite the development of so many sophisticated teaching aids, and despite the scorn of some theorists, the blackboard remains a necessary and fundamental requirement in any history room. Of the wide choice available the roller board seems to give maximum con-

2 For a suggestion on how to make a book trolley see pp. 41–2.

venience in use and greatest writing area, while it takes up comparatively little space. One refinement to be recommended is a strip light to illuminate it from above. This can ensure clear vision and can eliminate the awkward shiny areas which so frequently seem to dog some pupils' efforts to see straight. Such a light will also allow the board to be used during the showing of filmstrips and slides.

The physical arrangement of the classroom should be such as to encourage the use of projectors. It should be possible to show two or three slides, or a picture on an epivisor, without disrupting the lesson. To fulfil this condition every classroom in use as a history room should have power points, black-out, a permanent screen, and access to an equipment trolley.

Each history room needs to be supplied with power points. Two should be considered an absolute minimum, one at the back and one at the front of the room. Four would be more helpful, and it is worth recalling that additional power points can be easily fitted. In addition there should be radio and T.V. sockets. If a class has to tramp off to the assembly hall to watch a twenty-minute television programme the chances are that television will not be used.

To darken a room sufficiently to show colour films curtains are preferable to blinds. They can be drawn quickly and easily, and they allow the windows to be kept open. They have the additional advantage that they can be in gay colours and can help to create a pleasanter atmosphere in the room. With a little self-help the cost of darkening the room can be kept to a minimum. Would the needlework department be willing to make up the material into curtains? or would some of the parents? If so, then fixing a proprietary curtain rail should not be beyond the ability of most schools. With such cooperation the cost will be reduced to the cost of the materials and the final result will be as effective and quicker than waiting for the L.E.A. to do the job. If even this is too expensive it might be possible to lay hands on some stage flats to put in front of the windows, but this will certainly be cumbersome and will not be entirely effective.

Ideally each room should also have a permanent screen sited so that it may be seen absolutely clearly from the back of the classroom. If one has not been built into the room's facilities adequate improvisation should present no difficulties. White emulsion paint on a wall or on a piece of hardboard will give an excellent surface for slides or films in black and white or colour.

For schools which have no darkened rooms, and no prospect of achieving any in the near future, a somewhat inadequate daylight screen may serve as a substitute but despite manufacturers' claims

experience suggests that they are really effective only with comparatively small groups of pupils, those at the sides and towards
the back of the room receive only a very blurred image.

As an absolutely last resort, when all other tactics have failed to
result in the provision of even a daylight screen it is possible to
improvise one (see Fig. 8). The basic requirement is a long-sided
box, open at each end, and a large sheet of tracing paper. Cover
one of the open ends with the tracing paper, to form a screen. Take
care not to crease it, and ensure that it is taut. Stand the projector
in front of and facing the class, place the screen in front of the projector with the tunnel of the box facing the class and acting as a shade
against the light. Project the picture on to the screen (see Fig. 9).

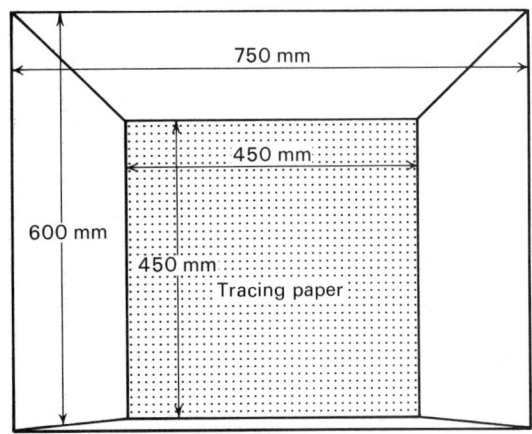

FIG. 8. *Making a daylight screen: view from the front*

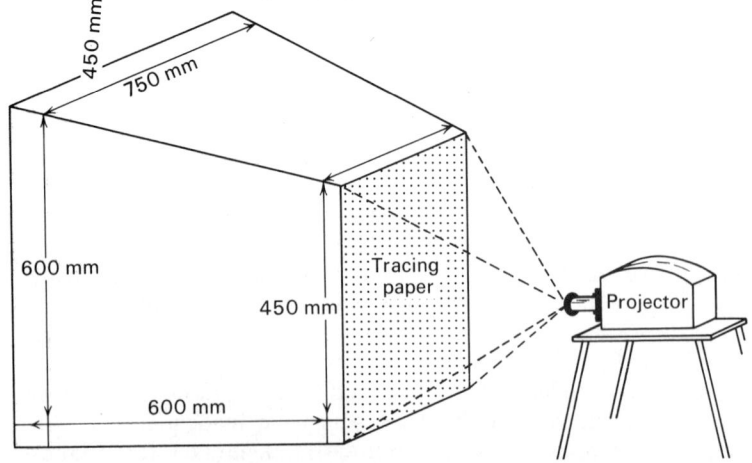

FIG. 9. *Making a daylight screen: view from the side*

As a refinement it is possible to manufacture a box making it funnel-shaped so as to increase the number of pupils who will be able to see something.

Such an arrangement will serve a very limited purpose. The pictures will not be good and the number of pupils who are able to see adequately will be comparatively few. Perhaps its most significant function will be to convince a headmaster of the need for something better and allow moral pressure to be put on him to finance adequate equipment.

If the basic criterion of ease of use is to be met then each history room will need a projection/equipment trolley. Nothing will inhibit the use of heavy electrical equipment more than the inconvenience of having to haul it about by main force, and nothing is likely to cause damage more quickly. There is a wide choice of such trolleys on the market, but our correspondents were able to suggest a means whereby one could be made from a desk by fixing castors to its legs. Should a higher trolley be needed two desks may be used. Remove the lid from the first desk and saw the legs and bottom off the second. Screw the second on top of the first and fit castors to the legs. (See Fig. 10).

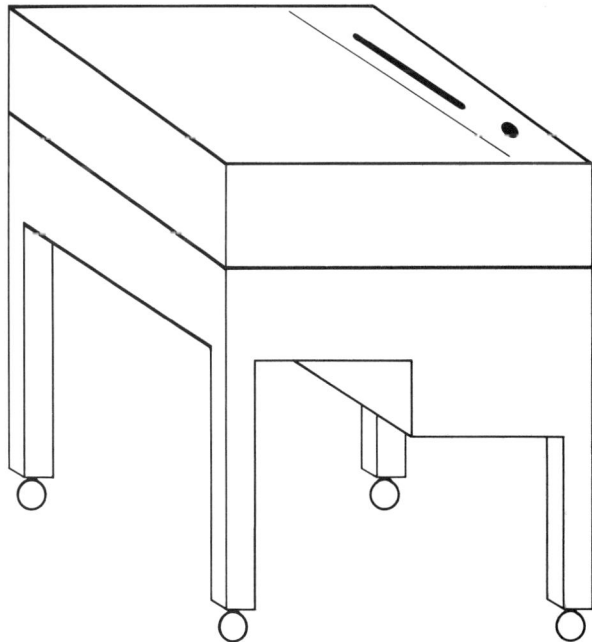

FIG. 10. *Making an equipment trolley*

Such a contraption will not only serve as a projector stand, but may also be used to store the projector, or a small tape recorder and films, slides and tapes. Indeed such is its versatility that it will serve equally well as a book trolley.

With rooms darkened and screen and trolley at the ready the department must have access to sufficient strip, slide and cine projectors to ensure that lessons can go ahead as planned and not have to be postponed because the essential piece of equipment is in use elsewhere.

Ideally each history room should have its own strip projector and, subject to the size of the school and the number of history teachers making use of the equipment, each department should have its own projector(s) and tape recorder(s).

Of all the teaching aids available the history teacher will probably make most constant use of duplicating facilities, with which he will produce and reproduce worksheets, assignments and source material. Except in the largest schools, it is probably too much to expect that the history department will have its own duplicators. It is not too much to expect that a head of department should use his influence to ensure that the best and the most up-to-date copying processes[3] are available within the school, and that he and his colleagues have a right to use them as they need, nor is it too much to expect that the department should have the sort of ancillary help which is usually available at present to the science and technical staff. It is not reasonable that the scientist should have help in organising and moving his equipment when the history teacher has none; nor is it reasonable that the history teacher should be expected, as he usually is, to be his own typist and to spend hours operating duplicating machines. It is indeed an appalling misuse of skill and energy.

### Display

Display facilities are also essential to the history room. There can be no good reason why the walls of the room should not be covered with display board, the bottom edge being 3 ft. 6 in. (approx. 1 metre) from the floor and the top some 8 ft. or 9 ft. (approx. $2\frac{1}{2}$ metres). This could incorporate softboard for pinning up charts, displays, maps and demonstrations of work (Fig. 11); an area of pegboard to take more substantial items, such as magazines, books and small display articles and models; a cluster board for magazines, documents, newspaper cuttings and individual pieces of work (Fig. 12).

[3] See page 70 for an assessment of these.

FIG. 11. *A wall display: the class are enjoying a historical quiz;
on the walls is a well-constructed display*

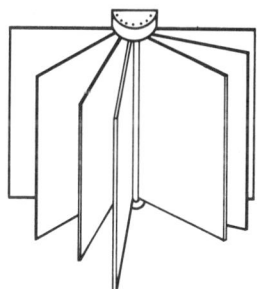

FIG. 12. *A cluster board*

Most of these points are illustrated in practice by the proposals
for a history room illustrated on page 32. These really are excellent
and may serve as an example to other local authorities.

No doubt the majority of teachers will have to manage with a
good deal less, but even in a classroom of modest proportions it is
possible to make some display space available.

A map stand is an invaluable piece of equipment which can be
cheaply improvised by mounting bulldog or Klemboy clips at the
front of the room, but *not*, wherever else they may be put, so that the

maps hang in front of the blackboard. Blackboard, screen and maps should be capable of being used simultaneously.

To provide board to which items may be pinned, sheets of block-board or softboard can be bought fairly cheaply. Mount them by plugging the wall, and if in doubt call on non-historian expertise. A wooden surround will prolong the board's life and give a more pro-fessional finish to the job. Should it prove impossible to take on this task of improvisation, displays can be mounted on card and suspended from the wall by Sellotape or wall clips. But preparing such displays will take more time than if the permanent facilities are at hand, and they will be in far greater danger of being knocked off the wall or accidentally torn. A problem of protecting displays al-ways exists, by whatever means they are mounted. One way to protect photographs, pictures, or documents is to Sellotape an acetate sheet over the top of them.

Display cases are a different problem. They are relatively ex-pensive to buy and take up quite a lot of room. Where it has been possible to organise a school museum the school ought to be able to supply the equipment needed, but for a departmental display it might be possible to lay hands on a spare cupboard (see above, page 34), the door panels of which can be removed and replaced by sheets of perspex. At least this will have the advantage of being usable either standing vertically or lying horizontally, or on its back. All that would then be needed would be some extra stands for displaying small objects. Alternatively the science department might have, and be willing to part with, some spare balance cases. If there is no cupboard to adapt, the simplest display area for models is a shelf. Given adequate width, about 2′ (600 cm), covered with a cheap laminate product, it could serve equally well as a work sur-face. Models on it, however, will be completely unprotected.

If it is anticipated, as it should be, that model making will indeed be used in teaching, then a sink with hot and cold water ought to be planned when the history suite is being equipped.

The facilities referred to in this chapter must be made available if the best teaching methods are to be encouraged. Where they are not available it will be unnecessarily difficult for the history teacher to do his job efficiently and effectively. This is considered to be so important that a number of suggestions have been made for their improvisation. Nonetheless it must be clearly stated that classroom space cannot be improvised; that it is the duty of the L.E.A. to ensure that space and facilities are available to its teachers; and that, where they are not available, teachers of history are fully justified in taking the initiative in demanding that the omissions be remedied.

# Methods and materials I

4

## Principles and criticisms

A principle generally accepted in teaching history is that any one method is likely to become progressively less effective the more it is practised, and especially if it is adopted exclusively. In the past, history teaching suffered from disregard of this, being often entirely based on one textbook simply because few alternatives existed. What is now available is a multi-media approach using many different types of books but including also artefacts, photographs, films, tapes, slides, source materials and so on, in overwhelming and sometimes confusing quantity. The obvious justification for using such variety is that spice is added to teaching, and the interest and concentration of the pupils tend to be prolonged. Moreover, such variety of methods heightens the effectiveness of learning, making acceptable the repetition in new contexts of matter already learnt (so reinforcing and deepening the knowledge), whilst at the same time creating many new paths to understanding for those experiencing learning difficulties.

Another principle is that the most effective lessons are those which have been well prepared, not only as regards the materials to be used – such as books, tapes, film strips and the like – but also where the aims of the lessons and the methods to be used are the result of careful forethought. Whilst a few lessons which drift according to the whim, fancy, and current concerns of pupils may turn out well (and may often be most valuable when spontaneously initiated or conducted by them), these are only a small minority; the general run of lessons needs to be seen as part of a syllabus or scheme of work in order to supply each lesson with a context, so preventing aimlessness and providing purpose. At the other extreme it is possible to over-prepare a lesson, which can feel like a steel corset to an inexperienced teacher if he is not prepared to jettison even his best prepared plan when this proves to be unsuitable. Ideally, a syllabus should be flexible, not inhibiting or restrictive, nor even strictly mandatory as regards the ground to be covered. Its principal object should be to supply a theme and to provide direction, and to make the planning and order of lessons and the choice of methods easier, so imbuing both teacher and taught with a sense of making progress and accomplishing something.

In theory, materials used in teaching history are subservient to methods and dependent on them; in practice, availability of materials may often seem to determine methods. For instance, if a particularly valuable tape-recording has been made, it may well be worthwhile to make time to include it; also, if no room with blackout exists in the school, then, however excellent a particular filmstrip, it cannot be used. Again, no teacher of history, however impressive his academic qualifications, is equally at home in every period of history, so it probably makes for sounder and more effective learning, if his teaching, at any rate in his first year, concentrates on those areas in which he feels most confident, although no teacher should confine himself to teaching only what he has learnt at college; he should keep his teaching alive by a willingness to experiment. Nevertheless, it makes sense if, for most of his time, he uses those methods with which he feels most happy, and with which his teaching is most successful, rather than that he should force himself, simply for purposes of variety, to use unfamiliar methods which he does not like and which may tend to nullify or undermine his good teaching. Quite apart from the fact that no old dog likes learning new tricks, personal elements in teaching, such as enthusiasm and conviction, are so strong, so intangible, and often so valuable that any loss in them may outweigh any gain by way of novelty of method. The criterion for deciding this point should always be the effectiveness of the teaching. For a teacher is primarily an organiser of learning situations, and any methods he uses are merely means towards this end, not in themselves of value except in so far as they lead to more efficient learning by his pupils.

Dividing methods of teaching history into traditional and modern types, with the implied assumption that the latter are preferable to the former, seems rather artificial and is somewhat misleading. There is not the same need to reform history teaching, either in the way or to the extent that mathematics teaching has been changed. But there is a desire for the provision of more suitable materials, to make the adoption of a variety of methods practicable, and much more thought required on the best use of these materials. The aims of history teaching have undoubtedly changed, in the same way as the writing of history has changed, to take account of modern interests and mores. In the past, emphasis was on the learning of factual information and on the promotion of worthy objectives by means such as inculcating national pride, drawing moral lessons, and providing examples of great men in whose footsteps pupils might be urged to tread. Today, concern is more with

FIG. 13. *Practical work by pupils: (a) Model of a Roman villa (b) Making a model of a parish*

the development of qualities of historical imagination, the encouragement of understanding and skills, and the use of facts to discuss issues rather than to ascertain right answers. But these changes of aim are no reason for disparaging traditional methods, which were only the means by which obsolete aims were pursued, and can serve new aims just as effectively. No history teacher need be put off from opting for the lecture-type lesson simply because it is traditional. To sit and listen attentively, although passive in the physical sense, is not necessarily so in the mental sense, for the mind can react wonderfully to the inspiring tale, and the result can be stimulating and enlivening without the need of any overt action by the pupil. The talk and chalk lesson has come in for much deserved censure because of considerable past abuse, when it was adopted almost to the exclusion of other methods and practised by those who were only poor performers. But the tale well told, provided the language and the idiom are suited to the listeners, is the one method of teaching which has universal appeal irrespective of intellectual capacities. From babyhood onwards, people like to listen to stories, and teachers of history need to talk to pupils, in the same way as parents are urged to talk to their children, to help to stimulate their imaginations. It is arguable that talking to the less academically able in this way is even more important than talking to the more academically gifted, for these latter normally have greater capacity to obtain some of their needs of intellectual stimulation through their ability to read books.

## Use of blackboard and roller board

One of the oldest teaching aids is possibly the blackboard, but its effective use, despite its familiarity and ubiquity, requires some skill. Care should be taken to ensure that writing on it is large enough to be legible even in the far corners of the classroom (Fig. 14). Pressing hard on the board helps, as also does the use of colours. Yellow contrasts especially well with a black background, but red, while making an excellent contrast on white paper, is disappointing when used on the blackboard. In lecture-lessons a good ploy to help induce attention is to write a series of points prominently on the blackboard as the lesson develops, accompanied, where suitable, by diagrams and quick sketches (Fig. 15). For instance, in a lesson such as *Methods of attacking and defending medieval castles* – which is a popular topic with young boys in secondary schools – quick sketches of weapons on the blackboard can be followed by the construction of models of scaling ladders, trebuchets, siege towers, battering-rams and mantelets by pupils in later classes or at home. Such models are easily made in balsa wood or cardboard, and the better ones, proudly exhibited on Open Day and obligingly presented afterwards by their young crafts-men to the history department archives or resources centre, serve well for demonstration purposes to other classes in future lessons as adjuncts to blackboard illustrations.

FIG. 14. *Using the blackboard*

Making diagrams of events and movements on the black-board is a convenient way of summarising lesson material. For ex-ample, when dealing with the war against the French Revolution, which reached a critical stage for Britain in 1797, the dangers and difficulties can probably be shown more clearly by means of a graphic drawing, as in Fig. 15, than by words alone. The danger of invasion was averted by Admiral Jervis' defeat of the Spanish fleet at the *Battle of Cape St Vincent* in February, and by Admiral Duncan's defeat of the Dutch fleet at the *Battle of Camperdown* in October, after the naval mutinies at Spithead and the Nore had been quelled in April and May respectively.

Such a diagram can be drawn on the blackboard during the lesson, or prepared on it beforehand if the loss in spontaneity is accepted, but in both cases the drawing is lost when the blackboard is cleaned. Less wasteful solutions are to use an overhead pro-

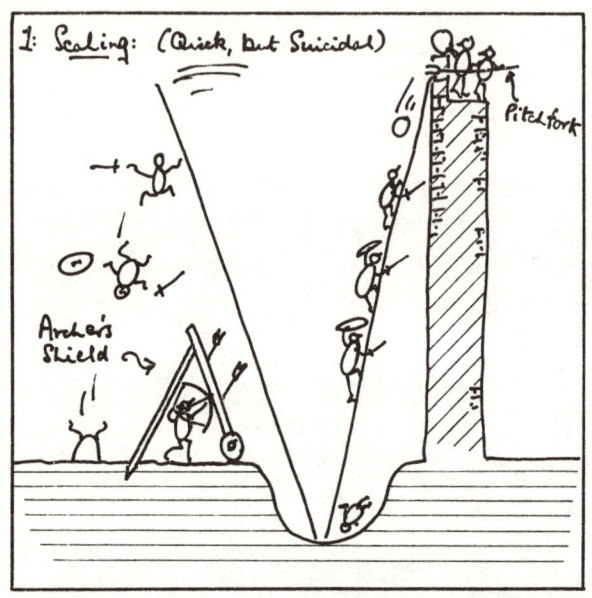

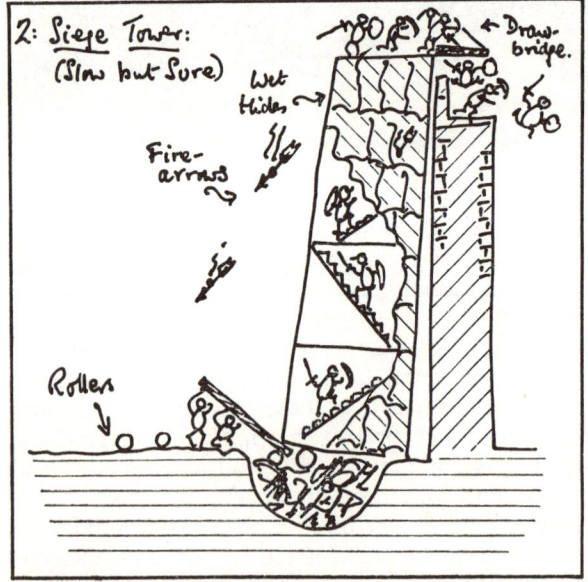

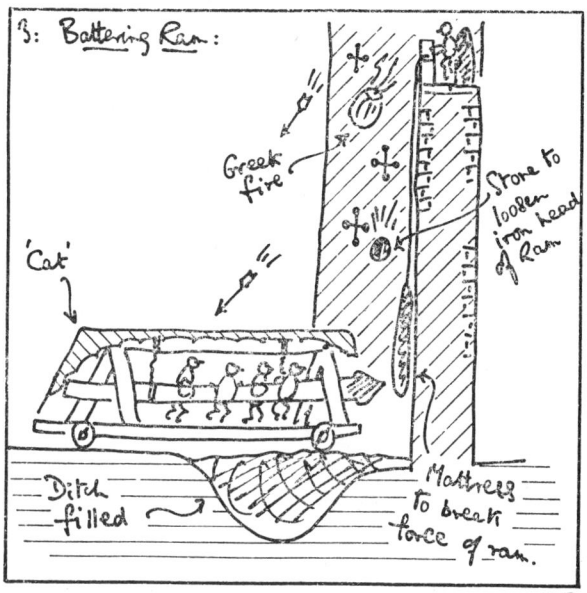

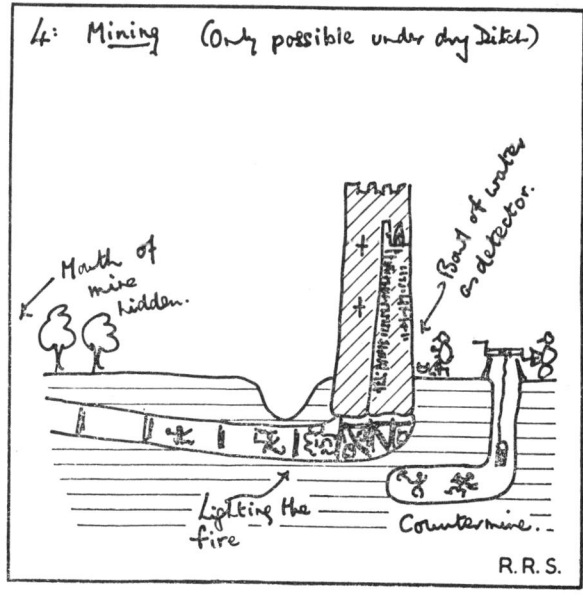

FIG. 15. *Blackboard drawings, illustrating medieval siege-methods, for first-year forms. On the blackboard the parallel shading would be solid colour; the figures would be differentiated from weapons, etc., by difference of shade*

jector or to draw the diagram beforehand on cartridge paper which can be stored in rolls for future use. Twenty-five-yard rolls take little space and may accommodate fifteen to twenty blackboard-size drawings, preserving them also in better condition than if they were on separate single sheets. Such rolls can be combined with the

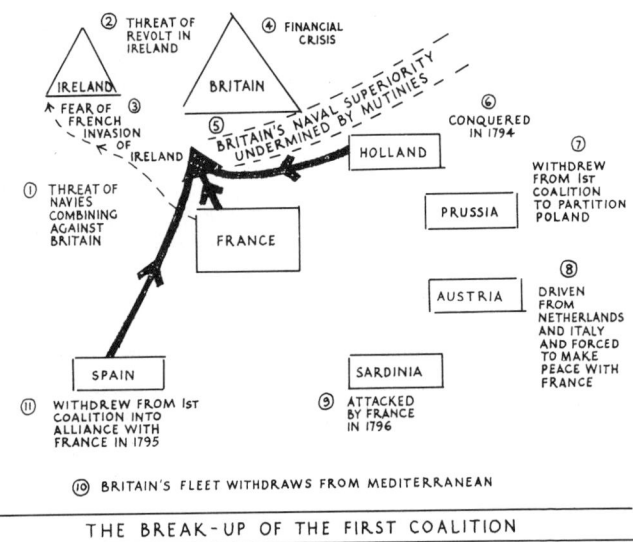

FIG. 16. *Sketch-diagram to illustrate the difficulties of Britain in 1797 –*
*a critical year in British history*

use of a roller board, which is basically a frame on which rollers are mounted just over a yard apart, around which the roll of cartridge paper can be wound. Writing on the cartridge paper with a felt-tipped pen is as easy as writing with chalk on the blackboard, and no blackout is needed. An important point to remember when drawing maps or sketches either on the blackboard or the roller board, is to make them large enough to be clearly visible – and all writing legible – everywhere in the classroom; to ensure this it is better to concentrate on a few simple specific points than to risk confusion by the addition of much detail. Colours are helpful, but their purpose is primarily to clarify drawings rather than to beautify them – a point which it may be worth stressing to pupils when they make sketch-diagrams in their project-files or exercise books. In this connection it is worth pointing out to pupils that coloured ball-point or fibre-tip pens are ideal for writing words on maps, but are less efficient than coloured pencils for shading.

## Use of group assessment

Although most teachers usually value their pupils' work by means of comments, grades or marks – sometimes even by all three – there is also some value as a method of teaching in setting pupils to assess and comment upon each other's work. But, before doing so, some simple preliminary guidance for pupils is desirable – in particular when asking them to assess other pupils' essays – some indication of what features to look for, what markings to make and what criteria to adopt. Here is a typical scheme, taken from a guide-sheet issued to sixth-formers in their first term.

*A short guide-sheet to the critical appraisal of an historical essay*
I.   Using a pencil, or a pen with ink of a different colour from that of the essay writer, write the following at the top of the essay:

MARKER:                SUGGESTED MARK OR GRADE:

II.   Read through the essay with the following points in mind:
   1. CONTENT
Put a small tick in the margin of the essay whenever the writer has made a good point or a telling comment, or used an apt quotation. Then compile on the back page of the essay a list of omissions, i.e. those points either essential or highly desirable, which seem to have received inadequate or no mention. Put crosses against errors of fact.
   2. RELEVANCE
Mark "R" in the margin of the essay where the writer is obviously wandering from the point. For example, if the title of the essay is concerned with the causes of a war, then matter describing its campaigns may be irrelevant.
   3. STYLE
Indicate infelicities of style, together with mistakes of spelling, punctuation and grammar in whatever way seems appropriate. Correct these where this is easy to effect. Give credit by means of ticks in the margin where there is a neat turn of phrase, and also where the form of the argument is convincing as, for instance, where generalised assertions are supported by particular facts, e.g. 'Pitt was a good judge of men; he promoted relatively junior officers such as Hawke and Wolfe who won victories over the French in 1759.'

III.   At the end of the essay write a helpful general comment about the essay, and suggest a provisional overall mark or grade for the essay based on the standards to which you have become accustomed.

Forming the class into a large discussion group – to talk on such questions as, for example, why enclosures took place – is another way of helping to ensure the participation of all pupils in what is going on, especially if the last part of such a lesson is used by pupils to summarise in writing the points made during the discussion. Alternatively, the class can be divided into a number of small discussion groups, each of which has first to debate and then to recommend, in writing, answers to questions such as, 'In what way can the United Kingdom government best help the preservation of the environment?' Some introductory remarks explaining the meaning and scope of such questions are called for from the teacher, and also he should make the cautionary stipulation that group recommendations must be supported by argument and facts and are not to be comprised merely of unsupported opinions.

In group work of this sort the hope is that the more able and voluble pupils, as well as being able to practise leadership in the discussions, will also be able to help the less talented and more retiring to take an interest in the subject matter and to learn from them. Moreover, the reading aloud of the final reports, either to each group for group criticism, or to the whole class for general assessment, can, if the atmosphere is conducive, be a valuable exercise, not only for the authors of the reports, but as much for those who make the critical appraisals. It is through listening to other people's work in this way, hearing it commented upon and having to criticise it himself, that a pupil can gain insight into how to improve his own work, and be encouraged to apply to it the criticisms which he has heard levelled at others.

**Use of reading aloud**

Reading aloud from a textbook by the teacher, or by pupils in turn around the class, is not likely to produce a very inspiring lesson, unless the passage has unusual interest or is exceptionally gripping. However, with the more academic pupils, if the teacher interposes his own thought-provoking commentaries and questions, the method may make useful training in critical thinking. Reading aloud by the teacher is justifiable occasionally, where the interest in the subject matter or the style in the writing are exceptional. For instance, extracts from the entry in Pepys' diary for 2nd September 1666 concerning the Fire of London, or from C. Woodham Smith's *The Reason Why* (Penguin Books, London, 1963), describing Lord Cardigan's charge at Balaclava (pp. 237–53) are so dramatic that, if read well, they can be appreciated as much by the sixth form as by the junior school. Pictures of the Fire, and a diagram of the Battle of Balaclava reproduced on the roller board or the blackboard, or projected from a slide or overhead projector, will add understanding and interest during these readings. Another way is to pre-record these readings on tape, which enables the teacher to ensure that the reading is a good one, and also ensures, by the adjustment of volume and tone controls when playing back to the class, that the reproduction is of arresting quality. But reading aloud from class textbooks, which, alas, are all too often uninspiringly written, rarely seems worthwhile. But there may be a case with the less academic pupil for a small amount of guided study of passages from textbooks, explaining the meaning of words and phrases as the reading progresses. This technique may help to improve pupils' vocabulary and to compensate for their reading difficulties while teaching them some history at the same time.

## Use of maps

Maps have long been recognised as an integral part of teaching history, and most modern textbooks include them. But historical atlases tend to be expensive so that it is difficult to justify each pupil being issued with one of his own, and one set, which can be shared between classes, may be the only feasible solution. An inexpensive atlas is Wheaton's *Atlas of British and World History.* More useful but costly are Philips' *Intermediate Historical Atlas* and Muir's *New School Historical Atlas.* N. Catchpole's *A Map History of the Modern World* is helpful, as also is Harrap's series of *Sketch-Map Histories* by G. Taylor, I. Richards and B. Goodson. Maps are of more value in some topics than in others, of course. For example, it can be quite dramatic to compare a population and production map of Britain in 1751 with one a hundred years later, important to know where the mountain ranges lie in relation to political boundaries in a topic such as the 1938 Sudeten question, and virtually impossible to understand the fifteenth- and sixteenth-century voyages of discovery without a map of the routes.

In this connection, it is worth remarking that it is not necessarily a waste of time for pupils to copy maps and diagrams from their textbooks or from the blackboard into their files or notebooks. Although not mentally very stimulating, it can be reasonably argued not only that the activity is surprisingly satisfying to the majority of pupils, but also that it is often only when compelled to draw maps and diagrams freehand that pupils gain sufficient incentive to observe them closely. In any case, most pupils delight in and learn something from copying of this sort, and it seems needlessly restrictive of those teachers who deny their pupils the pleasure and the opportunity. The main difficulty likely to be met is finding maps worth copying, because many of those in textbooks are often surprisingly and disappointingly inadequate. Yet the study of topics such as the Crimean War, the Indian Mutiny, and the Boer War calls for clear maps showing all the relevant detail without which a full understanding of the topics is hardly possible. One answer is for the teacher to draw and then to duplicate such maps on the spirit duplicator, or to make drawings for the overhead projector. If this is done, the need for an historical atlas for each pupil is even less. Commercially-produced wall-maps are of some value, but most suffer from being too small in scale and too confusing in detail. Irritatingly, they pre-suppose excellent sight, and two metres from a wall are often only a muddled blur. Too often they spend their lives unregarded, gracing classroom walls or uselessly gathering dust in stockroom corners. Some wall-charts supplied commercially are so anxious to be thought authentic that they fail to make any clear impact at all, whilst others use so minute a type, that they are hardly legible even close at hand. In these circumstances, it is certainly good advice to inspect such wall-maps before deciding to purchase them.

### Use of textbooks

The need for each pupil to have at his disposal more than one textbook cannot be overstressed. In this way he can be confronted with varying and sometimes opposed points of view, and perhaps with apparently contradictory facts. In an elementary way he is thus introduced to the problems of the use of historical evidence and can begin to understand the nature of history. Valuable exercises in collecting and arranging facts, reasons, causes, and opinions are made easier and more meaningful; the boredom deriving from the continual use of the same textbook through one or more school years, which is bad both for teacher and pupil, is avoided.

Though it is customary for each boy in a class to have a copy of one particular book, in order that certain common reading exercises, particularly for homework, can be undertaken, it is not necessary or desirable for the same additional history textbook to be held by every boy. It is far better to have sets of books in small quantities. The first six or seven pupils in the class can have one second textbook, the next six or seven another, and so on. If this cannot be done because of financial considerations, one other book may be shared between two, three or four boys. Books with a mainly chronological approach can be offset by books arranged by topics, whilst sets of source books are also useful. Contrasts in style, content, depth of intellectual approach, and arrangement, all help to keep interest in the subject fresh. There is much to be said for books which encourage selection because there is more in them than can be used; they become quarries for information.

The qualities to be looked for in choosing a history textbook for a class are that it should be accurate and up-to-date, and well written in a style and vocabulary adapted to the age of the reader. Books which also *look* up-to-date and attractive should be sought. A suitable textbook for junior and middle forms should be arranged in chapters of about ten pages each and be sufficiently full to engage the attention of the pupil for a considerable time. Far too many junior textbooks can be read from cover to cover by any intelligent child in a few hours, and thereafter become a bore. The book chosen should be clearly printed and should contain plenty of maps and illustrations. Here it may be noted that modern line drawings and photographs are more acceptable to the juvenile mind than reproductions of contemporary prints, however attractive these may be to the adult historian. All illustrations should be clear, absolutely correct in detail, should add to, summarise, or elucidate the text, and should appear where they are relevant. In his choice the history specialist will also, of course, be influenced by the special needs of his own syllabus.

Some teachers like textbooks with paragraph headings within the chapters, though others would think that this results in too rigid a presentation of material. Many feel that books consisting entirely of 'notes' or containing full chapter summaries in note form are to be avoided, but others think that, although a poor teacher can abuse them, such books can be of help to a good teacher if he uses them as a kind of dictionary and never sets work which the pupil may fulfil by learning a summary or making extensive use of it. For all textbooks a detailed index is essential, and this applies even to those used in the most junior of forms.

### Use of resources centres and museum loans

To assist teachers in the choice of resources some authorities, such as the I.L.E.A., have set up media resources centres, not for the loan of materials to schools, but where what is available commercially can be viewed by teachers who work for that authority. The I.L.E.A. Media Resources Centre (Highbury Station Road, Islington, London, N.1.) has a carefully catalogued library of books, records, tape-recordings, films, and film-strips, together with facilities for listening to tapes and records and for viewing films and film-strips. This centre enables teachers in the I.L.E.A. to see, grouped together under one roof, a comprehensive range of teaching materials for them to order by way of departmental allowances. Other areas have loan systems; Reading supplies facsimile reproductions of museum materials conveniently packed in brown suit-

FIG. 17. *Textbook illustrations: (a) Lloyd's Coffee House
(b) East India Factory, Surat*

cases, and obligingly delivers them from the museum to local schools on request. Reading Museum is fortunate in possessing much of the Silchester Collection, and its museum directorate is enterprising enough to have constructed many facsimiles of these. They can add much to lessons on Roman Britain, and since they are returned to the Museum after use, present no storage problems to schools.[1] If neither the L.E.A. nor the school has a resources centre, then a departmental one is desirable, where atlases, tape-recordings, film-strips, records, wall-charts, models, magazines and duplicated materials of the department can be stored ready for use. In addition, most teachers usually build up their own stocks of materials and visual-and-oral aids, in the same way as they accumulate their own personal libraries and notes, but help and cooperation in this field within a school department can obviously greatly increase the resources available to each member.

Such cooperative sharing also assists in the use of limited sets of textbooks and increases the possibility of using a wider range of books with the same financial outlay. Whilst some teachers manage without a textbook copy for each pupil, especially in the sixth form where the price of books is usually higher than elsewhere, most teachers prefer to use a general class textbook, supplemented by as wide a variety of topic books and other resources as is available and can be afforded. One common supplement is to issue pupils with sets of duplicated notes, but the value and wisdom of this depends largely on the quality of these notes and the ability of the pupils to use them. Where notes are dictated they should always be short and confined to essentials, for there is little interest evoked by mere copying. Some note-taking is necessary in many subjects, but nothing blunts a pupil's interest more quickly than a lengthy dictation lesson. Some copying of notes from the black-board may be justified, especially at the beginning of a course, as an example to pupils of how to compile notes for themselves, and where precise wording is important as in a definition or quotation. Pupils should be cautioned against the making of 'rough notes', unless these are to be used immediately for working-up into some essay or formal presentation. The trouble with many 'rough notes' is that they are often barely legible and lose their meaning very rapidly with the passage of time. In this connection, the ability to make notes, both on lectures and on books, is a useful accomplishment, and one in which every pupil can benefit from some instruction. If a lecture-type lesson is given, it is sometimes worthwhile collecting pupils' notes at the end of the period, not only as a humbling

[1] An article in *Teaching History* (Nov. 1971) provides further information on museum loan services.

check on the efficacy of the lecture, but in order to help pupils in the difficult art of note compilation by inspection and criticism of their efforts. Initially, pupils can be helped in this by the teacher writing on the blackboard the sub-headings of the points pupils should be recording as the lesson progresses, and also by him indicating verbally the points in his lecture of which he feels pupils should be taking a written note. In this way a framework is provided for them, but the notes still have to be inserted individually by each pupil. This ensures attention and is more valuable than just dictating notes, because each pupil still has to compose his own and is not just mechanically copying his teacher's.

Some advice should also be given to pupils on note-making from books – a procedure which often helps pupils to learn, clarify, and sort out material as they read it. The teacher could begin by constructing on the blackboard under the gaze of his pupils a note on a section of their class textbook. He can demonstrate to them where to choose paragraph headings, what to abbreviate, and how to use the various conventional note-making devices such as sub-headings, numbered points, indentations, paragraphs, underlines, and the use of colour for purposes of emphasis and discrimination.

The making of notes can be one of the most boring methods for pupils of studying history. At the same time, it is a most valuable technique to learn in its own right, and gives practice in sifting and sorting information into logical sequences and homogeneous groups – the basis, it could be argued, of any ordered system of acquiring knowledge.

## Use of a lesson-plan

A teacher also has to consider his own notes and lesson-plans, the preparation of which can entail a great deal of work. Here is an example of lesson-notes designed to cover two forty-minute class periods and one thirty-minute homework. The selection of the material to be presented is, of course, to some extent the personal choice of each teacher. Moreover, these notes are probably fuller than would be required in practice. Nevertheless, they provide some indication of the type of preparation which can be found useful. The age range of the pupils is junior secondary and the topic is 'Towns in Roman Britain'. The notes have been expanded to include some detailed explanation as to how the two lessons might be conducted:

*Previous topic*: The Roman invasion of Britain (Caesar, Claudian Conquest, Roman roads, Hadrian's Wall, etc.).
*Present topic*: Roman towns in Britain

*Material*: Wall-map of Roman Britain hung over blackboard. Photos, diagrams and maps as indicated.

Synopsis of introductory remarks:

No towns in Britain before the Romans. Roman towns were pocket-sized copies of cities in Italy. Built mainly in settled zone, south of Fosse Way (show this on wall-map). London founded about AD 61 at lowest point where Thames could be bridged. Burnt down in Boadicea's rising in AD 65. London the only town not to be destroyed or deserted in the fifth century when the Romans left Britain and the fierce, pagan Anglo-Saxons invaded this country and drove the Britons into the hills of the west and north, and settled on river banks in villages of wooden halls and mud and wattle cottages. Romans came to rule the Britons, unlike other invaders who came to replace them. Roman legions enforced peace over all the south of Britain for the first time. Romans stormed fortified hill villages like Maiden Castle, then deserted them and built towns at camps or where rivers could be forded. Procedure: Draw a sketch on the blackboard (see Fig. 18) using many colours of chalk, and describe each of the following features as they are inserted:

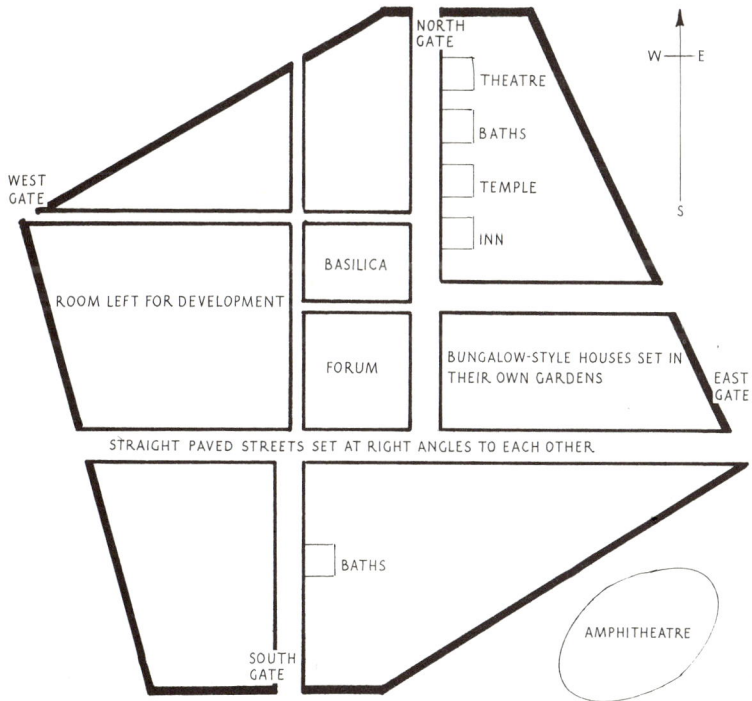

FIG. 18. *Blackboard sketch to show the principal features of a Roman town in Britain*

1. Walls around town (some still standing, e.g. Exeter, Colchester, Silchester).

2. Gates.

3. Amphitheatre (chariot races, bear baiting, open-air sports arena, outside town).

4. Theatre (one at St Albans – show picture).

5. Baths. (Romans taught Britons to wash but habit lost after fifth century. Our ancestors are the 'great unwashed' till development of modern sanitation.) These baths similar to present-day Turkish baths but social centres as well. (Show picture of Roman baths at Bath.)

6. Forum – market place and social centre.

7. Basilica – administrative centre, something like modern town-hall and courts of justice.

8. Streets. Paved, straight, set at right angles (similar in lay-out to a modern American city).

9. Temple (later there would be a Christian church, perhaps).

10. Inns.

11. Houses – detached, often of bungalow type, set apart, surrounded by a garden plot, stone built, windows with thick translucent glass, piped water with taps (aqueducts to bring water to town), drainage, mosaic floors, gabled roofs with slates or red tiles, plastered walls with frescoes, statues, round dining-tables, couches for reclining while dining, no chimneys or fireplaces in walls, doors with locks and keys, etc.

(1st lesson completed now by pupils drawing a copy of their own Roman town-plan in their exercise-books or files and labelling the features. Those who finish before the end of the period are asked to start reading the relevant chapter in their textbook.)

2nd lesson

1. Revise previous lesson by producing large wall-diagram of a plan of Silchester and pointing to features of the town. Explain that Silchester is the only Roman town in Britain fully excavated because no modern town has been built on the site. (Much of our knowledge of Roman times comes from unearthing their rubbish pits, often accidentally discovered when sinking foundations of large new office blocks – mention temple to Mithras found in London.)

2. Show aerial photograph of modern view of Silchester. The street plan can be clearly made out from the air. The crops in the present-day fields appear slightly darker where the roads ran.

3. Mention any local finds from Roman times, including any villas. Accept if any pupil suggests bringing some Roman coins to show the class. Pin up on the classroom notice-board a local newspaper cutting about a boy who found a piece of Roman pottery in a ditch at his home.

4. No complete Roman house found in Britain; often only the foundations and the heating-chambers with which larger town houses and villas in the countryside were equipped. (Put title, and draw rapid diagram (see Fig. 19) on blackboard, explaining while drawing.)

5. With the class looking at their textbooks, go through the illustrations in the chapter on Roman Britain (if any) commenting on them and emphasising the main points about each.

6. Any questions? (max. five minutes).

7. Allow class to make their own rapid diagrammatic illustration of hypocaust heating in a Roman house, possibly putting in the room a Roman wearing the ceremonial toga, together with a dining-table, fresco, couch,

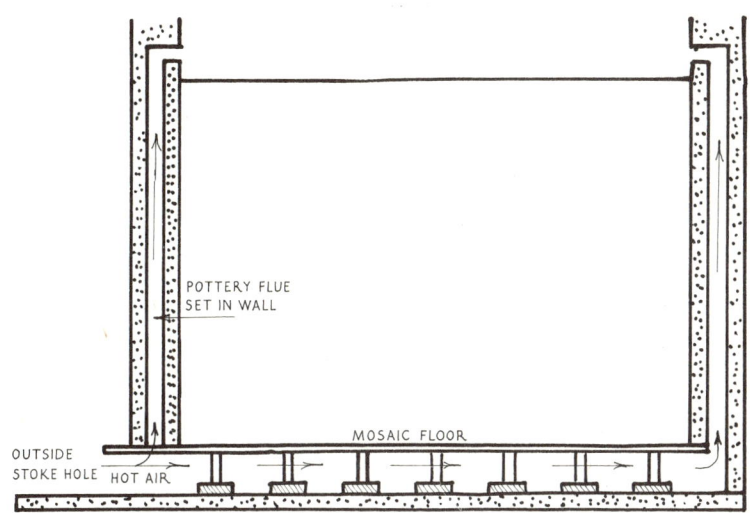

FIG. 19. *Blackboard diagram of Roman hot-air central heating system*

statue, etc., if pupils feel artistically inclined (allow about ten minutes for this).

8. Then set the homework: a composition on 'What a Roman town in Britain was like'. Explain briefly what is required in an essay with this title to prevent irrelevance.

9. Then, for the remainder of the period, ask class to finish reading to themselves the chapter in the class textbook on Roman towns.

If pressed for time, reading the chapter in the textbook could be set for homework instead of the essay, letting the class know that there would be a test next time of from ten to twenty short-answer questions based on the chapter and the work covered in class. If the reading prep. is set, normally the class would also be asked to finish any diagrams that any of the slower ones may not have completed, provided this does not make the prep. too long.

It might be objected that the pupils could gain much of the material information given in class by reading it for themselves in their textbook. The answer to this is that the textbook will approach the matter from another viewpoint, that it may not provide the same information that the teacher considers important, and that when reiteration takes place this helps to reinforce the pupil's learning. It is not just simple repetition, but repeating the information in different ways making use of many of the senses. The pupil is told about the amphitheatre, for example, in the first lesson; then sees it drawn on the blackboard in the diagram; then draws it himself in his own diagram. In the second lesson, he is reminded of it when observing the large wall-diagram of Silchester which is shown to the form; then he reads about it in the textbook; and, finally, he writes a composition including it, or prepares for a test in which one of the questions will mention it. He can hardly fail at least to have heard of a Roman amphitheatre after that.

### Use of drama

The use of drama in teaching history is often neglected, mainly because it is time-consuming, liable to promote noise and disorder with difficult classes, needs plenty of space, and lacks suitable scripts available commercially. (For a discussion on the use of drama generally see *Teaching History* (November 1970), pp. 303–6.) A solution may be for teachers to write their own playlets, or to promote play-writing by pupils, but resulting productions of the latter are unlikely to be notable dramatic successes. Many plays which are available tend to be concerned mainly with character conflicts, whereas history plays can also be used to describe historical movements – or famous battles – where the interest is not so much in the fate of individuals, but is concerned with an episode as a whole.

The dramatic method may lack the cutting edge of the lecture lesson in dealing with a topic, but the technique when used well can convey complex situations with economy of words in an exciting, easily understandable and memorable manner.

As an example of the type of dramatic playlet that a history teacher might devise, one for the 11–13 age groups is included in Appendix 1. While not neglecting action, the playlet is designed to produce some understanding of what happened in England in 1066, and especially of the sequence of events. It is followed by a twenty-question quiz, the purpose of which is to help induce attention during the play reading, and to serve as a follow up, reminding pupils again of much of the play's material.

# Methods and materials II

5

## Use of film

Films for history teaching suitable for showing in schools generally fall into three main types. First there are the big productions made for the cinema, of which old but famous examples are Laurence Olivier's version of Shakespeare's *Henry V* and Robert Bolt's *Becket*. This sort of film is hardly suitable for class use on account of its length, unless shown in sections when continuity is lost. Such films really require the use of the school hall and a complete afternoon or evening devoted to them. The second type of film comprises the numerous short instructional films such as *The Civil War in England*, *The Medieval Castle* and *The Bayeux Tapestry*. These films range in length from about ten to thirty minutes and devote themselves to a single theme, making good use of diagrams, dynamic demonstrations and instructive, if faintly amusing, animated arrows. They are suitable for use in class as integral parts of lessons, ideally being shown after rather than before work has been done on the topics they cover, so that what has been explained in class can be watched for on the film, and thus fixed more firmly in the mind. The film on *The Medieval Castle*, for instance, fits in well as one of a series of lessons on methods of attacking and defending medieval castles, demonstrating these more clearly and interestingly than can be achieved by other available methods. Moreover, group visits to castles are likely to take on a new significance; after viewing the film, pupils can hardly fail to have an appreciation of what features of a castle they should be looking for.

The third group of films comprises the larger number of short incidental films, some made by private companies, usually for advertising purposes, such as, for example, *The History of the Discovery of Oxygen* by I.C.I., others made by bodies with a social purpose, such as *English Criminal Justice: How the Law is Administered* made by Rank for the British Council, and films made by numerous agencies for all sorts of purposes and, perhaps most prominently, those made by the B.B.C. who publish a free catalogue (B.B.C. Enterprises Film Hire, 25 The Burroughs, Hendon, London, N.W.4). The quality and usefulness of these films varies greatly, so it is only prudent for a teacher to have seen the films and

satisfied himself as to their suitability for his purpose before order-
ing them for his pupils, or at least to have been given favourable
reports on the films from respected sources. A useful booklet is produced by the Film Committee of the Historical Association called
*The Use of Film in History Teaching* (1972) by N. Pronay, B. R.
Smith and T. Hastie, which gives guidance on the use of film, a
list of helpful addresses, and a short summary of catalogues available and a list of the distributors of films likely to be of interest to
history teachers, but does not include criticism of individual films.[1]

Many films may be hired by schools from the National Audio-
Visual Aids Library, Paxton Place, Gipsy Road, London, SE27
9SS, who also have some films, such as the *History of Europe since
1945* which are obtainable on free loan. There also exists a large
collection of historical films which can be seen free of charge at
the cinema of the Imperial War Museum, a facility of much value
for those schools close enough to London for their pupils to make
the visit.

### Use of tape-recorder

Films have probably been overtaken in popularity as an aid to
the teaching of history by the tape-recorder, now regarded as almost
essential by many history teachers who find it convenient and easy
to use, since it needs no special requirement such as blackout which
always limits the use of film. The best source of tape programmes
is radio and television, programmes recorded from the latter often
showing little loss from the absence of what is frequently merely an
intrusive picture. Television programmes may, however, need edit-
ing or re-recording using a second tape-recorder to eliminate silent
patches. Tape-recordings can also be made by reading extracts
from books with a teacher's own comments added, or composed by
groups of pupils who can gain much from the preparation of material
which they then record for general class use later.

An example of this use is the class group who made up a recorded
quiz based on a period of history which had recently been studied
by the whole class, each question consisting of a series of five progressively easier clues. Those pupils who wrote down the right
answer on hearing the first clue awarded themselves five marks;
if they got the right answers on the second clue, then they gained
four marks; but if they only gained the answer on the last clue,

[2] Such criticism can be found in *Feature Films and the History Teacher*
produced by the London History Teachers' Association and available from
the History and Social Sciences Teachers' Centre, 377 Clapham Road, London
SW9 9BT.

which was absurdly easy, then they could only score one mark. The advantage of this type of test is that it has similarities with a party game and borrows from that genre some fun to aid the learning process. Moreover, since some marks are scored by nearly everybody in each question, there is no sense of total failure or any lack of achievement, all pupils gaining the correct answer eventually by the time of the fourth or fifth clue. At the same time those who gain the right answer at the first or second clue often feel a sense of particular success, which reinforces their desire to continue with such work. A variation of this is to project slides on to the classroom screen, reading out progressively easier clues as to what the slides represent until everyone has the correct answer, scoring as for the tape-recorder readings.

The ways in which a teacher can use tape-recordings may conveniently be divided into five main groups:

(1) *The inspirational lead* – for example, Neville Chamberlain's broadcast at 11.15 a.m. on 3 September 1939, would be an arresting start to a lesson on the beginning of the Second World War.

(2) *The information tape* – for example, those made from the B.B.C. Contemporary History Series or from the B.B.C. *Scrapbooks*, which tend to be mixtures of narrative and reminiscence.

(3) *The dramatic reconstruction* – episodes from history, dramatised, such as those recorded from the B.B.C. *History in Evidence* series which is based on original sources.

(4) *The analytical discussion* – such as those produced commercially by Sussex Tapes, or produced in the school by a scholarship-sixth discussion group.

(5) *The school-made tape* – homespun productions, such as mock interviews, by the teacher or by his pupils. This use of the tape-recorder may be especially valuable with some less able pupils who often feel frustrated by their inability to communicate in writing, but may be surprisingly more confident when all they have to do is to talk.

A tape library in every school is highly desirable, either organised departmentally or as part of the school resources centre, or else located in the centres set up for groups of schools by some L.E.A.s. Such tapes can sometimes be loaned to a pupil who has missed a lesson through absence; he can take the tape home to play on his own tape-recorder, or, alternatively, he can listen to the tapes in class through a personal earphone without disturbing other pupils. Audio-distribution centres are in use in some schools, permitting six or more children using headphones to listen to the same tape, yet neither heard by nor disturbed by other pupils in the class. A tape-recorder can also be useful to a pupil who cannot write because of a sprained finger or other temporary injury, for he can use tape on which to record his essay. But it is inadvisable to permit many pupils to present their work in this form, if only because of the amount of the teacher's time that would be taken up in listening to them. On the other hand pupils may be encouraged to bring their own personal recorders to school to make their own tapes from the teacher's recorder; such a procedure enables pupils to have a record of their own for transcription at home later, and also, incidentally, often produces remarkably attentive pupils who seem as impressed by what has been recorded as they invariably are by what has been printed, as compared with what has merely been uttered.

There are two main types of tape-recorders. The cassette recorder is easy to load and to operate, is superbly portable, and can be battery operated. Unfortunately, it sometimes lacks sufficient volume. The deficiency can be compensated by using an external speaker, but this inevitably detracts from its portability. As yet, despite the overriding importance in schools of being able to hear clearly and listen attentively, architects do not design classrooms with sound quality or acoustic considerations primarily in mind, let alone with any thought of the effects in the room of sound produced by recorders. The result is that any cassette recorder of less than $1\frac{1}{2}$ watts output may be found to be inadequate. The other type of tape-recorder is the more robust reel-to-reel type, which has usually more power and sound quality, and is normally mains-operated. Teachers buying a recorder of this latter type for class use would be well advised to seek one which has an output of at least 5 watts. The Tandberg Series 15 (and subsequent models) can safely be recommended, for this recorder develops 7 watts through its internal speaker and 10 watts using an external speaker, which is adequate even for the school-hall. As it has a straight-through amplifier, it can also be used as public-address equipment.

### Use of episcope

Another important aid in the classroom is the episcope, by means of which the image of a page of any book can be projected on to a screen or wall of a classroom. The great advantage of using an episcope becomes apparent when the teacher compares the various ways in which, for instance, the sketch in the textbook showing the military campaign at Waterloo in 1815 could be shown to a class.

The teacher could:

(1) Make a photoslide and show it on the slide projector.

(2) Draw the sketch on an acetate roll and project it on the overhead projector.

(3) Draw it on the blackboard.

(4) Draw it on cartridge paper and wind it on a roller board.

(5) Draw the map on a spirit-duplicator stencil and roll off copies.

(6) Draw copies on a stencil for an ink duplicator.

(7) Produce enough copies of the book for each pupil to have one, or enough for groups of three or four pupils to have one.

(8) Hand round the book open at the appropriate page to each pupil in the class in turn.

(9) Try to show the map to all his pupils simultaneously (which would inevitably provoke a scrummage).

(10) Project the page by episcope on to a screen or wall.

If numbers 8 and 9 are the least satisfactory methods, number 10 is the one entailing the least inconvenience for the teacher. The American firm Vu-Lyte produce an episcope which throws a bright picture on the classroom screen in only semi-darkened conditions. The viewing field is at least ten inches (25 cm) square, which means that the instrument is capable of projecting a sheet of paper of up to this measurement. Although blackout is desirable, the episcope can be used in a classroom with sufficient light left on for a class of pupils to take notes and to make copies of the material projected. But episcopes are heavy to handle, tend to have somewhat noisy cooling-fans, and never produce an image even half as bright as a slide-projector or overhead projector. When they are moved, there is risk of damaging their lamps, which in any case have a limited life of between thirty and fifty hours. Episcopes do not usually have a choice of lens; one with a longer focal length would enable teachers to operate it from the back or middle of a classroom rather than from the front of a class, which is obligatory at present and is a less advantageous position for the teacher who is concerned about the maintenance of class control.

### Use of overhead projector

No comparable disciplinary disadvantage occurs in using the overhead projector because its greater brightness of picture helps to induce attention. These versatile projection machines enable the teacher to face his pupils and project what he is writing, at the moment he is writing it, on to a screen behind and above him. He can use colour and prepare material on acetate rolls before the lesson, or on separate sheets which can be super-imposed upon one another for some effect. Cooling fans are fairly quiet although still somewhat distracting, but no blackout at all is required. Models with the latest three-element lens project a remarkably crisp and clear image. Commercially produced transparencies and overlays for overhead projectors are costly, but home-made or school-made products may be the answer. In this connection it is really worthwhile for every history teacher to become something of a technician, not only learning how to work apparatus efficiently but also how to make materials himself. But this does not obviate the crying need of most history teachers for more technical and secretarial assistance, without which the use of many materials and equipment becomes unacceptably burdensome. In any case, however produced, overlays can be used to produce action-pictures on the magic-lantern principle enabling, for example, the workings of Newcomen's Atmospheric Engine to be demonstrated. L. W. Cowie's overlay maps of Germany, 1815–1945, are expensive, but an excellent and clear way of showing the development of Germany with the use of the overhead projector.

## Use of copying machines

Copying machines are an important adjunct for every history teacher. The spirit duplicator, because of its supreme ease of operation, is a first requirement, for it will produce up to a hundred clear copies of anything written on its inexpensive stencil. By varying the carbons, a mixture of colours can be obtained, and if the final product is rarely superb, the ease and speed with which it has been produced more than compensates. Outline maps for pupils to insert into their own files and fill in individually are easy to produce on the spirit duplicator.

For use with a typewriter, an ink duplicator is to be preferred, for it gives a clearer result. The number of copies obtainable runs into thousands and, by using a stylus and a backing sheet, teachers with steady hands can write as satisfactorily on ink duplicator stencils as they can on spirit duplicator sheets. Other copiers tend to be more elaborate; the chemical diffusion transfer copiers require a sink and water supply nearby, and the electronic duplicator, which will make a stencil in black and white from just about anything including photographs, is much more expensive both to purchase and to run. Most large schools have copying facilities centralised and handled by specialist administrative staff, and this makes the production of such materials more convenient and less subject to stencil and paper wastage. It also preserves the machines from injurious handling by inexpert staff.

### Use of video-recorders

Live television and radio broadcasts are familiar in most schools, and articles in *Teaching History* for May and November 1970 serve as useful guides. A remaining problem, however, is reconciling the timing of television broadcasts with appropriate history periods. Video-tape recorders, and especially the colour cassette ones, are an answer to this, for they are of a convenient size, and simply record from and play back through a normal colour television set merely by plugging into the set's aerial socket. They enable any television programme to be recorded at one time and played back at a more suitable or convenient time. They can also be used for closed circuit television purposes, displaying close-up pictures of, for example, flint tools, pottery pieces, and bone fragments found on archaeological sites for all pupils to see simultaneously. Other uses of the video-tape recorder include filming, either of a topic such as the French Revolution (excellently done by sixth formers at one school where a twenty-minute film was made from still pictures), or of an outside item such as a group visit to a local castle. Such a film not only provides good educational experience for the film-makers, but can be relayed to other classes at school, showing possibly an exciting item such as a portcullis actually being raised with, as bonus interest, Joseph Bloggs of Form III doing the winding. But one current operational drawback to the use of video-recorders is the relatively high price of the tapes. The preservation of video-tapes for future use on the same scale as is now possible with aural tapes would make the cost of using the video-recorder prohibitive, with the present unfortunate result that often valuable video-tape material has to be erased in order to make room for other television programmes to be recorded on the same tape.

The video-tape recorder also enables the history teacher to make his own television programmes, and all that is needed as equipment is a television camera, a video-tape recorder, an easel and a television monitor. The compilation of the film script will probably offer the most educationally valuable part of the film-making process, needing to be planned in three parts – vision, narrative and sound – each of which offers scope for historical research and consequent learning. There is no need to use pupil-actors, as the documentary approach, relying upon photographs, maps, diagrams and print, can be most effective. Up to 200 separate pictures is quite a reasonable number for a thirty-minute programme, but by zooming the camera lens in upon details, one photograph can sometimes be made to serve a number of television pictures. Letter transfers can be used for names and captions, while plastic squares, circles, stars and arrows are available commercially from such agents as the Visual Aids Centre, High Holborn, London WC1; these are useful for attaching to maps and diagrams.

Making such a film, whether the topic be a dramatic one such as the French Revolution or the Battle of Trafalgar, or one relying mainly on diagrams and drawings, such as the extension of the franchise, the film-making process automatically imposes upon pupils a natural discipline demanding teamwork and attention to detail, both educationally desirable – and the whole procedure can also be great fun, if somewhat costly.

Such financial considerations rarely limit the use of aural tapes, which are now inexpensive, especially those required only for the recording of speech as opposed to the more costly ones desirable for recording music. But there still remains the irksome problem of the Copyright Act of 1956 which seems needlessly and wastefully restrictive, permitting schools to keep recorded educational radio programmes (other than Open University programmes) only for one year (and radiovision programmes for three years), after which, strictly speaking, they should be destroyed.

## Use of film-strip and slide projectors

Film-strip and slide projectors are well-established aids to history teachers, but some blackout is normally required when using them, and even allegedly daylight projectors benefit greatly from some room darkening. The strips are produced commercially in abundance, but frequently include some frames which most teachers find that they would not themselves have chosen. Strips can, however, be cut up and the separate pictures put into slide holders, and in this way choice of visual material is decided by the teacher. But the task is time-consuming and may best be left to the school's ancillary staff, if available, as may the making of slides by photographing illustrated material (providing copyright laws are not infringed). By taking a 35mm camera on holidays, many teachers supplement school slides with their own snapshots of historical sites they visit; alternatively, if photography is not a teacher's bent, most monuments, such as Stonehenge or Audley End, for instance, sell sets of colour slides which are likely to give clearer pictures than amateur slides. But by whatever means slides are obtained, it is advisable to compile written notes to accompany them, or to write briefly on the frame of each slide what it represents. Hand-viewers for pupils using slides for individual project work can also be useful when numbers involved are few.

## Use of recorders and pre-recorded tapes

Tapes and records are, of course, talk unrelieved even by chalk. A. J. P. Taylor produced a series of three records which contained six twenty-minute talks on *Six Prime Ministers*, and in these he maintains attention by sheer lecturing skill. But even his lectures are inappropriate with junior secondary pupils or with other than academically-inclined pupils, and recorded history discussions between experts such as can be heard on Sussex Tapes are expensive and often of a dauntingly high level. Audio-Learning Ltd, 84 Queensway, London W2, produce similar taped history discussions but recordings from Open University programmes are sometimes notably simpler and more suitable for upper forms. In practice, nearly every history teacher really needs his own personal recorder so that he is in a position to make recordings from radio and television as they arise when he is at home, for it is a common experience to find that many of the best programmes are broadcast only at a late evening hour when all good pupils are asleep.

A magazine supplied to most schools is *Visual Education* (the official magazine of National Audio-Visual Aids in Education, 33 Queen Anne Street, London W1M 0AL), which describes the latest developments in teaching hardware. A useful address for all history teachers to know is the National Audio-Visual Aids Centre, 254–256 Belsize Road, London NW6. Here all the latest audio-visual aids are tested and may be inspected by teachers, but they may not be purchased here, although the staff of the Centre will always advise teachers where they can be obtained and how much they cost. The Centre publishes a free catalogue of all its audio-visual equipment and it would seem highly desirable for all history teachers to have access also to the following three catalogues, which are revised every other year and may be purchased from the Centre:

(1) Part 2 of the *National Catalogue of Films, Film Strips, etc.* (this section covers multi-media material on history, social studies, etc.).
(2) *A Catalogue of Wall-Charts.*
(3) *A Catalogue of Records and Tapes for Education.*

Pre-recorded tapes and records are widely used in history teaching today and some packages are offered combining slides with tapes or records, the latter serving as commentaries to the slides. But the teaching quality varies enormously and it is advisable to sample the goods before purchase rather than rely on any description. However, the following can be recommended: the Apollo Society's *History Reflected* series of long-playing records produced by Argo (Decca Record Co., 115 Fulham Road, London SW3), which has some useful titles including *Agincourt, Elizabeth I and the Armada, Charles I, Liberty-Equality-Fraternity, The Great Exhibition* and *World Wars I and II*; Discourses' record by A. J. P. Taylor on *The Bolshevik Revolution* (10a High Street, Tunbridge Wells, Kent); and Wren's Educational Record Library's talks on *Wales and Her History* and *Keir Hardie and The Rise of the Labour Party* (Wren Records, Llandybie, Wales). B.B.C. Publications (39 Marylebone High Street, London W1M 4AA) are producing an increasing number of historical records including such titles as (1) *History 1917–1971*, (2) *Richard and Blondel*, (3) *Drake around the World*, (4) *The Coming of War 1939*, and (5) *Ghandi*. Discourses also supply a record entitled *Chamberlain and Munich*. The Decca Record Co. has a series called *People, Past and Present* with titles which include *Pepys, Queen Victoria, Mary Queen of Scots* and *Charles II*. Records accompanying slides are produced by Audio-Visual Ltd, 5 Rosemont Road, Hampstead, London NW3; they include a useful historical set entitled *London*.

### Use of magazines, stamps, posters and music

Illustrations and series booklets can be of great help, especially with the use of an episcope. In this connection *Pictorial Education*, Purnell's *History of the Twentieth Century, Look and Learn, Knowledge*, BBC/Time Life's *History of the British Empire, History Today* and various historical newspapers are all valuable examples. *Then Ltd*, 28 James Street, Covent Garden, London WC2 E8PA, have put together, in the form of a journal, one year at a time from Britain's past; this includes contemporary diaries, letters, photographs and articles. Their journal for 1901 is a particularly good example. *Peter Way Ltd*, 28 James Street, Covent Garden, London WC2 E8PA, reproduce single issues of newspapers from the past. Their reproduction of *The Daily Herald* for 1 October 1938, is useful when dealing with the Munich Crisis. Allen and Unwin produce a number of four-page mock newspapers for years of great moment between 1493 and 1914. These are ideal for lower and middle secondary pupils, with easy-to-read articles, advertisements, stop press items and pictures – not genuine source material but the next best thing to it.

Use can also be made of posters, cartoons, postcards and photographs. The Imperial War Museum, for instance, has available a large number of reproductions of photographs taken during the Great War. Educational Productions Ltd, 27 Maunsel Street, London SW1, produce a poster called *Communication in Stamps* of interest to philatelist historians.

Contemporary music helps create the atmosphere of a period of history in many different ways, from playing the *1812 Overture* to accompany the story of the Moscow Campaign, to playing a recording of *Deep Lancashire* by the Oldham Tinkers in lessons on the growth of the textile mills in the Industrial Revolution. Other examples are *La Marseillaise* for the French Revolution, and *Oh What a Lovely War!* songs from the Great War. That marvellous piece Mars, the opening movement from Gustav Holst's suite *The Planets* composed in 1914, seems almost prophetic of the carnage to come, and many have felt that the syncopated rhythm and frenzy of Ragtime was a reflection of the changing world in the early twentieth century. See *Handbook for History Teachers*, pp. 673–87, for other suggestions on ways of introducing music into the teaching of history.

## Use of debates

Planned debates and talks by pupils are a means of introducing variety into lessons, but spontaneous discussions can also frequently become valuable. They sometimes arise from a question on current events which, if the teacher wishes, can serve as an excuse for sketching in the background to the affair. For example, trouble in the Middle East resulting in some headlined Arab–Israeli incident could be used to paint in the earlier history of Israel. Incredibly, there still exists some reluctance by some history teachers to talk about recent history, but most feel that tracing in the background to current affairs is an important responsibility of the history teacher, especially because of his belief, which he is inclined to use as justification for the study of the subject as a whole, that an appreciation of the past is a help to an understanding of the present. Re-enactment of past trials and war campaigns can also stimulate interest. In particular, prepared debates on subjects such as the 1832 Reform Bill, the views of the two sides in the American War of Independence, and the repeal of the Corn Laws are excellent ways of acquainting pupils with the division of views.

## Use of games

Games, such as Diplomacy, are an interesting diversion, but probably better played out of school in the History Society than in school in the classroom situation. They do not entertain all pupils, and may be difficult to play with large numbers or in a small space. Whether gaming is more educational in the wider sense than playing chess may be questioned, but for the dedicated few they have undoubted attraction. One drawback is that simulations of past events give little freedom for manoeuvre if they are to remain historically accurate. This can be overcome by playing games where players take freer roles, such as anonymous Merchant Adventurers for example, or attempt to act out a problem such as one of those which have plagued Ireland's history. *Games and Simulations*, a booklet published by B.B.C. Publications, is useful to those wanting to know how to play war games, as is the article in *Teaching History* Volume 1, No. 4 (November 1970), 303–8.

Charades is a miming game traditionally played at Christmas; it can occasionally be fun in a history lesson – historical clues and themes being obligatory, of course. The compilation of crosswords with historical clues, and their solving, can provoke interest, although such is more an end-of-term diversion than a regular teaching method. A more serious method requires pupils to construct test questions. This is not an easy task – as any G.C.E. examiner will readily confirm – and can be a valuable exercise. These may take the form of a list of questions on a topic or on a textbook chapter, carefully worded to admit of only one word or single phrase answer. A still harder task is to ask pupils to set questions requiring paragraph answers, but to be worded in such a way that the answers produced are analytical rather than factual. If the teacher then gives a test to the class selecting questions from their own compilations, on this occasion at least he will not be blamed by his pupils for asking the wrong questions, and the work of compilation will be seen by all as a fair and sensible, if unusual, method of preparation for the test that follows.

## Use of projects

Projects are a favourite method of teaching, because they keep pupils happily and gainfully employed at their own pace and in their own way, and seem to ease slightly the burden of taking the initiative in teaching. Their educational value is variable and arguable, but only when casually and improperly conducted can they be said to be soft options for the teacher. But such learning as does attend the enormous efforts pupils are liable to put into their projects is often incidental, slipshod and superficial, and if an examination question is asked relating to a pupil's project it is depressing how frequently it must be of the 'write anything at all you have learnt from your project' variety. Considerable guidance is usually necessary if projects are to have much value, and assignment sheets and work cards, coupled with the provision of adequate resources, are often essential. Merely to instruct pupils to do a general project on *Fashion*, for instance, and to leave them to get on with it, is to invite regurgitated passages from books and thoughtlessly-copied diagrams. It is much better to set a more specific and challenging task which requires research, such as 'Describe and illustrate trench warfare on the Western Front in the Great War and explain why it continued for so long'. The time set in which to perform a project can also be significant, for too long can mean that it drags, while too short may mean a very sketchy production; in any case a definite date for its completion is advisable. A useful guide for assessing topics is to mark them under the following six headings: relevance; amount and accuracy of detail; power of the illustrations to communicate; variety of sources and use made of materials; depth of analysis; and presentation of the whole. But many teachers abjure such arbitrary divisions and prefer to mark, if at all, simply on general impressions.

Projects can conveniently be divided into four types; wall-charts, project-booklets, special enquiries and model-making, in each of which group or individual work is possible. Wall-charts and models often make useful display items for teaching future classes and can be added to the school or departmental resources centre. Project-booklets are less useful in this respect, and can vary enormously, from work that looks good but upon analysis consists merely of interminable copyings, to original enquiries imaginatively presented. Some project-type work can be done in special enquiries by pupils recording interviews on tape or in notebooks of, for instance, grandfather's part in the General Strike of 1926, or his life in the trenches in 1917, or even just mother's reminiscences of her life at school in 'the old days'. These are first-hand testimonies to history which can be as valuable evidence as any other. Such oral history, as it is called, can take the form of a *This is Your Life* compilation, or it can be the result of interviews where the questions have been carefully planned beforehand. Grandparents often have a surprising affinity with their grandchildren, and are frequently pleased to have the opportunity to help provide materials to assist their grandchildren in the compilation of a history file on some national event which they can remember from their early lives. Another form of project is to take some local area, or perhaps just one building, and attempt to write a short history of it. This has the merit that original sources can often be consulted – the parish register if the building is a local church, for instance – and the nature of original sources, as contrasted with secondary works, is clearly demonstrated.

## Use of worksheets

The use of worksheets or cards with history projects is a method which helps pupils to work at their own pace and to sort out what they have to do in their own time. Probably the best arrangement is to give a lead lesson on a topic, followed by an assignment to each pupil which combines information and questions with references for materials. Such work of pupils should be regularly checked, because some pupils inevitably fall behind if this is neglected. Critical praise is required and possibly a markbook entry made whenever the work is presented. Textbooks may be allowed out of the classroom upon entries being made in a loan-book where the pupils' honesty and discipline standards are high enough but, where these are suspect, it may be prudent and save losses if drawing, deductive work from notes, and work from duplicated sheets is set for homework, leaving bookwork for class periods. A useful article on the use of worksheets and workcards can be found in *Teaching History* (May 1969).

For candidates taking external examinations it is advisable to prepare a sheet with full details of the period upon which they are to be examined, examples of the types of question papers they may expect (including, most importantly, the wording of the rubric), and possibly a selection of previous questions so that format and difficulty can be assessed individually by the candidates. It is a useful axiom with examination papers that familiarity helps to breed not contempt but confidence. In addition, a list of topics should be given, possibly accompanied by page references from one or two of the textbooks which have been recommended, for many pupils are quite unaware, not only of how to study and how to set about their work, but how much they should aim to cover in a given period of time. In this connection it is perhaps a pity to label all poorly performing pupils as non-academic, because lack of academic interest is not always an inescapable aspect of their natures, but sometimes means that they have never been instructed properly in what academic study really involves, and may therefore be a reflection as much of insufficient teaching as of inherent disability.

## Use of programmes

One way of helping such poor learners is programmed learning, but as a method of teaching history generally it has not so far been a commercial success. However, the technique may have value for a history teacher seeking a different approach, and the writing of programmes will inevitably and wonderfully increase, not only his knowledge of the topic, but also his ideas on how to present it. One simple linear method of programming is to duplicate sheets of factual material, followed, after every two or three sentences, by a question based on an understanding of the material immediately preceding it. The correct answers can appear staggered out of phase, in a column on the right, so that, when a cover sheet is placed over the paper, the answer to the first question is not in view until the second question is revealed. The merit in this method is that there are regular and frequent pauses in the acquisition of new knowledge as a check that what is read is being assimilated and understood. The questions also help to prevent the almost mechanical 'reading on' which occurs sometimes. But the price paid is that concentration and the free flow of the mind is interrupted by intrusive questions, often annoyingly and disconcertingly. The pupil often comes to resent them and to find the pattern tedious; for, if the questions can be correctly answered, then they seem unnecessary; and, if incorrectly, then they are not a reinforcement to further study but a setback. Nonetheless a simple linear learning sheet on the Spanish Armada of 1588, for instance, is straightforward to compile and may, through novelty at any rate, have something to recommend it. Here is an example:

Learning sheet on
The Spanish Armada, 1588                                    ANSWERS

---

*Frame 1*

The Duke of Medina Sidonia was the unwilling choice of King Philip II of Spain to lead the Armada against England as replacement for the able Santa Cruz who had just died. Though suffering from seasickness, Medina Sidonia led his 130 ships up the English Channel maintaining a strong crescent formation, diligently keeping to the instructions Philip had devised.

Qu. 1 Whom did Medina Sidonia replace?
Qu. 2 What strong formation did the Spaniards maintain in the English Channel?
Qu. 3 What complaint did Medina Sidonia suffer from during the voyage?

---

*Frame 2*                                          ANSWERS

When the Armada, with 19,000 soldiers on board, reached Calais, the
Duke of Parma with his army of    1.   Santa Cruz
30,000 men, which Philip had in-  2.   Crescent
tended should be taken on board and 3.  Seasickness
transported to invade England, was not
ready.

Qu. 4  How many soldiers would the
       Spanish Armada have carried
       to invade England if Philip's
       plans had worked?

*Frame 3*

etc.                                    4.   49,000

Although the questions are inevitably somewhat trivial, the
material progresses logically. There is, however, a tendency, perhaps
inevitable, to concentrate on factual information, on telling the tale
rather than on attempting to analyse the situation. Moreover, when
pupils eventually become bored with stopping to give answers, they
are likely to skip the questions and treat the sheets simply as pages
of a conventional textbook. Only with the employment of elaborate
teaching machines, which require correct answers being given to
frames before they allow pupils to proceed with further frames, can
cheating be eliminated. But it may be that some cheating, or at any
rate intuition, may be an integral constituent of learning, which is
not always linear and may at times be more accurately described
as a process of inspired leaps. In programmed learning the pace is
measured, so it is perhaps better suited for teaching tasks which
are closed – like how to service a lawn mower for instance – than an
open-ended subject such as history, which hopes to foster discrimination and judgement. More sophisticated programmes, both
linear and branching, can be compiled for use with such machines,
but similar objections still apply. *The Waterloo Campaign* by P.
Thornhill (Methuen, London, 1965) is a programmed learning book
and is an example of the difficulties which can be experienced when
applying this method to teaching history.

## Use of team-teaching

Unlike programmed learning, team-teaching has proved highly successful in the teaching of history. One variation is for three parallel
forms to be gathered together so that, while one of the three teachers
leads the lesson, another operates all the visual and aural aids, and

the third is available to assist individuals who may be in difficulty. In another variation, where two teachers are allocated to one large set, one teacher conducts a conventional lesson, while the other sees one or two pupils at a time in another room to discuss work with them individually – a valuable and personal tutor function which is rarely possible where the ratio is one teacher to one large class. Another form of team-teaching is to put two parallel forms together, and for their teachers to take opposing views in a mock argument, for example, on the rights and wrongs of the trial of Charles I. The teachers can also form a panel or combine as a double-act to analyse questions on an exam paper, criticise essays, comment on film strips, or even simply to answer questions from their pupils. Another method is for the whole group to be addressed by one teacher for part of the session, then for it to divide into 'follow-up' discussion groups led by the teachers available and, lastly, for all to come together again in full plenary session for a report back of the views of each discussion group and a final summing up of the proceedings. Such a method not only provides variety, and mitigates against boredom, but gives an opportunity for each pupil to contribute to the discussion in his group, and provides the possibility of arriving at some consensus of opinion in the final summing up. Team-teaching can also cross subjects, from a fortnight's study devoted by several departments to a topic such as the *Industrial Revolution*, to a full term's integrated project, such as *Man's effect on the Lake District*, involving most of the departments within the school and much field-work outside it. One college of education sends out groups of students for team-teaching together in schools for half of their teaching-practice term, an enlightened procedure which enables the students to help each other over their mistakes and difficulties. Team-teaching is not only of benefit to pupils and to teachers in training; it also helps experienced teachers, who otherwise often teach in isolation in their classrooms, with little cross-fertilisation of ideas or techniques.

## Use of museums and displays

One charming characteristic of younger pupils is their liking for bringing items of historical interest to school to show to their history teachers. This practice can be exploited by setting up in the classroom a glass-cased history museum in which these articles can be deposited safely and viewed clearly. One such museum included such disparate items as a flint tool from the Stone Age, a small plastic representation of a mammoth from a breakfast cereal packet, a piece of a Roman tile, a model of an Elizabethan house (painstakingly made by a pupil who was proud to see it displayed), an early eighteenth-century coin from Sir Cloudesley Shovel's wrecked flagship *Association* which had lain on the seabed off the Isles of Scilly since 1707, and a Second World War civilian gasmask. Such content is incredibly diverse, yet each item, properly laid out and labelled, can form the basis of some informal and incidental learning. A much more extensive museum has been created at Longsands School, St Neots, where appropriate accommodation has been spared. The advantages of such a museum for history teaching are described in *Teaching History* (November 1971).

History teachers can also often make good use of classroom walls from which much unconscious learning can take place during the moments before and after formal lessons (or even during them), when gazes wander distractedly. Points to watch about classroom displays are:

(1) Change the material when its purpose has been served.

(2) Ensure that all writing is printed large enough to be read at least from the centre of the classroom.

(3) See that each item carries a message, and is not just a decorative picture but succeeds in informing, explaining and educating.

One idea is to compile a class newspaper encouraging pupils to bring to school for inclusion in it historical clippings, illustrations and other items they have culled from newspapers and magazines. Such activity creates the semblance of useful learning activity and should not be dismissed as mere window dressing, for some pupils will assuredly read and benefit from some of the items displayed. Similarly, with the construction of history models, such as the commercial kit that, after assembly, produces an authentic, ready-to-paint Spitfire, some real learning probably takes place. In any case, making such models is creative, and it is not unreasonable for some time to be spared in history for such a popular activity. The educational value of such modelling is disputable; but there may be a danger in taking a rigid approach to methods in teaching; what matters is the quality of the learning taking place, and this is not always easy to assess. Who can tell, for instance, how much in terms of stimulation to the imagination and in disciplined control is gained by the pupil apparently idly fashioning his balsa-plank into a Viking longboat?

# Primary source material

**6**

## Definition and uses

During the last decade, there has been an upsurge in the availability of published primary source material, and in the readiness of teachers to use it. This trend may produce two opposite, but equally unwelcome, reactions: that of the teacher who embraces 'sources' uncritically as the answer to all his problems; and that of the sceptic who, in reaction against what he senses is becoming a shibboleth, equally uncritically dismisses them as merely the latest band-wagon, a conspiracy between publishers and 'educationists' designed to seduce him away from 'real' history teaching. The teacher who uses them properly will find that he has at his command a most valuable asset.

What is primary source material? We would define it in the widest possible sense, as anything which puts one into direct contact with the past. Thus it embraces far more than pictorial, cartographic or documentary evidence either in its original form or, more commonly, in edited and filmed, printed or otherwise reproduced selections. It covers such things as all artefacts (coins, stamps, tools, furniture, etc.), buildings, archaeological sites, tombstones, memorials and oral recollection. Contact with such material can therefore come in an equally great variety of ways: from a random conversation with one's parents about their past experiences, from watching a programme on television, from a visit to the local museum or art gallery, battlefield, archaeological site or parish church.

In considering the use that can be made of this material in teaching history, one has to move cautiously. If we are to argue that, with certain reservations, the use of such material can be valuable in inducing proper historical training, it especially behoves us to think critically about its use, lest we are untrue to our own profession. It would be dishonest to pretend that pupils can use sources in the way in which a research historian does. The amount and range of material which a pupil can handle will be extremely limited, and what he does with it will be largely determined by the teacher, whose preparation will of necessity short-circuit a number of functions which are an integral part of the research historian's

*TIMES OFFICE, Thursday Morning, 11 o'clock.*

We again stop the Press to insert a copy of the
**LONDON GAZETTE EXTRAORDINARY,**
THURSDAY, June 22, 1815.

### DOWNING STREET, June 22.

Major the Honourable H. Percy arrived late last night with a dispatch from Field-Marshal the Duke of Wellington, K. G. to Earl Bathurst, his Majesty's Principal Secretary of State for the War Department, of which the following is a copy:—

Waterloo, June 19, 1815.

MY LORD,—Buonaparte having collected the 1st, 2d, 3d, 4th, and 6th corps of the French army and the Imperial Guards, and nearly all the cavalry on the Sambre, and between that river and the Meuse, between the 10th and 14th of the month, advanced on the 15th and attacked the Prussian posts at Thuin and Lobez, on the Sambre, at day light in the morning.

I did not hear of these events till the evening of the 15th, and immediately ordered the troops to prepare to march, and afterwards to march to their left, as soon as I had intelligence from other quarters to prove that the enemy's movement upon Charleroy was the real attack.

The enemy drove the Prussian posts from the Sambre on that day: and General Zieten, who commanded the corps which had been at Charleroy, retired upon Fleurus; and Marshal Prince Blucher concentrated the Prussian army upon Sambref, holding the villages in front of his position of St. Amand and Ligny.

The enemy continued his march along the road from Charleroy towards Bruxelles, and on the same evening, the 15th, attacked a brigade of the army of the Netherlands, under the Prince de Weimar, posted at Frasne, and forced it back to the farm house on the same road, called Les Quatre Bras.

FIG. 20. *A printed primary source*

work. Thus, even the illusion of laying bare the bones of history may be difficult to maintain. One might go further, and say that, if the illusion were created, then pupils would have an even falser idea of how history is written than if they had never seen a document. However, the argument that, because pupils cannot use sources in a way the research historian does, no attempt can or should be made to stumble, however tentatively, in that direction, is rather unconvincing. Few of our pupils are going to be authors, but this is no argument for not introducing them to the skills of good writing, however incomplete their probable eventual mastery of those skills.

Work based on primary source material can make a valuable contribution to the encouragement of genuine individual thought,

Fig. 21. *A source of history: Abbeydale Forge, Sheffield*

so that the pupil is trained, 'not so much in the art of historical investigation as in the art of thinking historically'.[1] Skilfully used, such work can promote speculation and discussion about a source's origin, meaning and purpose, and thus lead to a greater readiness in pupils to question and criticise standard authorities – textbooks and teachers. Pupils can begin to recognise conflicts and connections between different pieces of evidence; to detect bias and inconsistency; to evaluate material in terms of its authenticity, relevance and completeness; to discriminate between fact and opinion; to assess different interpretations of the same evidence; to formulate their own hypotheses backed by reference to evidence, and to recognise that such hypotheses are merely opinions. Such work, at the highest level, can begin to instil some idea of what history really is – its qualitative aspects, its essence, as opposed to the more usual quantitative approach of merely covering a part of the factual content of the subject.

There is a danger of expecting modes of thought beyond the capacity of one's pupils, but there are ways in which even younger pupils, and those of limited ability, can be introduced to some of the basic source materials of the historian in such a way as to learn something about the nature of historical evidence and to practise at least some of the crafts of the historian, even if on a very crude and humble level. Most pupils are capable of exercising simple research skills, many of which are simpler in practice than might be imagined from the terms by which one describes them. The level of thought, the nature of the material, the problems dealt with, must all be carefully determined to suit the pupils' abilities, but the exercise of care in these respects, combined with thoughtful guidance by the teacher, can lead to the pupil's regarding himself as being involved in the study of the past rather than being merely the passive observer of the results of that study by others.

Primary source material has humbler, but still worthwhile, uses. First, though it is wasteful simply as a means of finding out about the past (if one's concern is simply to cover a particular topic, one does it better by other means), it does provide proof and illustration of what is in the textbooks. Textbooks, for the most part, deal in generalisations, and it is often useful to illustrate the general by reference to a particular example. This can have the added advantage of producing a readier understanding of a difficult concept. Both the meaning and the impact of 'enclosure', for instance, would be more fully grasped by reference to a local enclosure award

1 Report of American committee on *The Study of History in Schools* (1903). quoted in *Handbook for History Teachers*, W. H. Burston and C. W. Green (Methuen, 1970), p. 97.

## 68 Instructions for producing history text-books: Dr. Frick, Reich Minister of the Interior, 1933.

'As today a full third of all Germans live beyond the frontiers of the Reich, the history book must not confine itself when it deals with German history to the area *now* included within the German frontiers, but must keep before the student the fortunes of our tribal kin who live beyond the frontiers . . . Stronger emphasis than before is to be laid on the greatest achievement of the medieval Germans, the re-conquest of the area east of the river Elbe . . .'

## 69 An order from the Reich Minister of Education, Dr. Rust, January 1935

'Teachers are directed to instruct their pupils in the nature, causes and effects of all racial problems, to bring home to them the importance of race . . . for the life and destiny of the German people, and to awaken in them a sense of responsibility toward the nation . . . pride in their membership in the German race . . . and the will to co-operate in the racial purification of the German stock.

Racial instruction is to begin with the youngest pupils, in accordance with the desire of the Fuehrer "that no boy or girl" should leave school without complete knowledge of the necessity and meaning of blood purity".'

FIG. 22. *A history teaching broadsheet*

than by a general discussion of 'the enclosure movement'. Furthermore, the contemporary example speaks across the centuries in a way that no generalised account can. It makes the past more vivid

(*ic*) *Richard Riley or Royley, senior, of the City of Lichfield, silk weaver,* (*1674*)

| INVENTORY | £ | s. | d. |
|---|---|---|---|
| In the hall or house | | | |
| One table, two joyned formes and a cubboard | | 13 | 4 |
| Foure dishes and other pewter | | 8 | 0 |
| Bacon 6*s.* 8*d.*; andiron, fireshovell and tongues and other implements in the sayd hall or house with a Bible 3*s.* 4*d.* | | 10 | 0 |
| In the butterey | | | |
| Brasse kettles and potts | 2 | 10 | 0 |
| In the shoppe | | | |
| Three loomes with silke and workeing geares | 1 | 10 | 0 |
| In the parlour | | | |
| One featherbed with bedstid and furniture | 1 | 10 | 0 |
| One cupboard, table, presse, trunckes and other things with linnens within them | 3 | 0 | 0 |
| Two dozen of bothoms[1] and other implements | | 10 | 0 |
| In the chamber over the house and shoppe and entrye | | | |
| Two bedstids and a trundle bedd, with a featherbed and flockebeds and furniture | 2 | 10 | 0 |
| Three dozen of botthoms and haire sifes | 2 | 5 | 0 |
| Woodden ware and other lumber | | 13 | 4 |
| Foure barrells, and verges[2] in some of them | | 10 | 0 |
| One hackeney[3] saddle, yarne, toe, course wooll and other odd things | | 16 | 0 |
| Corne and cheese | | 13 | 4 |
| Four payre of sheetes | | 10 | 0 |
| In the backeside and barne and at doore | | | |
| Mucke, hey and implements £1; two piggs £1; two hives of bees 5*s.* | 2 | 5 | 0 |
| Five cowes | 10 | 6 | 8 |
| Twentey sheepe, young and old | 5 | 0 | 0 |
| Hard corne, pease and barley upon the ground | 10 | 0 | 0 |
| Clothes and money in his pockett | 2 | 6 | 8 |
| | 48 | 7 | 4 |

[1] a skein of silk
[2] vinegar made from crab apples
[3] a riding saddle

Fig. 23. *Local history source book*

and immediate. In so doing, it has the added advantage of bringing home the fact that, in a number of very mundane ways whose very mundanity strengthens the impact, the past was different. Textbooks sometimes do not do enough to correct the natural assumption that the past was essentially similar to the present, an assumption one has to exert oneself to remove. However, this task must be handled with care; there is little value, for instance, in allowing pupils to be diverted from a real task of investigation by giggling over oddities of expression; one wants to convey the impression that the past was different, not that it was merely quaint.

A final use of this material lies in the fact that, especially with younger pupils, it can arouse interest and stimulate the imagination. To handle a Stone Age axe-head, to don a gasmask, or to see a facsimile of the death warrant of Charles I, can have a dramatic impact whose long-term effect as the remembered moment will be immense compared with the small effort or time involved in thus colouring a lesson. It is, however, important to distinguish in this, as in all other uses, between different types of primary source material. One should not expect a reprinted, edited document to have a dramatic impact unless its content is unusually arresting and well presented to the class. It has no inherent dramatic validity to pupils simply because it is a primary source. The genuine article, however – a newspaper, an artefact, a tombstone – can produce real excitement of itself, not so much for its content as for the form in which it comes.

## Sources of sources

### Limitations

Though the total amount of primary source material available is enormous, its range is somewhat restricted, and the character of what is provided has certain limitations.

There is not a great deal of documentary material available from non-British sources, and the argument often used to explain this situation, that much of the value of source material would be lost by the movement away from authenticity involved in translation, is true only for that limited area of work which places a premium on authenticity. If one is studying a document for what it tells one rather than a means of stimulating the imagination by the form in which it comes, it does not really matter that it has been translated.

A second limitation is that of period. There is not a great deal easily available for use from before about 1700, for problems of language, handwriting and phraseology before that date seem to pose insuperable obstacles. But again, translation and transcription would obstruct the purpose of the work only in those instances where authenticity really mattered. Conversely, there are some times when authenticity is the only material factor, and on these occasions a useful purpose would be served by showing a facsimile document even if almost all of it were impossible to decipher. A Domesday extract, Magna Carta and Charles I's death warrant are cases in point.

Most of the good work that has been done on source material in recent years has been confined to social, economic and local history, and there is not much outside this field for forms below about O level standard. Even at the higher level, books of collected documents on political history are, with minor differences, much the same as they were 30 years ago, and show little of the enterprising approach to be found in the sphere of social and economic history.

Types of pupil, as well as types of history, have been somewhat neglected, and most of what is available is perhaps too difficult for many pupils. The average and the less able need more consideration from the publishers of primary source material. Failing that, as with all his work, the teacher must adapt the basic provision to his own particular needs. But though the teacher can do that, he is very pressed for time, and more could be done to help him. A useful purpose would be served by the production of kits showing teachers how to use particular schemes based on primary source material, and there are some indications that publishers are becoming aware of this need.

Teacher education has not kept abreast of pupil education, and it is asking a lot to expect teachers to be able to handle quasi-research projects when their own historical training involved no such work. Some University Departments of Education, particularly those who have pioneered the production of Archive Teaching Units, and many Colleges of Education, have done sterling work in teacher training of this sort, but the needs are still great, and are not fully met by simply referring teachers to articles on the subject, useful though these are.

So much for what is not provided. The main point to remember about what is provided is that no source is unbiased. A primary source no more monopolises that elusive thing 'the truth' than does a secondary source,[2] and the teacher would do well to remember that, in this respect, the only value in using primary sources is that they help us construct our own hypotheses about the past instead of merely repeating someone else's.

This inherent bias is compounded by the fact that most material for school use has already been heavily edited, and is particularly unbalanced. There is a natural tendency to be highly selective, and to choose that which is sensational and perhaps uncharacteristic of the norm. Furthermore, the sources we use are probably unrepresentative of the vast majority of people. The teacher must be aware

[2] See E. H. Dance, *History the Betrayer – A Study in Bias* (Hutchinson, 1960).

of these limitations and correct them, if only by pointing out that they exist. It would be wrong to limit oneself to using only what is as reliable as possible – which is, in any case, a search for the unattainable. The teacher should be prepared to employ any original material, so long as he is aware of its nature and purpose and takes them explicitly into account. For example, Disraeli's paragraph on the girl miners in *Sybil* is a valid primary source, even though – perhaps because – it is propaganda. It is not merely valid; it is very useful – so long as one recognises it for what it is, and differentiates between it and, say, the records of a nineteenth-century Parliamentary Commission of Enquiry into conditions in the mines. Similarly, Orwell's *The Road to Wigan Pier* is a perfectly acceptable source on miners' work, lives and homes in the 1930s – again, provided one recognises its original polemical purpose and consequent limitations.

## National publications

A huge amount of varied material is readily available in print, and teachers wanting a complete guide should consult publishers' catalogues and the books and articles listed in the last section of this chapter. What follows here is merely an attempt to discuss a selection of the published material available.

In assessing the quality of the available material, the teacher must be sure of his objectives. What is the age and ability-range of his class? What purpose does he want the material to serve? Is it to provide merely the initial stimulus? To serve an illustrative purpose? To be the main basis for coverage of the content of a particular topic? To provide the material for more intellectual exercises on the nature of evidence? Does he want a fully structured scheme of work which may require only minor adaptations to meet the exigencies of his own situation? Or does he merely want some raw material which he can absorb into his own method of approach? What form is the pupils' work going to take? These and many similar questions should determine his choice of publication and will influence his judgement of it.

The most common type of publication is that which merely reprints a collection of documentary material, with little or no commentary or programming for class use. Such books have a valuable purpose, perhaps particularly with older and more able pupils, but – if only for financial reasons – they would best be located in a library, for occasional reference use by individual pupils or by the teacher in a particular lesson. Basic textbooks of all sorts increasingly contain a good range of primary source material for illustrative purposes, and the teacher can always isolate these illustrations and use them more specifically if he wishes, and this can be a reasonably satisfactory substitute if one cannot afford the more ambitious source books and packs.

The chief growth point in the market is in the production of collections of source material on particular themes. Jonathan Cape's *Jackdaw* series rightly enjoys an esteemed reputation as a pioneer in this field, but later entrants have learned from the *Jackdaws'* limitations and offer something which is much more carefully and usefully designed. It may well be that the publication of M. Devitt's *Learning with Jackdaws* (Cape, 1970) is an indication that Cape is learning from its younger rivals.

T. Edwards' *Hitler and Germany 1919–39* (1972), in Heinemann's *History Broadsheets* series, is a good example of the 'improved *Jackdaw*' approach. It loses something in authenticity, but more than compensates for this by the amount and imaginative variety of content, thoughtful organisation and instant practicality. Another example of much the same approach is provided by the resource packs produced by the B.B.C. to accompany their *History in Evidence* radio programmes, which are designed for the first three years of the secondary school. For middle forms, Macmillan's *Exploring History* series has much to recommend it. The level is fairly elementary, the provision of work cards breaks the back of preparatory work, and the number of items provided makes each kit quite easy to use with a class of thirty pupils. Their particular value lies in giving individual experience in examining, and making deductions from, evidence.

Evans' *History at Source* volumes (general editor J. M. Thomas) provide a large and imaginative range of facsimile material on particular topics, impressively reproduced, but there are no assignment sheets, and much work awaits the teacher if he wishes to use them for anything but occasional illustrative or display purposes. Visually less authentic and impressive, but much cheaper and easier to use, are two series published by the O.U.P., both of which are edited, and processed for fairly immediate use, with considerable skill. They are *Society and Industry in the nineteenth century* (ed. K. Dawson and P. Wall, 1968–70) and *The Transport Revolution* (ed. R. Tames, 1970–1).

Among the most impressive recent publications are Longman's *Secondary History Packs* (general editors C. Barham and B. Williams), an ambitious series which welds a wide range of primary source material into a coherent scheme of study on various aspects of British social and economic history since 1700. The aim is to research through the content provided in such a way as to master both matter and historical method. Though the scheme is highly structured, one can easily adapt it to different uses, and the amount of teacher guidance given will be welcome to those whose complaint about most such publications is that they require an unrealistic amount of time before they are ready for classroom use. The publishers' claim, that these packs provide 'a resource library which may be adapted to different attainment levels and a variety of approaches', is quite justified. Of similar basic conception to these are Yendor Books' *History Resource Packs,* each of which provides the teacher with enough material for a large class working in groups, pupil-instruction sheets on the use of the material, question-sheets, a teacher's sheet, wall-charts and a tape. This sort of publication is likely to become increasingly common, and the intending purchaser needs to be sure of several points before committing himself. How much inherent complexity is there in the organisation of the classroom use of these materials? To what comprehension levels are the materials appropriate? How durable are the materials, given the robust handling inherent in their design?

For somewhat older pupils, Arnold's *Archive* series (general editors C. P. Hill and G. Fell) is excellent. The booklets are reasonably priced, imaginative in their selection and attractive in their presentation of material, and they provide a useful introduction in which the extracts are linked together into an examination of the broader context from which they are drawn. The study-direction is looser than is the case with the series discussed above, but, as one moves through the age-range of pupils, one needs gradually to ease away the supporting framework and free the individual pupil from the constrictions of a structure which is necessary for him at a younger age.

At a higher level and suitable only for fairly good sixth form use, are Longman's *Seminar Studies in History* (editor P. Richardson), which provide a deep discussion of particular topics with references to the documents appendix worked into the text.

Books and packs of predominantly written material form the chief corner of the market, but by no means the only one. The B.B.C. has produced some very good recorded material, such as *The Age of Steam, For Johnnie* and the *Scrapbook* records, and the Apollo Society's *History Reflected* series produced by Argo is imaginative and effective. However, more recorded memories would serve a useful purpose. Music is no less a source-material than the written or spoken word, and many topics could be well illustrated by, or even studied through, the music associated with them. Perhaps one of the best examples of this is the American Civil War, whose songs

– available on record – afford considerable insights into the nature
of that conflict.

There is much more available in the way of pictorial source
material. Studio Vista's *Visual History* series (editor J. Simmons),
containing reproductions of photographs and original maps, is
good. On a more ambitious level, the E. P. Group reproduce historical manuscripts and records on microfilm. Macmillan's *History
Class Pictures* (ed. G. Lay) are based on a fine idea – pictures linked
with questions and related documentary extracts – but are indif-
ferently executed, as the pictures are so often crude reconstructions.
Filmstrips and slide sets too often display similar faults, or contain
pictures which convey no information and cannot be usefully
employed, and this is one area where there is a need for the same
kind of careful selection and presentation, with work-study guides,
as have now been practised in the field of written source material.
However, not all filmstrips are so poor. *The Bayeux Tapestry* (Visual Publications LH1/LH2, 1967), for example, is very fine, and
opens up a number of interesting opportunities for work based on
it. Other good Visual Publications filmstrips are those in the series
*Looking into History, People of Other Days*, and *English Architecture*. Nicholas Hunter, of Richmond Road, Oxford, is another
filmstrip publisher whose work combines authenticity and usefulness. Reproductions of paintings deserve more attention than they
perhaps usually receive from history teachers. The Imperial War
Museum, for example, sells postcard-sized reproductions of many
of the works of the official Great War artists, and these can be most
effective aids to a study of that War. Many school art departments
have a reasonable stock of reproductions which they might be prepared to make available to their history colleagues.

## Local publications

Whereas the general publishers concentrate almost exclusively on
publishing primary source material of a national or international
character, local bodies concentrate on more local material. It is in
this area that the most notable advances have been made in recent
years, and this is as it perhaps should be, since, in the words of one
of our correspondents, 'local source material is far more popular
than source material from other areas or from the national scene'.
Such material has an obvious value to the teacher whose syllabus
specifically includes local history. Indeed, his work would be arid
without it. But one does not have to be a 'parish pump' history
teacher in order to employ local source material, nor does large-scale

employment of it necessarily imply undue parochialism of approach. A lot of national history could well be approached through and illustrated by the immediate locality. It might then begin to make rather more sense. A good teacher always relates the unimaginable to the known, and in history we frequently personalise, in order to enhance interest and to bring the material within range of comprehension; so why not localise the national similarly?

So vast has been the expansion of the work of various local bodies that all one can do here is to touch on a few activities and refer the reader to the last section of this chapter, where he will find information on where to look for further details. Probably the best work that has been done is in the field of Archive Teaching Units. Certain County Record Offices, most notably Essex, were early pioneers in this field, but activity within it has now spread out to include an increasing number of County Record Offices, University Departments of Education, local branches of the Historical Association, libraries, museums and – perhaps most encouraging of all – local history teachers' associations. It would be invidious to single out any by name; suffice it to say that there can hardly be an area of the country that is not served by at least one, and probably several, of the above agencies.

Archive teaching units enjoy several advantages. They are usually devoted to subjects of local interest which have a national significance, and thus lend themselves to both purely local and locally-illustrated national work. In the latter, the points at which one's own locality can be integrated with the syllabus are necessarily limited, and it is an asset, therefore, to be able to obtain an archive teaching unit about Peterloo from Manchester, about the General Strike from Newcastle, about the Pottery industry from Staffordshire, about smuggling from East Sussex, and so on. Alternatively, one can obtain folders on the same theme – say the Poor Law – from widely different parts of the country, so that pupils may discover regional differences in, say, the application of the 1834 Poor Law Amendment Act. Another merit is that the production of an archive teaching unit usually combines the energies of archivist, research historians, College and Department of Education lecturers, practising teachers – and, very often, students and pupils. A balance of skills is thus brought to bear on the task, ensuring that the finished product is both academically and pedagogically sound. No doubt as a result of this, its composition is generally superior to similar nationally produced publications. The contents, wide-ranging and imaginatively selected, are adequate for a large class, and lend themselves to a study both of sources *per se* and of the particular historical topic, in both cases aided by study-guides.

## *The individual teacher*

The teacher who uses primary source material cannot just expect the sources to come to him ready packaged for instant use. He must himself be a 'source of sources', if in no other way than that of selecting and adapting what the market offers to his own particular circumstances. He may even dismiss all available sources as inapplicable to his own situation and bravely launch out on his own, producing his own source-booklets and archive teaching units. However, limitations of time, money, resources and expertise will almost certainly prevent all but a very few from succeeding in such an enterprise. The teacher is better advised to confine his energies to adapting what is available, organising it for easy use and supplementing it from his own experience and local facilities. If he is more ambitious, he would serve himself and others best by contributing his efforts to a local body, such as those listed in the previous section.

Published material varies widely in the help it gives a teacher, and teachers vary just as much in the extent to which they welcome help that, of necessity, cannot take particular circumstances, predilections and foibles into account. Perhaps the best publications are those which include a selection of varied material on a limited theme, suited to a fairly narrow age and ability range, and accompanied by some form of study guide. The teacher then has a more manageable task both in selection of material to be used (and of local additions to it), and in amending the methods of use to the requirements of his own particular situation. The groundwork has been done for him; only the system is personal.

Despite the activities of multifarious agencies, the vast bulk of primary source material lies unused unless Mohammed goes to the mountain. It is not, and frequently it cannot be, published. Historical sites, artefacts, local newspapers (e.g. all numbers of the *Hampshire Chronicle*, dating from 1772, on microfilm in Winchester Public Library), personal recollection – all these, if they are to be used, require original movement by the teacher.

If he moves at all, it is most commonly in the direction of the local Record Office. Record Offices vary in their cooperation with teachers. Many are very good indeed, not only producing archive teaching units and other aids, but offering visits, reprographic facilities and the services of an archivist who will visit the school and, for example, teach the sixth form to read the secretary hand. Essex's appointment of a Schools Service Officer and provision of a pupils' room with ancillary services and staff, are indicative of a promising development in the field of Record Offices' recognition of the invaluable service they can provide to schools, and of the need for some specialist liaison between raw material and teacher.

The responsibility, however, is reciprocal. The teacher himself must be knowledgeable about and skilled in using the materials he intends to employ, before he lets his charges loose on them. In this, as in all other respects, much preparatory work is essential. We would do well to heed the advice given in one school's advisory booklet: [3]

*Seeking specialist help*

In any work with primary sources you will need to ask for the help and advice of experts. They will usually be very busy people, so prepare your ground thoroughly before consulting them. Do not worry them with vague questions, try to be as specific as you can and only ask for help when you are stuck. Above all, do not regard asking an expert simply as an easy alternative to reading something for yourself, and remember always to be polite and patient.

You may go to the Local Record Office, but you should, if possible, call in, write or telephone first to arrange a convenient time and to give the archivist some idea of what you will want . . . At a museum, if you wish to arrange a specific appointment, you may be shown objects which are not normally on view in the showcases, but, once more, you must go knowing precisely what you want to see, why you wish to see it and how to use it to further your knowledge . . .

If you go to interview someone with expert knowledge, you must again prepare for your visit by working out exactly what questions you wish to ask, and, if necessary, write them down. You must write to ask for an appointment at a time convenient to the person you wish to interview, explaining in your letter the reason for your request and giving an outline of the work you are doing and the points you wish to raise in the interview.

One of the most common problems facing the teacher using primary source material is that of reproduction. Obviously the retention of as much authenticity as possible is desirable, and dog-eared duplicated sheets are a deterrent. Few schools will have the resources available for photographic reproduction, but local teachers' centres, Record Offices and other bodies frequently have such facilities.

Although pleas of shortage of time and money are very real, the problems they pose are not insuperable. It is quite easy and inexpensive to build up a reasonable collection of transparencies, enlisting the aid of a colleague if one lacks the necessary skills oneself. Similarly, there is no great difficulty in amassing a collection of postcards on a given theme or period, which one could then organise into a 'line of development' or 'patch' kit, bind the selected cards together, and opposite each picture write brief comments drawing attention to salient features, referring to relevant secondary sources,

3 *Projects in History: A Guide for Students*, by John Higham of the Nelson Thomlinson School, Wigton, Cumbria.

and setting exercises. Too often, perhaps, defensive pleas about time and money are merely covers for lack of initiative, though certainly one would like to see more realistic provision of reprographic facilities in many schools.

## Oral source material

Although oral testimony has always occupied a place amongst source material in the teaching of history, only recently has it acquired a recognised status of its own. Work undertaken in various universities includes a systematic study of the potentialities of oral history, a collection of memories of particular events and subjects of a representative sample of older men and women, and the promotion of this particular branch of historical activity in schools.

This is not the place to enter into discussion of the academic credentials of this relatively new specialist area, though it is worth pointing out that nothing more nor less is claimed for it than is claimed – with perhaps less demur – for more generally accepted or orthodox historical sources. Of course, personal recollection is prone to inaccuracy, selectivity and distortion, but this does not invalidate it as an historical source. It simply means that the resultant information must be treated with caution, just as one would similarly treat diaries, letters or newspapers. Those who are sceptical about the use of tape-recorded oral testimony should ask themselves whether they have the same reservations about the oral evidence given before, say, nineteenth-century Select Committees and Royal Commissions.

Neither is this the place to discuss the particular problems and techniques involved in drawing up a questionnaire, and then in interviewing people from it. Clearly, this is a sophisticated and delicate operation which is best left to experts – or, if done, undertaken only after careful preparation. Teachers interested in the subject should consult the references given at the end of this section.

The values of the tape-recorded recollections of our senior citizens are many. They can lend immediacy and personalisation to an otherwise dry or remote topic; they may vividly illustrate both the degree of change that has taken place since the early years of this century, and – sometimes – the surprising similarities between our own age and a past era; above all, perhaps, they can bring to the study of social and economic history in particular the voice of the common man, whose historically valuable experience otherwise goes with him to the grave – for, even today, poor men leave few records. In this last connection, oral testimony can act as a useful counter to the belief that history is concerned only with great people. Both the whole recollected life of a single individual, or a particular theme seen by a number of people from different perspectives, can provide imaginative insights into the life-style and experience of a past generation, and bring one into contact with the 'inner' history – the essential, living reality which is often such a refreshing contrast from the casket in which historical study too often inters the past. Finally, oral testimony can reach far back, when elderly people recall the memories and experiences of their parents and grandparents. The span of this source material is certainly not confined to the twentieth century – nor to national history.

Teachers could either use the recorded sources currently available or attempt a little original work of their own; for example, a number of interviews could be conducted on the subject of a particular local incident, or of a national event having local repercussions – the Great War, the General Strike, the Depression. Some schools might even begin to build up a bank of original material resulting from tape-recorded interviews, and this can be transcribed and organised under different headings, thus making it capable of a number of different uses. The Cambridge 'A' level optional project allows the submission of tape-recordings, and some pupils doing this paper might be encouraged to undertake a piece of late nineteenth- or twentieth-century local research which could draw heavily on personal recollection.

Teachers interested in this field of activity should subscribe to the journal *Oral History*, details of which are obtainable from Dr Paul Thompson, Reader in Sociology, The University of Essex. Issues numbers 4 and 5 contain a full discussion of the nature, possibilities and problems of this specialised branch of primary source material. Also of help are two articles by John Whyman, Lecturer in Economic and Social History, Rutherford College, the University of Kent: 'Oral History and its possibilities in Schools' (*Kent Education Gazette*, LII, No. 1 [June 1971]) and 'By word of Mouth' (*Sound and Picture Tape Recording* [April 1973]). Mr Whyman has also produced a 'Memorandum on Techniques and Questions in Oral History', copies of which are obtainable from him, and has been instrumental in encouraging the involvement of schools in Kent in the use of oral sources, in the hope of producing at some future date a number of tape-recorded teaching aids.

## In the classroom

There is little point in simply distributing the contents of a *Jackdaw*, allowing time for browsing, and then collecting them in again.

Similarly, on a visit to a museum, very limited profit is likely to accrue from merely telling pupils that they have fifteen minutes to look around a particular room. Undirected contact with an arbitrary selection of material is of very little value, and is historically unsound. Before engaging in work of this sort, the teacher has to address himself to certain questions. What exactly is the point of the given exercise? What precisely is it intended that the pupils learn from it? What role does primary source material play in it? Why use any such material? Why use this particular material? What are its limitations? How is it going to be used in detail, to serve the intended ends? Experienced teachers probably cope with these problems intuitively, but the newcomer to the profession would be well advised to build such questions as these overtly into his preparation. Even at its most incidental level of use, primary source material – like anything else – requires careful prior thought. The 'dramatic impact' use can be squandered unless the teacher has given thought to precisely when and in what manner to spring the rabbit from the hat, and has considered how best to sustain and capitalise on the imaginative stimulus thus administered. The use of an item of primary source material for supplementary illustration, equally should involve similar preparatory thought, as well as consideration of the question, Is this the best illustration I have available for my purposes?

More extended use of source material obviously requires more extensive preparation. It would be useful here to draw a distinction between the occasional special lesson based on primary material built into an otherwise perhaps fairly conventional syllabus and mode of approach, and the extended scheme of work based largely on primary material. Teachers persuaded of the value of the latter, and reconciled to the slower rate of work it entails and to the consequent need to abandon the traditional syllabus sprint through several centuries, may be in a minority; but most teachers should be ready to consider the value of accommodating occasional 'primary source material lessons' within a traditional syllabus, at minimal disturbance, and potentially great profit, to it. Of course, the purposes of these two approaches – though overlapping at points – will be different, and thus the preparation involved will also be different.

It does not greatly matter, for instance, precisely what sources are selected for a special lesson built into a conventional scheme of work on, say, transport in the eighteenth century, if the purpose of the lesson is to illustrate a general feature, such as a turnpike trust award, by a local example, in order to strengthen the impact of the general by particularising it. Nor would it matter in similar circumstances if the purpose were to introduce pupils to certain basic historical skills by discussing the nature of some contemporary evidence on this subject. The only important criterion for selection of material in such conditions is its suitability to the age and ability of the pupils concerned. But if one were basing one's whole study of a given topic largely on primary source material, so that the material was the main source of content as well as a vehicle for the inculcation of certain skills, then of course very careful thought would have to be given to the question of its selection.

*Single lessons*

A useful exercise for introducing pupils to the skills of drawing and presenting organised conclusions from evidence, and to the initially disturbing fact that the same evidence can be used to lead to very different conclusions, is to devise an entirely imaginary situation such as the following:

> Here is a list of objects found in the pockets of a jacket. What can you reasonably deduce from this evidence about the owner of the jacket?

Once the basic skills have been grasped by such work, which to be fruitful should allow time for extensive analysis and discussion of different answers, the teacher could then begin to apply them to more genuinely historical situations.

Another exercise, therefore, could be to ask pupils to report an incident seen by the whole class, or alternatively, to study different newspaper accounts of an incident. This could demonstrate how widely contemporary accounts often differ. The precise use of such work would vary according to the level of ability of the class. One might confine oneself merely to discussing the obvious differences, such as direct contradictions; or one could advance to a more subtle level and examine the selection, arrangement and presentation of material – the less overt forms of difference and subjectivity.

Another stage in such work would then be to apply the lessons so far learned to incidents in the period of history currently being studied. For example, examine and discuss different eye-witness accounts of the Battle of Lexington in the American War of Independence.

A different use of the occasional primary source material lesson is that which aims not so much at the – perhaps rather self-conscious – inculcation of historical skills, but at merely doing a conventional job by other means. That is, one teaches primarily 'content', but bases a whole part of it on primary and particularised, rather than secondary and general, sources. For example, a good

introductory lesson on the history of the U.S.A. could take the
following form: each pupil has before him a map of the U.S.A. On
the blackboard, or hanging before the class, is a large blank outline
map. The teacher, by carefully directed questioning, gets the class
to deduce major themes in the outline history of the U.S.A., such as
original settlement patterns by colonising powers, from a study of
the place-names on their maps, and, on the outline map, he gradually
builds up the picture that emerges. Another example of a similar use
of this type of material is a lesson in a scheme of work on the Great
War which uses duplicated extracts of poems distributed to the
class to illustrate such aspects as the horrors of the trenches, the
change of attitude and mood towards the War, the 'credibility gap'
between the front line and the home front.

### Schemes of work

Building a scheme of work around primary source material may be
putting the cart before the horse, but many teachers feel that to
build such material as a main ingredient into a scheme of work already selected for other reasons than the mere availability of the
requisite source material has much to recommend it. For example,
a teacher who is convinced of the value *per se* of devoting a term, or
even a year, to local history could well then investigate the possibilities of building much of his work around primary material. However, he would be well advised to guard against undue parochialism
by employing either generally relevant primary or secondary sources
which deal with the national context, or primary sources from other
areas – preferably ones which differ in some fundamental respects
from his own. What do they know of England who only East
Anglia know?

A scheme of work centred on a study of the Industrial Revolution in one's own locality could employ the following resources:

| | |
|---|---|
| *Local* | Industrial – archaeological sites |
| | Record Office |
| | Museums |
| | Newspapers |
| | Transparencies taken by members of staff |
| *Other regional* | The relevant University of Newcastle Department of Education Archive Teaching Unit |
| *National* | Relevant *History at Source* folders and *Jackdaws Then and There* booklets (Longman) |
| | Nicholas Hunter filmstrips |
| | G. D. H. Cole *Common Ground* filmstrips |
| | A basic textbook on the Industrial Revolution |

A good idea would be to build up as complete a kit of primary source material as possible on one local example of each main industry – a turnpike trust, a canal company, a coal mine, a railway. Schemes such as this take a lot of time to develop, and a good method is to combine the energies of all members of the department so that they concentrate on one particular topic at a time, to build up and organise the necessary materials. It is wise to absorb material gradually, using it first for occasional, illustrative purposes, and then expanding its use as the amount, and experience in using it, build up.

The scheme outlined above is not so much local history *per se*, as national history based on local examples. There is, however, much to be said for purely local history, where the source material forms the essence of the work, rather than playing a secondary, mainly illustrative, role. It can be argued that the complexities of national history are such that no collection of primary material on it can satisfactorily be made the basis of a sound historical exercise, and becomes merely another sort of textbook.

One scheme of work that came to our notice illustrates the exploitation of a particularly fruitful major resource in the local area. The school, in the vicinity of Hadrian's Wall, devotes the summer term of the first year to a study of the Wall and associated features. The emphasis in the work is upon archaeological method, the selection and weighing of evidence, and imaginative but authentically-based reconstruction of the past in creative writing which cannot be done by slavish copying from secondary sources. An additional bonus to such a scheme can be the development of environmental appreciation and concern. The whole enterprise is a good example of imaginative and thoughtfully-structured expansion out from a primary source material base which, because it touches on so many different facets of Roman Britain, can be made to develop along a large number of different lines of enquiry. The Wall itself, and relevant museum objects and documentary extracts, provide the basic material, and general classwork is followed by individual projects.

The word 'project', like 'sources', tends to stimulate a Pavlovian response. It is viewed by some as the automatic passport to success; to others, it is anathema. The word has acquired connotations which need to be prised away from it, if one is to consider it afresh, and there is a need to do so, uninfluenced by stereotyped attitudes. This may simply be a case of putting old wine in new bottles, but if that makes teachers more inclined to concentrate on judging the content critically, instead of giving an instant response to the packaging, it is a worthwhile exercise.

Any scheme of work involving primary source material in a major way is almost certain to involve individual project work. If this is to be worthwhile, it requires very careful thought and planning, and others might well copy the example of the school involved in the Hadrian's Wall work, which, in the advisory booklet referred to earlier,[4] gives guidance on such matters as choosing a topic, how to begin work, sources, seeking specialist help, fieldwork, making notes, writing up and presentation. The section on sources contains the following advice:

Secondary sources pose questions and suggest the answers as well. When working with primary sources, you yourself must think of the questions you wish to ask, and then use the evidence in the sources to try to find the answers. It is best to ask very simple questions at first: 'When did the idea of the Carlisle Canal first get raised? What had to be done before the canal could be begun? How was it constructed? What were the difficulties? How long did it take? Who supplied the money?', and many more questions of the same type. Some of your questions may prove unanswerable – there may be no evidence or insufficient evidence for a reliable answer. New questions may (and should) suggest themselves as you work, but it must be stressed that it is no use going to study any primary sources until you have framed some questions in your own mind.

There are two checks you must make before writing up the answers to your questions. First, you must make sure that the evidence is reliable – is it accurate and impartial rather than hearsay, gossip and propaganda? Check, if possible, with a different piece or pieces of evidence. Ask yourself why the evidence was made . . . if possible, you must ask questions that were not in the mind of the person who was the author of the document you are studying . . . Secondly, you must check that you are not simply finding the answer you hoped or expected to find and ignoring inconvenient or contradictory evidence.

Using primary sources is not easy, but once you have had some practice in the techniques you will find it rewarding, and you will enjoy tackling the historical detective work that is truly the most exciting part of the work of the historian.

Another school bases some of its work in the third year on collections of local documents which have recently been donated to the school museum. One scheme exploits the possibilities presented by the election returns for parish constables in the period 1908–30, which list occupations as well as names:

PARISH CONSTABLES

*Introduction*

Constables have existed since the Middle Ages. For centuries their duties were not confined to maintaining law and order, but included taking charge of the parish armour, stocks, whipping-post, pillory and ducking stool. They also collected the county rates, paid out rewards for catching vermin, attended fairs and even punished people who stayed away from church. In other words,

---

[4] See footnote p. 97.

at a time when most of the people of England lived in villages, the parish was the administrative unit of the country, and the constable was the only local government official that most people would see in their daily lives.

You can get some idea of a constable's duties in Elizabethan England from reading *The Elizabethan Village,*[5] pp. 65–71.

The office of constable was a compulsory one – when chosen a man had to serve – and as it was an unpopular job, a man would usually serve only for a year at a time. Until the eighteenth century it was usually an unpaid job. Before the seventeenth century a constable was usually appointed by a manorial court: after this date he was appointed by the justices of the peace.

In the nineteenth century, with the rapid growth of towns, different methods for organising local government had to be found. Gradually, the responsibility for tasks such as maintaining law and order and collecting rates passed from the hands of the parishes to other local government bodies, but the duty of supervising the welfare of the poor remained, even though parishes often grouped themselves into 'unions' supervised by Boards of Guardians. Thus the constables still had a job to do. This explains why in these documents you will find the parish councils, vestries, and overseers of the poor mentioned as being those responsible for choosing constables, although still the J.P.s are shown to be the men who put the final signature upon the documents and therefore legally appoint the constables.

In 1929, local government was re-organised once more and the Boards of Guardians were disbanded. Responsibility for caring for the poor no longer rested with the parish, but passed to the local councils. This explains why in these documents the signature of the clerk to the council appears at this date.

*Research tasks*

1. Check your series of documents. They should all relate to one parish (named on the top line) and they should be in order (dates on the third line down). Some years may be missing.

2. Take a piece of paper and prepare it so that it looks like the attached form.

3. Starting with the earliest document for your parish, list the constables' names in column A, their occupations in column B, and place a tick for each of them in the column relating to the appropriate year.

4. When examining each form that follows, do not rewrite the name and occupation if you have met the name before; merely place a tick in the appropriate year column. But if a new name appears, add it to the list just as you did in Section 3.

5. If a change in a man's occupation occurs, place an asterisk in the appropriate year box and make a note of the change as a footnote when you have completed the chart.

*Follow-up tasks*

1. As stated in the introduction, in days gone by men did not usually want to serve as constables for more than a year, as it was seen by many as a waste of time and money. Does your chart suggest that this was the case

---

[5] A. J. Fletcher, *The Elizabethan Village* ('Then and There' series, ed. M. Reeves, Longman, 1967).

in the early twentieth century? Most of the constables were still unpaid. Can you suggest why the same names keep re-appearing in successive years?

2. Do you notice any years when the list of names varies considerably, and can you suggest why a variation occurs?

3. What do the lists of occupations tell us about the character of the area and how people made their living?

4. See if you can pick out occupations mentioned which suggest that new trades and industries are coming into existence.

5. In the introduction many different duties carried out by constables were listed. Find out who carries out these duties today.

6. We do not know enough about what these constables mentioned in the documents had to do as part of their duties. A few of these men will still be alive. You may know them or their families. A few polite enquiries as to the memories and duties of these men could reveal much that would help us. If you are able to help in this way, please mention the fact.

It can readily be seen how this work can lead to some promising discussion on both the history that can be learned from the documentary material, and on the nature of historical evidence. Note also how the introduction sets the particular work within a broader historical context, and how clear the instructions are. Pupils are made to think about and use the conclusions that may emerge from the analysis, and there is interesting scope for the use of personal recollection.

Schemes of work based on old newspapers can employ them as general mirrors of their age. Another use is as contemporary illustration of one particular subject. For example, a study of 'Flight' in one school, based on the secondary source *Flight* by M. N. Duffy (Blackwell, 1967), was enriched by reference to extracts from articles in national newspapers. This facilitated detailed 'patch' treatment of particular episodes such as Bleriot's cross-Channel flight, and, by covering many more points of detail than a more general source could, lent verisimilitude to reconstruction of such episodes in written and dramatic form. With older or more able pupils, one could extend the potential of this scheme, and compare different newspaper accounts as a basis for some work on historical evidence.

A C.S.E. scheme, on the history of the American Black Man, illustrates some of the problems raised by this kind of work. The material used is wide-ranging, imaginatively selected and stimulating, but poses a problem of balance which arises primarily because this is a historical topic that is still a burning contemporary issue. It is all too easy to be one-sided in one's treatment of such a delicate subject, to imagine that there is only one side to the question, and to judge the institution of slavery by current mores. This difficulty is compounded by the fact that most of the best material is hostile to slavery, and a reasoned defence is neither as spectacular nor as conceptually easy as a vivid description of the hardships of slavery on a – perhaps untypically – harsh plantation, or of the sadistic punishments meted out by a particular overseer. It may therefore be that a subject such as this is too large and poses too many problems for it to be built around primary source material. However, such material could still be used, but as illustrative rather than as fundamental matter, and with the explicit aim, essential to the use of all such material, of establishing direct contact with the past and appreciating its uniqueness, rather than merely reinforcing current attitudes and opinions.

Many schools have something of a post-examination problem with their older pupils, and it is often possible to arrange a fairly extensive scheme of fieldwork in local studies which can be geared to individual skills and interests and employ primary source material work in a major way. A village survey, for example, could include work on the following:

1. *Parish records* (the omnicompetence of parish officials up to the early nineteenth century makes such records a mine of information on a wide variety of local topics).

2. *County Records* – e.g. Tithe maps resulting from the 1836 Tithe Commutation Act; turnpike trust records; inventories and wills.

3. *The church fabric and contents* – e.g. memorials, monumental brasses, list of incumbents, graveyard. Work based on these sources could involve listing as much statistical material as possible (e.g. from gravestones: recording name, date of death, age at death), with a view to attempting some analysis of, for instance, continuity of settlement, life expectancy at different times, size of population at different periods. Often such work serves the purpose of revealing questions requiring further research elsewhere – for example, why did so many people die in a given year?

4. *Modern survey* – e.g. comparison of graveyard findings with existing electoral roll; land-use and land-ownership maps; map showing each building and coding it by (a) age, (b) use; survey of communications serving the village; analysis of inhabitants by (a) occupation, (b) age group.

It should be stressed that such work must be preceded by very thorough, detailed and careful preparation, and must at all times be seriously and purposefully directed. It may be advisable to build up to such a scheme over a number of years, gradually extending the scope of one's operations and feeding material into the scheme as a result of practical experience, some of which may be gained from employing parts of the scheme occasionally in normal course work.

It is essential to obtain local permission for much of this work, and to retain local good-will. In that connection, it is worth stating that the interview and the questionnaire have become perhaps too obtrusive in recent years, and should not be used lightly. Individual privacy is increasingly intruded upon from a growing number of directions, and we should think very carefully before adding our unwanted attentions to those of market researchers, salesmen, social surveyors and the like.

Fieldwork, of course, need not be so extensive as in the village survey outlined above. Neither need it be so analytical. The single visit to a site which has some bearing on current work is the most common form of extra-mural historical activity, and the emphasis can sometimes be put on an appeal to the heart rather than to the head. A gifted talker taking a class round the magnificent landscape garden at Stourhead can, with the help of the stimulus received from the location, make the past live, and get beneath its skin. Being 'on location' can thus facilitate the imaginative leap into the past, the suspension of disbelief which contributes to the development of an intuitive sense of a past age. This we sometimes neglect in our concern for transmitting its content. We often act capably as the pall-bearers of the past; we perhaps think too seldom of trying to revive the corpse.

Mention of the gift of tongues raises the question of individual aptitudes. We often pay attention to differing skills and abilities among pupils; less frequently, among teachers. The use of any material depends not only upon the particular school, its locality and the opportunities it offers, and the individual pupils in question; above all, it depends upon the teacher. What is brilliantly successful in one pair of hands can, in otherwise identical circumstances, be a dismal failure in another's. The teacher must consult his own interests, skills, weaknesses and personality, and shape his work and approach accordingly. One therefore cannot give him a blueprint; one can only try to set down a number of thoughts and ideas for him to consider adopting and adapting to his own individual style.

## Primary source material in examinations

### Internal examinations

Obviously, if a teacher bases quite a lot of his work on the use of primary source material, any internal examinations that occur whilst this work is going on will be based on it. However, there is much to be said for some accommodation of such material within otherwise conventional examinations.

Three types of question that can be based on this material are as follows. First, the question which seeks to test not so much the content of the work done as the skills and methods it has been designed to foster. For instance, What is the difference between a primary and a secondary source? What are the advantages and limitations of each? What are the respective merits and limitations of 'a' and 'b' as sources of evidence for such and such a subject?

More common than this sort of question is that which seeks to test comprehension of source material handled in recent work. This might take the form of a documentary extract followed either by a series of fairly specific questions related to particular phrases used, judgements made, attitudes struck, etc.; or by one more general and more open-ended question, such as 'What light does this throw on the condition of roads in the eighteenth century? Giving reasons, say how far you agree with it.' A variation on this type of question would be one which, say, listed extracts from the speeches of Joseph Chamberlain and required the pupil to use these to indicate Chamberlain's attitudes, aims and policies at different times in his career.

A third method is to set two or more contrasted primary extracts on the same subject, and to require the pupil to comment on the discrepancies.

Whatever the precise nature of the examination, particular care should be taken over two matters that can easily be overlooked. First, one should allow time for reading the examination questions. This is particularly important when the questions include perhaps fairly lengthy documentary extracts, and put a premium on a careful scrutiny of them. Second, it is essential to ensure that the material employed is integral to the question and not merely incidental. The questions must essentially be based on and result from the material, and should be incapable of being answered except by close reference to it. Too often, one finds that there is no essential connection between the material and the question, and that the latter could stand alone. For example:

Read the following extract from Leo Tolstoy's *What Then Must We Do?* (1886); then answer the questions which follow:

'In that house two women hardly manage to wash up all the crockery for the gentlefolk who have just had a meal, and two peasants in dress coats are *running up and down stairs* serving coffee, tea, wine and seltzer water. Upstairs a table is spread: they have just finished eating and will soon eat again till midnight, till three o'clock, often till cock-crow.

Some of them sit smoking and playing cards, others sit and smoke talking liberalism; others move about from place to place, eat, smoke, and *not knowing what to do* decide to go out for a drive. There are some fifteen healthy men and women there and some thirty able-bodied men and women servants working for them.'

    (a) Describe the conditions of life in nineteenth-century Russia of (i) a serf, (ii) a landowner's family.
    (b) When was serfdom abolished in Russia?
    (c) Why did its abolition not reduce revolutionary fervour?

There is, in this example, no essential connection between the primary source material and the questions. The inclusion of the former is artificial and unnecessary (even misleading), and seems little more than a hypocritical genuflection towards prevailing fashion. If the extract were to be used properly, better questions might be as follows:

(a) Comment on the contrast between the two italicised passages.
(b) Why might some of the 'gentlefolk' be 'talking liberalism'?
(c) What implied criticism is there in that phrase?
(d) On whose side do you think Tolstoy's sympathies lie? Give as many reasons, drawn from the extract, as you can.

If, as has been urged, the material is integral to the question, this of course necessitates clear prior thinking about the precise purpose of the question, which is obviously not going to be simply a test of knowledge. It is necessary to determine the exact skills that it is intended to test, and then to select the material and frame the questions accordingly.

*External examinations*

As with internal examinations, so also with external, there is considerable evidence of growth in the use of primary source material. This is especially true of the C.S.E. Mode 3 examinations. The 1972 Regulations of the North Regional Examination Board of the C.S.E., for instance, explicitly state that project work should be 'primarily concerned with methods of research', and that a principal aim is 'to encourage pupils to look for information not only in books but using all available sources'.

    At G.C.E. O level such an emphasis is relatively rare,[6] but it reappears in various guises at A level. Two examining boards in particular encourage such work for A level. The Cambridge optional

    [6] Southern Universities Joint Board have a 'Looking for History' alternative at O level; it is concerned with 'the exploration and interpretation of the visible evidence of history around us, making use of the material available in libraries and museums and of historical monuments'.

project paper requires extensive use of primary sources by candidates, and is an attempt to stimulate something approaching original historical research. The Joint Matriculation Board Syllabus C is based largely on a study of primary documents. However, it should be pointed out that the Cambridge project is an optional extra for which usually only the better candidates are encouraged to enter, and that the J.M.B. paper, in the opinion of one of our correspondents, is 'very difficult, and heavily weighted against the mediocre candidate who can be drilled to perform satisfactorily on a more orthodox paper, and thus achieve a higher grade'.

Examining boards which set recommended reading lists for A level special subject papers usually include in them a fair range of primary material, and it should be stressed that a critical scrutiny of evidence ought to be a normal part of any self-respecting sixth-form course, whether or not the examination explicitly requires it.

It may be argued that, unless one's syllabus covers an unusually short period, one simply has not the time to use primary source material for anything but occasional, illustrative purposes. This argument needs to be strongly refuted on two grounds. First, there is available now a large number of primary source booklets (e.g. Arnold's *Archive* series; Longman's *Seminar Studies in History*), use of which can easily be built into the teaching of an A level course in such a way as to contribute to the coverage of the syllabus at the same time as paying more than passing attention to the cultivation of proper historical skills. For instance, the *Archive* booklet on *The Reform of the Lords*[7] covers that topic at least as well as any other source in common use, and much more thoroughly than even the most substantial textbooks, and covers it in such a way as to bring the pupil face to face with the sort of historiographical problems to which even the weakest A level candidate should be gently introduced. Even if one feels that one can afford no more than an occasional lesson for what might mistakenly be regarded as such luxuries, a very worthwhile lesson can result from a carefully thought-out use simply of the cartoon end-papers of any of the *Archive* booklets. Cartoons, incidentally, can provide a very quick and useful means of testing an understanding of issues, a good cartoon being a terse expression of the essence of a particular situation. Opposed cartoons, also, can be especially useful.

A more general argument against the non-user of primary source material at this level is that good, even if only occasional, explicit use of it can have a valuable 'fall-out' effect. A level history is not merely sequential; it is cumulative. It is not just one damned thing

[7] Ed. R. D. H. Seaman (1971).

after another; it is one thing on top of another. This developmental aspect – especially at its conceptual level – can be greatly assisted by the judicious, if irregular, use of primary source material.

## Useful publications on primary source material

Perhaps the best source of information and guidance is the journal *Teaching History*, published twice a year by the Historical Association, and an essential aid to any history teacher. Many of the articles are concerned with primary source material work of one form or another, and even those which are written with a particular age-range in mind are capable of adaptation to other ages. Indeed, one of the significant advantages of this kind of material is that it is capable of being used across a wide age and ability range, since – unlike most textbooks – the raw material is infinitely adaptable to widely differing circumstances. Articles of particular usefulness are as follows:

B. G. E. Wood, 'Archive Units for Teaching' in Vol. 2, No. 6 (Nov. 1971) and Vol. 2, No. 7 (May 1972) – these articles contain most exhaustive, classified lists of available material.

M. Bryant, 'Documentary and Study Materials for Teachers and Pupils, Part 1 – Survey' in Vol. 1, No. 3 (May 1970); 'Part II – Theories and Practices' in Vol. 1, No. 4 (Nov. 1970); 'Part III – Practices – Research or Claptrap?' in Vol. 2, No. 5 (May 1971).

G. Jones and D. Watson, 'Archives in History Teaching – Some Problems' in Vol. 1, No. 3 (May 1970).

F. P. McGivern, 'An Approach to Archives and Local History' in Vol. 2, No. 5 (May 1971).

J. Hancock and H. Johnson, 'Archive Kits in the Secondary School' in Vol. 2, No. 7 (May 1972).

A particular value of *Teaching History* is that each number lists the addresses and activities of local History Teachers' Associations, many of which are active in the field of primary source material work.

Other useful journals, which often contain helpful articles on this subject, are *Amateur Historian* and *History* (in the latter, see J. Fines, 'Archives in School' in Vol. LIII, [Oct. 1968]).

A. Jamieson, *Practical History Teaching* (Evans, 1971) contains two chapters on source-work which show the variety of materials and methods that can be employed, and has a number of useful references. G. R. Batho contributes a sensible discussion of sources in the *Handbook for History Teachers* ed. W. H. Burston and C. W. Green (Methuen, 2nd ed., 1972). There is a very useful chapter,

'Documents as a basis for method', in M. Keatinge, *Studies in the Teaching of History* (Black, 1910).

This list is a mere tithe of what is available, but the teacher who pursues any of the references listed above will find more exhaustive bibliographies awaiting him there.

# 7 Written work

## The importance of written work

For many students of history written work is of central importance; for others it has a minor yet still indispensable role. At one extreme is the university open scholar whose skills in the writing of history will owe something to intelligent teaching as well as to his own talents. At the other extreme is the student who will be entered for no external examination at all and who may find it difficult to fill in blanks in sentences provided for him. For the latter type of student forms of expression other than the written word will often be more appropriate. He may be as much superior to the open scholar in devising display board illustrations, in compiling, as a member of a group, programmes using audio-visual aids, or in model-making, as the scholar is to him in written work. On the other hand, though these alternative methods of communicating ideas have their uses, more so in schools perhaps than in the kind of employment in which most school-leavers find themselves, the ability to communicate ideas on paper clearly and persuasively is so basic a skill in so many phases of adult life and work that training in written work ought not to be by-passed altogether, even for those with no talent for it.

It can be argued, however, that, while it is accepted that students should learn at least the basic skills in writing, this training ought to be the responsibility of the English department; consequently history teachers should confine themselves to the more congenial work of making their subject entertaining and, in small doses, informative. One answer to this is the long-established maxim that all teachers are teachers of English; it is a sound view. Secondly, history needs to give students something more than a casual interest in the more picturesque activities of our ancestors, and the knowledge that, for instance, the Battle of Hastings took place before the Battle of Waterloo. If it can do no more than this then it hardly deserves the name of history at all, a fact tacitly recognised in some recent changes in nomenclature in the subject at school level. If history in schools is to be taken seriously it needs to give students opportunities for individual assessment of evidence, however simple their judgements may be. This cannot be achieved solely by oral work. There are many occasions where written work not only gives practice in a skill of great value in everyday life but is far and away the best method for enabling most students to express their personal judgements about historical situations more thoughtfully, coherently, and freely, than many can orally. Group discussions and activities have a value of their own but the sovereign virtue of written work is that it generally enables a student to develop his own ideas at his own pace, slow though that may sometimes be. At the same time it is recognised that there are almost illiterate pupils for whom conventional written work destroys any interest they may have in the subject. This does not mean that they never write at all. Writing the script for a tape, writing articles for a newspaper (centred on a historic event or year) for a wall-display, and writing an imaginary log-book for an explorer's voyage, are examples of written work which they can undertake. Their work must be written in rough first, and checked by the teacher, so that the final product is perfect and associated in the mind of the writer with success rather than failure.

So far the value of written work has been expressed at least in part with reference to those whose command of vocabulary, grammar, and clarity, is so uncertain that it is a major achievement by their teachers if, by the time these students leave school, they can make themselves intelligible in the use of the written word. That this should be so more than a hundred years after the teaching of the three R's in schools was considered to be a reasonable objective is a dampening thought. There are, however, many secondary school students who are capable of far more than constructing simple sentences grammatically expressed. Once the needs of these more able students were given too much attention; now there may be a danger that some of them will be given too little. This would be a pity since their role in preserving high academic standards is valuable both in schools and later. There is the attitude, of course, that written work, which is of crucial importance to these students, is merely a utilitarian aid to passing examinations. This is a narrow-minded view. Training in written work is undoubtedly useful in preparing students for examinations but its value is not limited to that. 'So much of what we agree to be valuable about History in its widest sense finds its best expression and combination in written form' wrote one correspondent. When it is well taught written work gives training in clarity of presentation, in persuasiveness in argument, in balanced judgement, in attention to detail, in intelligent assessment of evidence, and in literary skill. It may well be that there is no other subject in which these qualities of mind are so fully exercised collectively as in history. Clearly the usefulness of these qualities is not confined to passing examinations, nor even to producing better historians; they have a wider relevance in developing skills of general value to the individual and to the community. In short, the student is learning a craft and few educational processes give greater satisfaction to teacher and taught alike.

## A-level history

### Essay writing

In judging what he hopes to achieve by written work in his school the history teacher should first consider what the final product of this work is to be. This will give shape and purpose to the training throughout the school. Most students leave before they are seventeen and specific guidance for them, at their appropriate level, is given later in this chapter. There still remain many thousands of A-level candidates for whom skill in written work is of pre-eminent importance. Since their needs in this respect are more complex than those of other students, yet still, in part, set the standard for most other written work – it is not only in A-level work that relevance and factual accuracy, for instance, are required – an examination of the qualities of a good A-level essay may be of value. There would probably be a large measure of agreement that the following list comprises most of the essential features:

## 1. Relevance

Relevance is the *sine qua non of* any successful essay. The line of argument to be taken in response to the question needs to be firmly established in the introduction, possibly even in the opening sentence. Each paragraph should be a development of a particular facet of the argument, and the conclusion should be crisp and convincing. Close study of the significant words and phrases of the question is an essential preliminary; so is a paragraph plan. Relevance may well be strengthened by explicit reference at intervals to crucial words in the question, if failure to do so is likely to create the least uncertainty in the reader's mind over the direction of the argument.

## 2. Factual accuracy and thoroughness

The tendency to be encouraging in marking essays is a sound one but factual errors should be given short shrift by the marker. Students have to learn to treat facts with respect. Carelessness over facts easily verifiable from books ought not to be lightly tolerated. Secondly, philosophical disquisitions are no substitute for the generous array of precise accurate facts which are an essential feature of any good history essay.

**3.** Wide range of ideas

An elementary oversight in this respect is the failure to realise that a general question, for instance 'Was Joseph II's reign a failure?', involves both foreign and domestic policies. Usually, but not always, students avoid this mistake. More frequently a major aspect of domestic policy is omitted. Omissions are less likely if, depending on the question, the following policy sectors are considered – the administrative organisation of government at central and local level; the power and activities of the legislature; economic and financial policies; relationships with the Church, nobility, bourgeoisie, and working classes; social policies; the armed forces; the judicial system. Mnemonics are not to be despised since, especially in a timed essay, it is easy to miss out a major branch of policy. Teachers sometimes devise these mnemonics for their students but they can create their own. The danger with a mechanical aid is that it will be used mechanically. This can be avoided if the student learns never to suspend his attention over relevance; he, therefore, selects from the knowledge brought to mind by the mnemonics merely those sections which relate to the question being answered. The wide-angled approach may also be evident in the ability of the student to place his topic in its national, international, and historical context, and in his awareness of influential trends of thought, always assuming of course that he uses his knowledge for a relevant purpose.

**4.** Persuasiveness

Mechanical regurgitation of facts is not a habit encouraged by A-level questions and those students devoted to the writing of lengthy narratives have to learn to reshape their thinking accordingly. Perhaps the simplest way of achieving this is for the student to think of the essay as an argument, in which, however, he has the unique advantage of being able to develop his own point of view without interruption from the reader. At the same time the student needs to be conscious of the fact that he is not writing merely for his own edification but in order to convince the reader of the soundness of the arguments used. If he can imagine the presence at his elbow of an invisible sceptical critic he will begin to develop the self-critical approach which every writer needs.

**5.** Historical awareness

This is not a quality which is easy to pinpoint, nor consequently to teach, yet its importance is self-evident. It springs in part from scepticism, leading to a realisation of the fallibility of much of what passes for evidence, and of the fallibility of historians in their interpretations of the past. It finds expression in writing in an approach which takes very little for granted, which is always ready to make a fresh examination of conventional wisdom, and which refuses to regard the work of senior historians, however distinguished, as being necessarily the last word on any given subject. The student who has such a critical approach should of course be prepared to be judged by the same high standard himself. Another indication of the historical awareness of the student is his ability to distinguish between the significant and the incidental. Confronted with an array of facts on, for instance, some aspect of domestic policy, students differ quite widely in their ability to disentangle those facts which are influential upon historical decisions, or events, from those which are subsidiary or ephemeral. Practice in this skill by group study of selected passages of historical writing is one means of achieving progress in this important matter. The ability to see connections, comparisons and contrasts is also to be encouraged. Made parenthetically, to prevent the essay from becoming diffuse, these references widen the scope of the discussion by placing the immediate issue within a broader context of general historical understanding. Historical awareness is evident, too, in extreme wariness over the use of absolute words – 'all', 'never', 'first', and so on. One further indication that the student has benefited from historical training lies in the care he takes to ensure that every assertion he makes is reinforced as strongly as possible by intelligent use of supporting evidence.

### 6. Stylistic effectiveness

To say something is one matter; to say it well is another. Literary skill is not merely an incidental extra in writing. It permeates the whole fabric of the essay, and, since it is a skill, it can be developed by training. Some of the features of the good A-level history essay which have been mentioned so far – such as persuasiveness, for instance – pre-suppose stylistic skills since style is a habit of thought as well as a collection of verbal techniques. It is the latter which are more easily taught, but in mastering them the student also begins to develop an awareness of words, of the ideas which they represent, and an observant attention to detail; this experience is as important in historical as it is in literary training. Among the qualities which add to the stylistic effectiveness of an essay are these: a mature vocabulary; the use of punctuation as a positive aid; a readiness to create, or to borrow, the striking phrase; the skilful blending of quotations into the body of the essay; the antithetical sentence, balancing opposed or complementary ideas; a logical flow of thought from sentence to sentence and from paragraph to paragraph; an eye for vivid and enlightening detail; and compactness of expression

– desirable in itself, and more so still in an examination system where the time given for answering questions is short.

Obviously, unless the teacher himself has a clear conception of the requirements of a good essay his students have only a remote chance of developing the requisite skills themselves. Precept is more effective when it is reinforced by example and it is a stimulus to the class and teacher alike if he occasionally writes a timed essay himself alongside his pupils and on the same terms. There is no better way of understanding the problems of essay writing. The marking of many essays is not a complete substitute for the first-hand experience of writing one oneself. If the teacher is confident enough to depart still further from the safety of criticism to the risks of performance, and is willing to make his own essay as well as those of his students the subject of discussion, the exercise will be additionally enlightening. It is by discussion of this kind, by offering suggestions, and by encouraging each individual advance as soon as it occurs, that the more subtle skills of written work, such as the power to argue persuasively, to see events in a wide context, and to make style an ally, develop.

The qualities of a good A level history essay listed above do not emerge spontaneously and instantly in any student. Regular practice in essay writing is essential but a sense of proportion needs to be kept. Sixth formers, taking at least two papers in each of three A level subjects, and with some claims on their time by minority subjects, cannot give their essay writing the thought it deserves if they are overloaded with this kind of work. Nor should history teachers, nor any others for that matter, adopt the childishly arrogant view that their own subject is the only one of any consequence for those whom they teach, thus giving themselves some imagined prescriptive right to monopolise the working time of their students. Two essays in three weeks, one in European and one in English history, for instance, are ample. Essays can be written at home, particularly in the first year in the sixth form, in class with the help of a few brief guiding notes, and lastly in class without notes.

Essays written at home should not be of an inordinate length. New entrants to the sixth form quite commonly have the illusion that the quality of an essay is decided predominantly by its length. These long essays, often a matter of mere copying from books, give very little practice in selectivity and provide more physical than mental exercise for the writer. This point needs to be made firmly to avoid wasted effort. It is well worthwhile, too, considering the desirability of indicating to students a maximum – and minimum – length for essays. A useful variant, either for revision or when time is short, is for the student to make a brief analysis of an essay question instead of writing it in full. The introduction, however, does need to be written in full to show the tone and the line of argument to be adopted in the essay. After this it is sufficient to give paragraph headings and, under each heading, a mixture in brief itemised form of key points, quotations, significant incidents, and so on, followed by a conclusion also written in full. This method incidentally makes a good basis for discussion. Another variant is the one paragraph 'precis' essay containing the essence of an answer shorn of supporting evidence and comment. This method is useful in training students to search for the heart of a question. Nevertheless, the best practice is that which most closely resembles the examination situation in which the student has to write four full answers in three hours, without any help from books. The mock examination – a misguided title but too well known now to be changed – provides one occasion for practising the requisite skills, but is insufficient on its own. Nearer the time of the A-level examinations some class periods should be used to give candidates further experience in writing timed essays; if the periods can be so arranged, a double period during which two answers have to be written is better practice than two single answers in separate periods. In the early stages of this practice students can be allowed to make use of a single sheet of notes containing details of significant quotations, detail, or comment, to give them some guidance while writing, the questions having been given in advance; compiling such a reference sheet is a useful form of revision in itself. In the later stages the student must rely exclusively on his own memory and intelligence as he will have to do in the examination itself. Although practice in the writing of timed essays is important the methods suggested should not be used with obsessive frequency; teachers who fall into this trap merely dull the responsiveness of their students at a time when they need to be at their best.

Collective and individual discussions of essay work are important but need to be managed with discretion. The prepared comments based on the teacher's own observations from marking the students' work are valuable; so, too, is the discussion which arises from them. The limit of usefulness is passed when discussion continues inordinately on trivialities which can be settled by a stroke of the marking pen in the essay or by discussion with individual pupils. This latter activity is at least as valuable as group discussion. The view that learning is not taking place unless the teacher is lecturing his pupils must by now be defunct, or nearly so. The pattern for a period occasionally may be, for instance, that the teacher hands back corrected essays to a group and makes a few brief general comments on the work. Work is then set involving the selection of material on a theme, or introductory reading on a new subject, or simply the widening of knowledge of the variety of material available in books, journals, and pamphlets. So long as the dimensions of the room make it possible for this work to continue undisturbed the teacher can then use the opportunity to see each student individually about his written work. A few minutes spent with each is more influential in reinforcing the better features of students' work, and in eliminating the worse features, than reliance on the marking pen alone. It is a practical and significant matter in this activity that student and teacher should sit side by side where both of them can see and discuss the essay concerned in comfort.

These individual discussions follow marking which needs to be as detailed and as prompt as possible if it is to be fully effective. The symbols used, so long as they are time-saving and understood, are of no consequence, but it is important in marking to be specific in indicating the good features of an essay as well as the bad. Marking which consists exclusively of criticisms scattered dramatically in red biro across the essay does more to gratify the marker's ego than to help the student. Sarcasm is equally out of place; and if the marker believes himself to be a wit he needs to be certain that others think so too. These cautions need to be borne in mind; at the same time it is obligatory to point out weaknesses in the work of students. Common faults, particularly in the first year sixth, are irrelevance, a narrowness of approach leading to omission of a major sector of policy, inaccurate or ill-judged statements, purposeless introductions, loose organisation of paragraphs, padding, clumsy expression of ideas, and mistakes in spelling and grammar; blunders in punctuation are particularly common. But there are good features, too, which equally need to be indicated as they occur, not merely left to a general favourable comment at the end. If, for instance, the student writes a sparkling opening sentence, an effective introduction, uses vocabulary, source material, and interesting and significant incident well, shows understanding of underlying trends, and makes frequent shrewd comments of his own, then the marker should acknowledge these good features by a comment or symbol at the point where they occur. Elimination of mistakes is valuable but it is positive marking which contributes most to the growth of a student's confidence and skill. Whether marks or grades are given, whether sub-divisions are made giving assessments for style, content, and so on, are matters of minor consequence on which teachers will follow their own whims. The more important issue is that marking should be detailed and helpful.

One device to improve essay writing is for students to tape-record a selection of their best essays; after A level is a good period of the year for this. A useful collection can quickly be assembled in this way. Playing back a taped essay of a post-A level student to those in the lower sixth approaching the same topic for the first time is a useful means of providing a realistic standard at which to aim. Students are closely interested in seeing how one of their near contemporaries has tackled the subject, and the method stimulates discussion more effectively than the high-powered academic talks commercially available on tapes – although these have their uses in other ways. Another method of self-improvement is for the student to read aloud his essay to himself and to listen to the sound of it. This practice is useful for all, but particularly for those who find it difficult to express themselves well.

*Note-making*

The making of notes is another form of written work on which the teacher needs to give guidance. He will have done so before lower down the school, but the scale of notes required and the extent of individual work set new problems for the newcomer to the sixth form. Moreover, it will not be a waste of time to remind the sixth former in the early weeks of the course of the commonplace but important matters which he can easily overlook. The blackboard is still a useful aid to the teacher in showing students how notes can be organised. Ample use of heading and sub-headings, the itemising of information when possible, generous spacing both to give room for after-thoughts and to improve the lay-out of the page – not for its own sake but to facilitate learning – and for a similar reason, neat writing, are all to be encouraged as part of the essential training of students. Sometimes notes have to be made from oral lessons. The emphasis nowadays is rightly on individual work and group discussion rather than on lectures but there remain a few situations where a lecture is the most efficient teaching method for dealing with a particular problem. Providing background information as the prelude to the study of a new topic, or explaining an idea of special difficulty such as, for instance, the significance of the work of Sir Lewis Namier and his colleagues on the early years of George III's reign, are teaching situations where lecturing may well be required. Taking notes from lectures presents difficulties for students in choice, organisation, and neatness. These difficulties melt away if the teacher has organised his own material logically, has a clear unhurried delivery, stops to explain and, if necessary, to spell difficult words, and is sufficiently in touch with his class to sense the need to repeat an idea in other words, or to stop altogether for a time if he can see that the group is having to struggle to keep abreast of his ideas. Variations in the pace of delivery help, too, in indicating which parts of his comments are worth detailed notes and which parts are minor, possibly light relief incidents, which do not deserve to be diligently recorded. Approached in this way, notes can be taken directly while the teacher is lecturing, a time-saving device which students welcome. There are alternatives. The note-taking can take place in the second half of a lesson, after the teacher has lectured in the first half. Again, notes can be made in rough during the talk and copied up afterwards. The former method, however, drastically reduces the subject matter which can be dealt with in a period, while the latter method is a mechanical and time-consuming task.

It could be argued that duplicated notes might be used as a further alternative. Their double disadvantage is that they provide no practice for the student in taking notes efficiently from a lecture, a skill which some at least find valuable in higher and further education, and, secondly, while the compilation of duplicated notes may involve considerable mental exercise on the part of the teacher, the use to which they are put by the student may be casual and superficial precisely because, unlike intelligent note-making, duplicated notes make no direct demand on the student's own ability to grasp and synthesise information. There are, however, a few situations where the use of duplicated notes may be justified. They may be useful in saving time since students cannot deal with every topic they are expected to master by individual research and discussion. They may be essential in making available to students source extracts and articles in journals where shortage of copies as well as of time makes it impossible for every student to have first-hand contact with the subject-matter.

The great bulk of a student's note-taking will, it is hoped, be from books rather than from lectures. The notes need to be a response to a specific theme of a wide-ranging nature rather than a general narrative. 'Make notes on the reign of Peter the Great' is a worse instruction to a group than 'Make notes on the theme "Was Peter the Great an imitator or a creator?".' Choosing the question for note-making requires careful thought. It needs to be one which involves consideration of every major aspect of a new subject, while, at the same time, requiring students to be alert over relevance. The general points, previously made, about neat organisation and generous spacing of notes still hold good, of course. Textbooks will generally be the starting point. There should be a mixture of these – the differences of emphasis being in themselves a source of discussion. No notes should be made until the complete section has been read. The student who starts making notes from the first page he reads and who continues to accumulate them as he reads will collect unwieldy notes with the significant and insignificant points lumped together indiscriminately. The more efficient method is to jot down page references to material which looks as if it may be useful then, after the reading is completed, to select for detailed note-making only that material whose value is still evident when the topic has been seen as a whole. The next stage, in which shortage of time may be a very limiting factor, is to collect notes from documentary material, biographies, articles in journals, and any other source which suggests itself. Judicious use of the contents and index pages, wherever possible, is a useful time-saver in this work; students do not always readily grasp that it is not obligatory to start to read every book at page 1, nor, indeed, to start reading even a chapter from its beginning. The notes made should always include the name of the author, the title and, if significant, the date of the source.

*Documentary analysis*

The analysis of documentary evidence is a form of written work which provides excellent and interesting training for the student. English history, particularly from the eighteenth century onwards, is quite well provided with books of documents on constitutional, economic, and social history. Slim books of documentary extracts on miscellaneous subjects spanning a period of a hundred years or more are of little value, but sufficient books of adequate length and substance are now available to make possible intelligent study of source material. The Archive Teaching Units issued by County Record Offices, by some universities, and by the Historical Association, have notably strengthened this aspect of school work. (See p. 95.) The training provided by these units in working directly from copies of documents is invaluable; already there are several topics on which the student can see a useful conspectus of the evidence himself instead of having to rely on the second- or third-hand comments of specialist or textbook historians.

In organising written work involving documentary analysis the teacher may sometimes be helped by the handbooks issued with many Archive Teaching Units in which questions on the documents are provided. He may very well, however, prefer to prepare his own worksheet and may sometimes have to do so. Detailed study of a single document is sometimes justifiable; more often the questions can be more significant if they deal with a group of documents with a logical unity. There is not much point at this level in the purely factual question. The aim is to encourage deductions from the evidence provided, though attention will also need to be given to the understanding of terms which are not now part of everyday language. Training in this kind of written activity leads by a natural progression to project work where the student, with minimal guidance from the teacher, chooses the theme and does the research on his own. The Cambridge Local Examinations Syndicate provides an optional project paper eminently suitable for this individual work. The stage where help from the teacher is most justified is in advice on the theme. Experience is needed to head off students from choosing vague project titles and to guide them towards a theme which is precisely delimited in date and subject matter, and which poses a question which has to be answered. The teacher's knowledge of the material available in the school and in the area is another highly relevant consideration in helping students to make a wise choice of theme.

### *Maps, charts and diagrams*

A good historical atlas and modern textbooks with a generous provision of sketch maps may make it unnecessary for the student to draw many maps himself and, since time is very limited, this is just as well. There may, however, be special situations where the sixth form student should draw a map himself – drawing a sketch map, for instance, to show the diplomatic and military situation in central Europe during the Seven Years' War may well be an instructive exercise. Moreover, some teachers take the view that A level candidates should be able to draw reasonably accurate sketch maps of the regions and countries studied as they were at the relevant time; this activity is likely to give students a clearer understanding of geographical factors in history than they can gain merely by looking at an atlas. Charts and diagrams are primarily valuable in economic history particularly since in the post-Clapham era economic historians feel it obligatory to pepper their pages lavishly with statistics. Visual representation of these statistics by the student himself in the form of graphs or blocks helps him to understand general trends more effectively than he can by studying pages whose readability may be on a par with that of a telephone directory.

### O level and C.S.E. history

A thorough understanding by the teacher of the characteristics of good essay work (see pp. 116–19) is not only helpful in the effective teaching of A level candidates; it also gives him the advantage of a long-term plan in the teaching of O level and C.S.E. candidates. Not all of them will go on to A level work but some will, and, for the rest, mastery of some of the skills mentioned will have a general educational value. Judgement is required in concentrating on the development of those skills in writing which are appropriate to the ability of the student. Candidates for O level and C.S.E. examinations certainly should be capable of relevance, factual accuracy, sensible paragraph organisation, and a reasonable flow of ideas. They are also often capable of finding and using interesting supporting detail from source material, for instance, and of disentangling significant from insignificant facts. Some progress can be made too in developing stylistic skills, particularly in encouraging the development of a more mature vocabulary, in blending smoothly together material from different sources, and in discouraging looseness in the use of vocabulary, phrasing, and punctuation. Detailed advice on these positive and negative features of writing is needed at frequent intervals, and the student needs regular practice, making an essay a fortnight essential. To attempt to implant the skills mentioned all at once is of course foolish. Each needs to be grafted into the training as the teacher senses that the majority of the group is ready for it. The size of the groups usually precludes the possibility of the regular individual guidance which can be given in sixth form teaching, nevertheless means can generally be found at the end of the school day to help those who are most likely to benefit greatly from individual attention; this includes both those who find progress difficult and those who find progress easy.

Training in the skills of formal essay writing bulks less large in C.S.E. than in O level work. There was some feeling among corresponding members that the all-important requirement in C.S.E. essay work is a lengthy recital of facts, and that other refinements, though no doubt welcomed when they occurred, are not expected. The C.S.E. examination, however, does not consist exclusively of essay questions; short questions, often of the multiple-choice type, are also provided with the expectation that C.S.E. students will have been well practised in using their powers of observation to assess evidence. The abundant availability of booklets, folders, wallets, and packs of source material, particularly on British social and economic history, gives ample opportunity for training in this activity. The amount of writing by the student is small but its value in providing historical training appropriate for the age group is clear. 'Hence the paradox', writes W. Lamont:[1] 'in reacting against the "academic" aridities of the conventional examination papers many of the C.S.E. papers moved closer to the academic criteria of the professional historian. C.S.E. candidates are increasingly being asked to reflect upon, and draw inferences from, raw material in the shape of graphs, cartoons, statistics, literary sources, and the like.' These words may be over-generous as a comment on the C.S.E.

[1] *New Movements in the Study and Teaching of History* (ed. M. Ballard; Temple Smith, London, 1970), p. 202.

examination as a whole, and over-critical of conventional examination papers, but there are clear signs that the approach of the C.S.E. boards to examining in history is, in some respects, having an influence on the G.C.E. boards. It could be added, too, that the imaginative accounts which C.S.E. candidates frequently write during their course, though at first sight far removed from the activities of the professional historian, do help to make the minds of students more aware of the everyday realities of the lives of preceding generations; in that respect at least their observation of the past is being made more acute; G. M. Young might well have approved. Here one example, easily adapted, must suffice to show an imaginative approach: 'Write a letter home to your parents as if you were an infantryman in the 1914–18 war describing life in the trenches. Make use of the following material – soldiers' songs, their attitude to generals, war-poetry, the conditions and layout of the trenches, weapons of war.' Questions of this kind are a far cry from 'Give an account of the reforms introduced by Gladstone's government of 1868–74', but it would be a bold spirit who would assert that the letter about trench warfare required less historical grasp and insight.

This is not to suggest, however, that one should leap impulsively to the conclusion that conventional O level questions are anachronisms, Canute-like survivals in an age of progress, having no useful part to play in training students in written work. We are governed by politicians, not by sociologists, and to ignore that everyday fact is merely to exchange one form of myopia for another. Questions on political history – and they do not have to be so stereotyped in their wording as they have tended to be in past O level examination papers – give students opportunities of gaining some understanding of the motivations for political decisions and of the practical problems and limitations which have to be faced in securing change; this is an important matter which is given very little attention in social and economic history. The point is, therefore, that in organising written work for O level and C.S.E. candidates the teacher should not concentrate exclusively on political or socio-economic history. The student will gain in understanding if he has some knowledge of both, though the proportions will vary according to the examination he is taking.

*Note-making*

Preparation for examinations in which memorisation plays a part inevitably involves the keeping of notes in a well-organised way. Whether note-books or folders are used is a matter for the teacher himself from his knowledge of his pupils. The use of folders and file-paper gives more scope for initiative and for the addition of material from a mixture of sources. If this is beyond the capacity of the students, however, and if they find the organisation of notes difficult and are apt to lose sheets of paper, then the notebook method is better. Even then, however, it is essential for students to be trained to space out their work well, to divide their notes into headings and sub-headings, to itemise their material when it is appropriate, and to leave spaces between one sub-division and the next so that there are a few lines left for afterthoughts, such as an apposite quotation, comment, or interesting illustrative detail. Guidance on headings can be given by the teacher in the first place, but later they can be evolved collectively by teachers and students; it is still necessary to add, perhaps, that note-making should be a follow-up to individual reading and to group discussion, not a replacement for them in which the student merely writes down as much as he can of the teacher's lectures. In the guidance which is given to students in note-making they should be made aware of the value of a three-way approach to a historical event so that they are trained to analyse it into its causes, its course, and its results, including its significance.

### Project work

The plentiful availability of booklets and similar material makes it possible to deal with many subjects as individual projects. Work sheets need to be provided for each student containing questions which will give him a clear idea of the major issues involved, while still giving him scope to use enterprise in finding material which may, or may not, support the information given in textbooks. The sources need to be indicated by the teacher and should include textbooks, topic booklets, and other appropriate sources, such as Archive Teaching Units, for instance. The teacher himself must have first-hand knowledge of the sources which he recommends. Generally this means that the sources will come from within the history department itself; public libraries may be useful but, unless the teacher is watchful, young students will base their choice of books from libraries merely on the title. The result is apt to be that in studying poverty, for instance, they may well choose S. E. Finer's *Life of Chadwick* or some other book much too erudite for their age. Some students like to illustrate their work with photographs, press cuttings, and sketches. These add variety and, sometimes, point to their work, but by this stage it is practice in the written assessment of a theme which contributes most substantially to their progress. In this respect setting a maximum word length for a project is desirable. In con-

junction with intelligently compiled work-sheet questions this helps
to eliminate the bug-bear of seemingly endless pages of mechanical
copying from textbooks which is one familiar way in which project
work can be abused. It is important too that the topic itself should
not be diffuse. 'Transport in the nineteenth century' would be an
unwise choice for a project: 'The Liverpool and Manchester Railway between 1824 and 1847' would make a more manageable and
instructive topic.

*Maps, charts, diagrams and cartoons*

Although atlases and sketch maps in books may often be useful
it may still happen that the only way to acquire a map to illustrate
precisely the points which the teacher wants to show is for him to
draw it himself and to duplicate copies. Duplicated map outlines
on which the student himself puts in place names, frontiers, and
brief information of the kind found in sketch-map histories are also
a valuable means of conveying and testing knowledge. Since in a
busy life teachers cannot always have duplicated maps instantly
available there is no reason why students should not draw the map
outlines themselves using tracing-paper, so long as the map is
reasonably large, and then supplying the information which the
teacher requires. In the process of drawing the political frontiers
of the Balkan nations in 1878, for instance, and the changes which
took place in these frontiers during that year, the student has the
chance to absorb more thoroughly than he can from studying a
map drawn by someone else the geographical features which are
vital to an understanding of the situation. The need to show physical
features is well illustrated in this 1878 crisis where, for instance, the
Balkan Mountains were chosen for military reasons as the northern
frontier of Eastern Roumelia. Indicating the major harbours in the
area in the Mediterranean and Adriatic would also be an advantage;
if the map is large enough the sketch-map method of brief comments
on the map itself is useful too. The use of charts and diagrams to
illustrate population changes, railway construction, and so on, is
another way in which the eye can be used to help the mind; modern
social and economic history books provide plentiful examples of
the ways in which this statistical information can be represented.
Another form of illustrative work which has been recommended is
the drawing of historical cartoons by the student in an attempt to
represent the essence of a historical situation. This is only suitable
for those who can draw reasonably well and even then requires a
talent for historical understanding as well as for art unlikely to be
simultaneously present in many students. Nevertheless, for those

who think the attempt is worth more than the result, and for those who, in the interest of variety, want to use every possible technique, the drawing of historical cartoons by students may be thought worthwhile; certainly, cartoons drawn by pupils with a talent for that form of expression make interesting material for display boards.

### Non-examination work

Under this broad heading there are two categories of student whose needs overlap to some extent yet are not wholly identical. One group consists of those who at some later stage will be taking a public examination; the other group consists of those who will not be doing so. In organising written work for the former group some account needs to be taken of the special importance which this work will have for them later. It will often happen, of course, that representatives of both groups will be taught together in mixed ability classes; this makes imperative, therefore, the provision of a generous proportion of individual work. Trouble taken at this early stage to develop habits of accuracy and relevance will mean that higher up the school more time will be available for developing additional skills.

Keeping to the point is an art which adults as well as students find difficulty in mastering; training in this respect of these young students needs therefore to be very elementary. Nevertheless, if the assignment is to explain why the Spanish Armada was defeated it needs to be made clear to any student who devotes himself to describing why the Armada was sent that he has to think what he is doing and to learn to pay close attention to the wording of the question. One of the by-products of historical training ought to be a habit of scrutinising words closely and thoughtfully. Many young students are quite capable of this if they are made to realise that it matters; equally, most of them are quite capable of being slipshod if they are allowed to feel that it does not matter. Moreover, the habit of studying words observantly strengthens literary as well as historical ability. These abilities, after all, do not exist in water-tight compartments: the boy who is careless in his use of English is unlikely to be notably vigilant in choosing significant remarks from documentary extracts, for instance. In discouraging spelling mistakes and carelessness over punctuation the history teacher is fostering an attitude of mind which is needed in his own subject too.

Another valuable characteristic of written work which can be trained at this level is enterprise in using lively and interesting detail to supplement the basic information in textbooks. There is a tendency at this age, and later sometimes, to venerate the textbook to such an extent that, while ample opportunity is given to read booklets and so on, these valuable aids are treated as entertaining diversions while 'real' history consists of that which is copied out of the textbook – a reminder that one does not have to be old to be reactionary. Greater familiarity with source material is leading to more intelligent use of information than was possible when students gained their knowledge exclusively from the teacher and the text-book.

A caveat needs to be entered that for this age group written work should be simple, varied and not too mechanically frequent. The formal question, based on the style of G.C.E. examinations, is in-appropriate. There are many alternatives – a Viking raid described by a Viking; a dialogue between two Jacobites in 1745, or rather more ambitiously, a playlet; compiling a nineteenth- or twentieth-century newspaper, using perhaps the commercially produced news-papers on great events as a model; writing the story of a family to incorporate the events, say, of 1533–53; the diary of a soldier in the Boer War; a letter describing the death of Cranmer. Each of these devices can be adapted to suit the period being studied. It is essential that written work of this kind should, as far as possible, be soundly based on fact and should show some historical understanding. The language used, too, should be modern, and neither colloquial nor pseudo-period. Furthermore the teacher has to be confident enough in his relationship with his class to ensure that his students give serious thought to this work, otherwise it can quickly degenerate into nonsense. Even with these provisos the purists may still feel nervous about straying from the straight and narrow path of formal work; narrow, however, it certainly is and by being so misses oppor-tunities for stimulating the imagination and interest of pupils who are very responsive to personalised accounts of the past. The accounts they write will no doubt be far from the truth; if so they are in good company, if historiography is any guide. Moreover, the effort of imagination to see the events of the past through the eyes of the past, so far as that is possible for anyone, is an attribute which no historian worth his salt would despise.

Just as the writing of formal essays is unsuitable at this stage so too is the accumulation of pages of notes. They serve very little purpose for these pupils. Occasional follow-up lessons in which, largely under the guidance of the teacher at first, a topic is broken down into its component parts by using headings and sub-headings are useful in giving practice in grouping ideas relevantly. Another method is to duplicate a framework of headings, based on the pupils' reading, which they themselves complete after discussion in class. It would be stultifying, however, if note-making were to become the major class activity.

*Projects*

The project is a form of written work where those who have enthusiasm for writing about the past can, to some extent, be given
their head, except that the teacher should provide an optimum length
of time for this work. The title needs to be wider than it is in more
advanced work. If a boy wants to launch out on the story of football
through the ages he will be able to find material much more easily
than if he wanted to write the history of West Ham United: the
specific topic requires a more mature approach. Biographies provide
suitable subject-matter too, particularly where, as for James
Brindley, Louis Pasteur, Madame Curie, and so on, the main interest
is not political. There are, however, always exceptions to take into
account in any advice about teaching methods. Nowadays, particularly, there are apt to be young pupils whose knowledge of local
archaeology or of railways, for instance, fits them admirably for the
writing of projects on topics which are more specific than those
generally set at this stage. The future open scholar, too, will undoubtedly be able to make intelligent use of the kind of material
found in Archive Teaching Units. In obtaining material for projects
recourse will often be made to outside resources, such as public
libraries, museums, nationalised industries and national organisations. The teacher should take seriously his responsibility in diminish-
ing the flow of vague requests with which these organisations are too
often plagued. For Oxfam to receive several letters from one class
saying 'we are writing a project on the history of food supplies in
the twentieth century. Please send us information' is a gross misuse
of the time of that organisation and an indictment of the inadequacy
of the teacher's preparation.

*Maps, charts and diagrams*

Drawing as an alternative to literary activity is particularly appropriate for younger students. It is a method with which they are
familiar from their primary school days, it is one in which many of
them take great pride, it gives variety and, equally important, it
remains a valuable method of instruction; it is of some relevance,
too, that those not gifted in other forms of written work can quite
often produce sketch maps which are both informative and a
pleasure to see. Tracing-paper, mapping pens, rulers and coloured
pencils are aids which will help even the most untidy to produce
reasonable sketch maps or charts. Ignorance of the location of places
is widespread. Simple map-work tasks such as drawing the route of
Hadrian's Wall or, from modern history, a map of Africa to show
the modern names and frontiers of states are a valuable means of

remedying this weakness. Sketch-maps to show the system of defences for Hadrian's Wall, patterns of immigration into Britain, and so on, are also recommended. There are, too, a few topics – architectural styles, for instance – where writing is of negligible importance at this stage and drawings are by far the best means of conveying the information required. The making of time charts is a traditional teaching method which retains its usefulness; the visual impression is a means, not easily secured otherwise, of giving students a sense of perspective about time – an important consideration in their work.

The kinds of written work so far described are relevant for those who will be taking an external examination at some later stage. They are also partly relevant for those who will not be doing so, but some adaptations will need to be made. Formal essays and note-making will play very little part in the work of these students. The purpose is to give them an interest in the subject rather than thorough training in the disciplines of reading and writing. Progress in these latter respects will probably be made most effectively in special remedial groups. It is admitted that without these disciplines interest may well be superficial and ephemeral. Nevertheless, a superficial interest is better than none, and may grow into something more solid with developing maturity in the post-school years. Written work is likely to be the least welcome form of activity for these students. A parallel, which may help in understanding their attitude, is for an academic to have it imposed upon him as obligatory that he should represent all his ideas in pictorial form. No correspondent, however, suggested that written work should be dispensed with altogether for any group in schools. Apart from any other consideration, written work is a means of providing variety of teaching method, a matter of even greater significance when the level of interest in the subject may well be very low. Imaginative work, projects and narrative accounts are likely to be the most successful methods.

Finding subject matter for imaginative work is no great problem, particularly as the syllabus for these students can be much more flexible than it is for those working for examinations. On the whole the topics of interest are likely to be from the border land between sociology and history and from modern times rather than from the pre-twentieth-century period, largely because it is easier, for instance, for a boy to understand the attitude and environment of a coal-miner in the 1920s than it is for him to understand the attitude and environment of an Anglo-Saxon villager. Obviously there are exceptions to this and intelligent opportunism by the teacher in relating imaginative work to films at the local cinema and to programmes and series on television and radio can help to widen his students' knowledge of the past. Classroom films and film-strips, photographs and paintings of historical interest, and artefacts, if imaginatively presented, can also be stimuli to lively written work (see p. 65). It is, incidentally, quite clear that to secure satisfactory written work from this group requires highly skilled teaching and the accumulation and expert presentation of a wider variety of material, as a preliminary to writing, than is needed for those who find writing easy. Inevitably this slower build-up before writing means that the teacher has to adjust himself to a very different pace from that at which work for examinations proceeds.

Project work presents particular difficulties for those who both need close guidance on written work and yet are apt to resent it. So far as it is possible the topic chosen should reflect the choice of the student rather than be dictated to him by the teacher. The teacher cannot be expected to be a universal fount of knowledge on every topic which appeals to the interests of his students but he should have enough general knowledge and organisational ability to show them individually how to examine their topics from a number of different aspects. In spite of the difficulties, and in spite of the fact that the project when completed will contain a plentiful crop of spelling and grammatical errors, and of colloquialisms, a project can rouse the interest of the slow learner in the distant or recent past to an extent which makes it well worthwhile as an occasional venture. Obviously the teacher will have to differentiate in his comments on completed project work between those who have genuine difficulty in using the written word correctly and those who are grossly careless, or, worse still, deliberately shoddy or flippant. He will have some pieces of work submitted to him which will make him wonder whether there was any point in setting it, but progress needs to be counted in individual not group terms in this context; there will be some whose interest in history and, to a minor extent, their skills in writing will have been increased by this project work. In marking this work, comments to show the teacher's appreciation of an interesting idea or detail, interspersed with judicious correction of the more blatant errors in English, and meticulous correction of factual errors, are the needs.

Whether a narrative account is an appropriate piece of written work depends on the class. Slow learners and very young students undoubtedly experience some satisfaction in recounting a narrative, and it is valuable for them to be given the time to think out their sentences coherently, as many of them can more easily in written than in oral work. There are, however, others, verbally quick but backward in writing, for whom writing down a narrative account based on what they have recently heard or read is likely to be neither interesting nor rewarding. They respond rather better to written work of the imaginative kind requiring the sorting out of impressions based on a mixture of material from different sources.

Skill in writing probably develops more slowly than any other for the slow learner. The most practical advice on this subject came from the collective view of the teachers of one school:

Regarding writing the motto should be little, often, and accurate. Accurate rather than corrected is emphasised . . . Notes for written work may be worked out orally; the notes may then be expanded into a piece of prose, orally; the prose is then written up on the blackboard for copying, sentence by sentence. Another method is to duplicate an appropriate note leaving out key words. Following the lesson these may then, with discussion and the use of the blackboard to ensure correct spelling, be filled in individually and the whole passage copied up into note-books.

These methods were described in the same letter as onerous and time-taking but plainly were thought to be worthwhile if any progress at all were to be made by the slow learner in his writing skills. The abundant guidance provided will give the slow learner the satisfaction, unusual for him, of producing written work sound in sense and English, and he can play a small part too in the oral work which precedes the writing up of the notes.

It was plain from hearing and reading the views of teachers that flexibility in method is essential in written work. The needs and interests of examination candidates, non-examination students, young students, slow and ultra-slow learners are clearly not the same: each category requires a separate approach. It is equally obtuse to make either the formal examination essay or the social documentary a Procrustean bed into which they all must fit. Underlying the differences of method, however, was the widespread recognition by teachers of the value of written work in giving students opportunities for self-expression and for deepening their knowledge and understanding of the past.

# 8 Tests and examinations

There is probably more misunderstanding about the nature, purpose and reliability of examinations than about any other aspect of modern education. At the same time, there is enormous pressure from parents (and indeed from some pupils) to increase and extend the system of public examinations, which are regarded as rites of passage; even school examinations are regarded by pupils with a kind of fascinated horror. Moreover, amongst those who ought to know better, marks once given in an examination are frequently regarded as sacrosanct and immutable, with all the awful validity of the tablets of the Decalogue, indicative not of a passing state of mind, but of the poor pupil's moral character, his future capacity, and his potential contribution to Western civilisation.

It is therefore necessary for the teacher to make it abundantly plain to his pupils that the test or examination, private or public, is intended to help the candidate; to show him the extent of his knowledge and to indicate his progress in a limited field at a definite moment or within a definite period; to measure his success in a highly specialised exercise; and that, if a mark is given in figures – as in school tests it usually is – this is only one way of indicating a grade of excellence, and is not intended as a comparison of his performance with that of other members of the group except in public examinations where it may well affect his life and future prospects, and where there is intense competition. In other words, examiner and candidate are on the same side, as it were; like teacher and pupil, examiner and candidate are engaged in a cooperative activity. An examination is not a game; it is a service.

It is necessary to emphasise this point as in present society the evils of examinations, which certainly exist, are stressed whilst their good points are not. Examiners try, when they set examinations and tests, to ask fair and simple questions within the grasp of the candidate; when marking the scripts, they give credit for every scrap of knowledge and every glimmer of perception; and they are pleased when a candidate 'does well'. They try to promote the welfare of the candidate, not always successfully; but often the candidates are their own worst enemies.

**Purpose of an examination**

Every test should have a clear aim or aims, which should be explained to the candidate before the test is taken. There is in fact a very considerable measure of agreement among teachers as to the qualities which can be tested and as to the merits of the work submitted in examinations in history. These qualities are (a) knowledge of fact, (b) assimilation and understanding of knowledge and (c) the candidate's powers of comment, i.e. appreciation or critical appraisal of the value of what he knows. This latter will include skills such as analysis, synthesis and judgement. The relative importance assigned to each of these qualities will vary according to the age of the pupil, and the presumed academic capacity of the group to be tested. It is obviously possible to devise tests in which factors (b) and (c) above are reduced to zero. This does not invalidate the test so long as factors (b) and (c) are also tested in additional papers. We are convinced that a capacity to remember important facts is an essential quality of the historian, and that examinations in history ought to test this capacity. In fact, it is not possible to devise an examination in history which does not test memory; even if the candidate is allowed to take textbooks and notes into the examination, or if the examination extends over a period of days, months or years (as some examinations do) the candidate must still know where to look and what he is looking for. One of the major principles of examining is that it is pointless to use a sledgehammer to kill a butterfly; if factual knowledge can be effectually tested with less effort, it should be.

Candidates display understanding in many ways, more or less sophisticated, more or less subtle. Obvious examples are the ability to get facts in the right order, to distinguish between cause and result, the avoidance of confusion of persons, countries, or centuries. These instances are cited because pupils so frequently get them wrong. No teacher and certainly no examiner will damn a pupil for an accidental slip; but the errors which follow are overwhelmingly common and repeated throughout script after script; pupils might really be encouraged to avoid them. Some are explicable: Pitt for Peel, Dutch for Danes (with particular reference to the Schleswig-Holstein crisis); some are due to difficulty in finding a convenient locution: 'Gladstone passed an education act in 1870' or worse, 'Gladstone passed the first Home Rule Act in 1886, but it was defeated in the commons.' Many, as we have just demonstrated, are due to a mental aberration which seizes candidates as soon as they are confronted with a date. It is startling (but not uncommon) for a candidate to date the outbreak of the Crimean War as 1754 in one sentence, 1654 in the next, and 1954 two sentences further on. Moreover, it is as well for the teacher to make sure that candidates understand what is meant by century and do not for instance write solely about the work of Tull, Coke, Townshend, Bakewell and the Collings brothers when they are asked to give an account of agricultural developments in the seventeenth century. Similarly, the most carefully drafted and simplified historical maps are by no means as clear to pupils as one would expect; and their knowledge of geographical locations, despite all the school visits and summer holidays, remains exceedingly hazy. Moreover, many pupils have great difficulty in understanding historical terms so embedded in the teacher's culture that he considers them self-explanatory. It is not a question of subjectively defined terms such as 'democracy' or nonce- (and nonsense) words such as 'suzerainty', but of simple names such as 'parliament', 'prime minister', 'empire' and the like. Nor is it safe to assume that the pupil understands anything by 'Labour' and 'Conservative' but baddie and goodie (or *vice versa*). It is even more unsafe to assume that the pupil knows anything at all about the Christian religion or has ever been inside a church.

No teacher and no examiner will ever penalise a pupil because their views differ. It has frequently been suggested that it is unfair to ask sixteen-year-olds for their opinions, presumably on the grounds that (a) they have not got any, or (b) if they have, their opinions are in any case not worth having, or (c) they will merely recite their teachers' opinions. In fact, the opinions of children, though sometimes unsophisticated, are by no means worthless; and we should welcome with delight any sign that the pupil is interested enough in the subject to think about it, and give him every encouragement to do so. Moreover, we must face the fact that, regrettably enough, most of the population of this country, present and future, will never open a serious history-book after the age of sixteen; and that therefore those of us who feel that history is a valuable and fruitful study must do our work early or not at all.

**Types of tests**

*(i) Oral questions and answers*

Every teacher makes more or less use of the Socratic method; but here we are concerned with oral question and answer not as a method of instruction but as a method of testing. The difficulty is twofold; first, the teacher is necessarily dealing with only one pupil at a time, so this is not really a class exercise and therefore extremely expensive in time; second, the more sophisticated forms are extremely difficult to mark, so that the pupil does not know how well he has done.

Oral question-and-answer round the class – the Madras system or 'moral steam-engine' of 150 years ago – means of course that the pupils can sleep in rotation as the question pursues its slow and winding way. Something is gained by random selection of the questioned, provided that the teacher can be sure that the selection is random, and that he is not selecting only those least or most likely to be able to answer. It is also possible to institute various refinements of the quiz: for instance, to divide the class into teams, and to allow correct answers to score points for the team; to keep a record, public or private, of those who fail to answer correctly, and if appropriate, to demand extra work. Oral answers need not be short. Pupils can prepare and deliver speeches on set topics – the teacher can mark by impression and explain his mark to the class – but however satisfactory this is as a method of instruction, it is still a very cumbersome method of testing. The teacher can supply an essay question; the pupils can be invited to supply a topic sentence for each paragraph – this can be written on the board – and can then make suggestions for factual material, paragraph by paragraph, to support the topic sentence. Each pupil keeps his own score. In an ideal situation, one may be able to arrange one's own oral examinations. At A level, this can be a particularly useful experience for the candidate, as a *viva voce* on his written paper. Lower down the school, a small group is required, familiarised with the technique and acquainted with each other, so that they are not shy or intimidated, and at least two members of staff, one to direct the discussion and one to observe and mark. It is usual to start with some kind of source material. This can be the pupil's own work, on which he may be invited to comment, or which he may be invited to expand, with others participating on the suggestion of the director, or, one hopes, spontaneously. Alternatively, use can be made of a picture, or a map, or a diagram, or of written material – say a ballad or a broadsheet – which pupils can be invited to explain. To do this kind of thing successfully takes a great deal of time – not only in the actual test, but also in its preparation – a great deal of experience, and a sympathetic disposition. It is sometimes claimed that this method will do justice to those children who have difficulties in written expression. It is probably true that kindly and leading questions will elicit from some less able or excessively nervy pupils a few facts which they would not otherwise remember and such techniques play a part in some C.S.E. assessments. On the whole though a fairer estimate of their capacity is gained from the teacher's recollection of their past efforts – a process sometimes known as 'continuous assessment'.

## (ii) Oral questions, short written answers

This is a technique familiar to every teacher; but there are certain points worthy of remark. In a short test of the kind we are describing the child must realise that the object is for him to discover what he knows and what lacunae remain. In the second place, the test must be so constructed as to have apposite questions with a clear answer. The arrangement of questions may be chronological or topical; it is frequently convenient to make the questions follow the order of the source material – textbook or notes – which is being tested. The pupil should be told how the test is going to be arranged. Another method is to dictate an essay question, supply the topic for the first paragraph and invite the class to write down – as briefly as they like – the support material they would use, then, of course, continuing with the second paragraph and so on.

The pupil should sometimes mark his own work, though he might more usefully mark the essays of his colleagues on occasions. This will show him a variety of interpretations, styles and techniques; just as important, it will reveal something of what takes place in assessment and help him to understand a mark. If the teacher always marks the work, the pupil will look only at the total, which is exactly what we wish to avoid. There are several methods of marking. The teacher can dictate the answers or write them on the board. If time is available, it is better to ask the pupils to supply the answers, either orally (in which case everyone finishes at the same time) or by reference to their textbooks or notes (in which case it is necessary before you begin the test to tell the pupils to make a note of the question if they are not sure of the answer). This allows for variety of answer.

A test of this kind is a blunt instrument. The teacher should not assault his class with it too frequently. On the other hand, one of the major lessons of history is that prolonged immunity from attack tends to breed an undesirable complacency. The teacher should ask only what the pupils really ought to know and should expect a high percentage of correct answers. It is as well to collect and record the marks, partly so that you can see what success you and the pupils have achieved, partly because it gives you an opportunity to commend the candidate where possible, and partly because the pupils like it.

## (iii) Written questions on source material requiring short written answers

These tests are not really suitable for general use in class, because they take up too much time; they may be used in examination papers, or for homework where powers of deduction in finding the answers to the questions set will be suitably tested.

One obvious source is a map; the advantage is that anyone can draw or trace maps and they are therefore cheap and easy to reproduce in quantity. The possibilities are: to indicate significant places by letters and ask the candidate to identify them, adding comments on their importance ('why should these places be included on this map?'); to indicate territorial divisions by different kinds of shading and ask for an explanation (for example, partitions of Poland, expansion of Prussia), including the date of the settlement represented, how it came about, what figures are associated with it and so on. A major advantage of this technique is that it does teach children to be concise. Adolescent girls, in particular, are convinced that examination scripts are marked by weight; in order to counteract prolixity, the teacher should sometimes lay down a maximum number of words. However, nothing should be done which may hinder the development of the young pupil into a fluent writer.

Another source is a photograph. The candidate can be asked to identify what is represented – e.g. an event (as blacklegs driving lorries during the General Strike) or building (the palace of Versailles) or other work of art (the 'Mona Lisa', the 'Rocket') or a domestic interior – the field is vast – and to comment under various headings which may or may not be phrased as subquestions. The examples given above are there of set purpose, because this is a very difficult exercise. All source questions tend to be more difficult than the examiner thinks they are, but this is the most difficult sub-species. Do not be afraid to make your questions leading and try to make them as simple as possible. Identification of architectural styles (or of techniques of repression for that matter) depends on the half- or sub-conscious recollection of a vast mass of data which pupils simply have not had time to acquire.

Cartoons are useful and many are readily available as illustrations in popular textbooks. The candidate may be asked to identify the occasion, and to indicate: the attitude of the cartoonist (or his public) to the events in question as revealed in the cartoon; what outcome the cartoonist thought probable; what actually happened; and why? The examiner must bear in mind that there is no point in using pictorial source-material or an historical map if the same information can be elicited without it. Frequently, after labouring for five or six hours to draft a question on pictorial material, one realises that the final version has eliminated the need for the illustration. There is no point whatever in using an illustration as a gimmick.

Documents – that is to say printed versions of state papers, Acts of Parliament, popular ballads, broadsheets, contemporary novels (and so on) – are also a possible source. (It should be borne in mind that what is said here relates solely to the use of documents in tests and examinations and not to their use in the general course of teaching; for which see Chapter 6.) The drawback is that, if the extract is extensive, it takes a long time to read; the original phraseology, vocabulary and syntax may be involved and obscure; in any case, if the original relates to foreign history, it was probably not written in English; one may, therefore, reluctantly have to abridge, modernise and translate.

The candidate may be asked to explain the meaning of some of the expressions used – a line reference is the most satisfactory means of identification; to explain the situation which produced the document; to explain the outcome; to comment on the importance of the document; or to give biographical details about the author; but here again it is frequently possible to elicit the same information by much more economical means.

A further variant is to quote certain historical catch-phrases, such as are the common resort of textbook-writers desperate for local colour, and to ask the candidate to ascribe and comment. The difficulty is that some are apocryphal and others distorted. Marie Antoinette's alleged remark about cake is a good example of the former; Mme de Pompadour's remark about the flood an example of the latter. Research in no more recondite a source than the Oxford *Dictionary of Quotations* on Bismarck's remarks on iron and blood is enlightening.

One can ask questions on set texts. This is more suitable as a sixth-form exercise, and even in that age-range should be used with care. Though there is a place for the enquiry in depth, one has constantly to bear in mind that what the majority of pupils require is a fairly broad conspectus of a significant period, either, if they are specialist historians, as a basis for more detailed studies later on or, if they are not, as ancillary to studies in the subject in which they are going to specialise; and that specialisation is for adults, and indeed is only possible as a consequence of a general education. The study of documents may be much more fun for the teacher than the repetition for the thirty-fifth time of his lesson on the progress of the German Reformation between 1517 and 1521; but that is not the point. Furthermore it is by no means easy to set significant questions even on set texts. One must not imitate the features of context or 'gobbet' questions so familiar in papers on English literature; nor must one drift into setting questions which would without significant alteration pass for 'appreciation' questions on English language papers.

### (iv) Objective tests

Although objective tests can be used without reservation in some areas of knowledge, the historian views them with some hesitation. In history, the standard generalisation, the unique answer, and the one-sentence description are viewed with suspicion. In addition to all this, objective tests in history drafted by experts in objective tests for the consideration of historians frequently display not only a profound ignorance of elementary history, but a complete lack of understanding of the way in which historians use words. Nevertheless, we believe these tests to be valid. In any case, valid or not, they are and will be extensively employed by examining boards which face increasingly heavy costs, so a few words of explanation will perhaps not come amiss.

There are many types of objective tests, but the most common is the multiple-choice, which is therefore the subject of the present discussion. It consists of a short question or statement, complete or incomplete (called the 'stem'), followed by four or five alternative answers or predications, usually identified by letters, of which one (the 'key') is correct and the others ('distractors') incorrect. The candidate is invited to indicate the key by blacking out, underlining or ticking the appropriate space on an answer-card in pencil.

The stem should indicate the nature of an answer. Thus the stem 'William I of Prussia was . . .' is unsatisfactory because it gives no clue to the nature of the predicate; a better effort would be 'The first German Emperor was . . .'. The distractors should not be obviously absurd; they should be similar to the key in length and phraseology, and one at least should be close enough to the key to give the candidate something to think about. Both distractors and key should form a syntactically and logically correct connection with the stem.[1] Thus the second stem given above might be followed by: A, Franz Josef of the House of Habsburg; B, William of Hohenzollern; C, Leopold of Hohenzollern; D, Albert of Saxe-Coburg. This example illustrates the difficulty of drafting this type of question.

---

[1] A quotation from a pamphlet on objective testing emanating from a large examining board is relevant here. After stressing the importance of grammatical accuracy, it continues: 'Opinions will be inappropriate to the stem if none of them are in the class of statement the stem requires.'

The most popular varieties of multiple-choice questions are:

(i) The correct answer (the stem is a question, key and distractors the possible answers):

Who commanded the French forces at the battle of Trafalgar?
- A Villeneuve
- B Rosily
- C Napoleon Bonaparte
- D Joseph Bonaparte
- E Massena

(ii) The stem an incomplete statement: as above, 'The first German Emperor . . .'

(iii) The best answer; this is a little more subtle. Candidates are invited to choose the best response from a number of contributing factors:

Which *one* of the following was the principal cause of the bankruptcy of the French Crown in the second half of the eighteenth century?
- A Court extravagance
- B Expenditure on foreign wars
- C Inefficient tax collection
- D Fiscal privilege
- E Over-centralisation of government

(Some would argue that this question shows the weakness and difficulty of this method, since a good case could be made for any one of the five points.)

(iv) Negative response:

Which of the following statements about Frederick II of Prussia is incorrect?
- A He is widely known as Frederick the Great
- B He enlarged the boundaries of Prussia
- C He instituted representative government in Prussia
- D He initiated economic and agricultural reforms
- E He changed the legal system of Prussia

An advantage of this type is that it does permit the examiner to start with a throwaway, which, one hopes, will give the poor candidate a bit of confidence.

(v) In a multiple-response type, one can invite the candidate to choose combinations of factors:

Two results of the 1931 economic crisis were that
- (i) The Trade Unions called a general strike
- (ii) A coalition government was formed
- (iii) Britain abandoned free trade
- (iv) The government increased unemployment benefit in coal-mining areas

Choose A if i and ii are correct
   B if i and iii are correct
   C if i and iv are correct

D if ii and iii are correct
E if iii and iv are correct

(And, of course, even now we have not included all possible answers.)

(vi) Or one can use several stems and keys and invite candidates to match key and stem; but in this the number of keys must be greater than the number of stems (or *vice versa*) or the final choice will be inevitable.

On the left is a number of treaties or international agreements, on the right a list of historical developments which were associated with these treaties. After each of these developments write the letter of the treaty to which it corresponds.

| | | | |
|---|---|---|---|
| A | Berlin | 1 | Napoleonic Empire broken up |
| B | Frankfort | 2 | German annexation of Alsace-Lorraine |
| C | Paris | 3 | France regains Alsace-Lorraine |
| D | Tilsit | 4 | Independence of Holland finally recognised |
| E | Utrecht | 5 | Britain becomes colonial power |
| F | Versailles | | |
| G | Vienna | | |
| H | Westphalia | | |

Of course, illustrations or documents can be used as bases for objective tests, and in so far as they are seminal they are particularly suitable; but the observations about source material in the preceding section still apply.

When a sufficient number of questions has been devised, all the questions are pre-tested. The setter is usually asked to grade his questions in order of difficulty; experience (admittedly early) shows that the grading is usually wildly inaccurate. The questions must therefore be tried on sample bunches of candidates, usually those who are going to attempt a (conventional) examination of the same standard. In the light of their response the questions are re-graded (or perhaps even rejected) and then finally assembled in examination papers of any desired degree of difficulty. This pre-testing is an essential part of the process and must be carried out on a really large scale. If it is not, the test clearly ceases to be objective.

It is therefore apparent that no teacher can set valid objective tests to his own candidates, or use them for internal examinations, or even, with any degree of reliability, invent specimen questions which will give his pupils a little training. Books of objective tests are published. Some training in the techniques of this exercise should certainly be given; a little, but not too much, practice will dramatically improve candidates' scores.

## (v) Answers of paragraph length

These figure in most examination papers up to O level in some form or other. The time-hallowed 'Write short notes on . . .' has now largely been displaced by other formulae; but they all mean the same thing. A possible variant is to ask candidates to define a selection of historical terms (e.g. Whig, prerogative court, impeachment) giving illustrations or examples where possible. One can try to introduce some unity into this ragbag by making each item an illustration of a theme – rebels, aggression, Imperialism, for example. If you include one or two jokers in the pack – for instance Star Chamber, Magnus Intercursus, the Second Act of Annates, Anne of Cleves, Fountains Abbey – you may induce in the candidate the revelation that his day out with Mum and Dad last Whitsun was a visit to a real place where real people really got evicted in 1539 and that what he was told in school really means something.

What the examiner looks for in a short answer is (a) that the topic should be dated by a brief reference to its historical context, (b) that its major features should be indicated and (c) that there should be some appropriate comment, particularly on the themes of causation and significance. Mere general knowledge will not enable the candidate to get by in this kind of question; but sound information and comment can score very high marks.

## (vi) Essays

Pupils always want to know how much they should write; one should tell them clearly what is expected. Essays which are merely transcriptions of the textbook are not much good as a test (of historical ability anyway) and it is best to encourage paraphrase by explaining to the pupils that they ought to try to write from memory even if they are finishing the essay for homework. As a matter of examination practice pupils should be encouraged to follow the line of the question in the construction of their answer; if they are asked (for instance) to comment on the domestic and foreign policy of Wolsey, there is really no reason why they should not deal with domestic policy first and foreign policy second.

It will perhaps be convenient to illustrate some of the types of essay questions by taking one topic – say Mary, Queen of Scots. First, obviously, is the pure narrative: 'Give an account of the career of Mary, Queen of Scots.' This will be a better question if we limit it by date to a significant period: 'between 1560 and 1568'. This has the further advantage of indicating clearly the identity of the first subject; it is always irritating to set a carefully contrived essay on the first Robert Devereux under the title of Earl of Essex, and to find the perverse candidate devoting his answer to Thomas Cromwell. If this happens one must of course accept his answer; the candidate cannot be made to pay for the mistakes of the examiner.

Secondly, one can add a rider to the narrative, inviting the candidate's opinion. 'Give an account of the career of Mary, Queen of Scots, between 1560 and 1568. Why was this period a critical one for her?' It is frequently possible, however, to elicit the same facts without asking a direct question – the question is, as it were, all rider. 'Why was the period between 1560 and 1568 a critical one in the life of Mary, Queen of Scots?' It is possible to be more direct, and still briefer: 'Do you feel sorry for Mary, Queen of Scots?' will elicit substantially the same factual response as the questions previously suggested. A serious objection to the last example, though, would be that it is subjective, and consequently invites a non-academic response even though based on evidence; but this is obviously without weight if the question is not intended for academic historians.

Thirdly, one can invite comment on a quotation, genuine or invented. The genuine quotation is perhaps better style; the trouble is that historical figures, or, for that matter, reputable historians so very rarely say what is convenient to the examiner. ' "The monstrous regiment of women!" What reasons had John Knox for this description of the reign of Mary, Queen of Scots?' is forced and clumsy; it is better, perhaps to invent a quotation: ' "A helpless victim of the intrigues and ambitions of others." Would you agree with this description of Mary, Queen of Scots?' – though even here the phraseology is not quite right, and 'intrigues' and 'ambitions' are not truly parallel.

Fourthly, comparison: 'Compare and contrast the religious policies of Mary, Queen of Scots and Elizabeth I'. This obvious example is a celebrated ancient monument; and some may well feel that the question is by this time so dilapidated as to be useless. But the age of a question is no bar to its use; it may be old to the examiner, but it will be fresh to its constantly renewed respondents.

Fifthly, the candidate may be invited to select:

Which of the following is in your opinion the most appropriate judgement on the career of Mary, Queen of Scots:

the female counterpart of the Renaissance Prince
a helpless victim of scheming politicians
an agent of the Counter-Reformation
unable to control herself, let alone her country
a truly romantic figure?

(One of the unsolved problems of this type of question is where to put the question-mark – it is better to formulate the question so as to render the question-mark unnecessary.) Theoretically, the advantage of this type is that you can provide something for everybody – hence the last two options in the example. In practice, alas, the intelligent and capable candidates will select the easiest option, whilst the less able who might have written about Mary and Bothwell will attempt a discussion of the concept of the Renaissance Prince.

Selection can be encouraged by questions more economically phrased: 'What were the main factors which led to the downfall of Mary, Queen of Scots?' Candidates should be encouraged to reflect upon the significance of the word 'main'.

Sixthly, the examiner can invite contradiction: 'What did Mary, Queen of Scots gain from her domestic policy?' The obvious answer is nothing, and one hopes that the candidate will give it. A negative reply is frequently acceptable and candidates should be encouraged to consider its possibility; at the same time, even on entrance papers for Oxford and Cambridge, not all questions are designed to be provocative, and the candidate who finds himself writing for the fifth successive time, 'This is a silly question, because . . .' should pause to reflect.

Finally, we come to the class known as 'guided' or 'directed' essays, where the candidate is provided with some sort of material to work on. In fact, because you tell the candidate what you want him to tell you, this attempt to help does not always succeed; and, as in other branches of education, both academic and moral, the candidate prefers to be left alone to get on by himself (or at any rate, without his teacher poking his nose in). The guidance can be factual – a useful locution here is 'What is the connection between the following events . . .?' – or causal – 'Study the following notes on . . . and explain what resulted from this situation' or consequential – 'Explain how and why the . . . came to have the following consequences . . .'. One can give a series of (short) self-contradictory quotations from the speeches of a politician at various stages in his career, and ask the candidate to explain. One may quote an appropriate extract from a history-book and ask the candidate to expand it; coffee-table history-books, old textbooks, or the works of the less reputable nineteenth-century historians are useful here. One example may be quoted:

'George III was ignorant, self-confident and obstinate; to him does Great Britain owe the loss of her American colonies, the failure to pacify Ireland, the delay of parliamentary reform, and the long continuance of the slave trade.' Explain the above statement. Do you agree with it?

The difficulty is that these questions tend to be non-selective;

while the fact that some material is given is no handicap to the good candidate who has a mass of material at his disposal, in effect the candidate who knows a little is equated with the candidate who knows nothing. Moreover, the question is necessarily long, and frequently wordy. Unless the question is very carefully set, the answer will degenerate into a series of short notes.

## (vii) Project work

It is presumably possible, in theory, to examine at school level theses, reports on projects or other extended essays. The question here is what qualities we are examining. In so far as the pupil has copied most of his material out of a book (and where else can he get it from?) we are clearly not testing his memory of fact. We may be testing his capacities for construction and appreciation; but these qualities can be more easily tested in other ways. It may well be that there are pupils who are good historians but bad examination candidates, either because they work slowly, or because of the panic feed-back reaction self-induced by the word examination; but in this case it is easier to test them by asking for short essays, done if they choose without time limit, with access to sources, and in non-ritualised conditions. For less able children, a personal project, in a file, forming an integral part of structured course work and counting a reasonable percentage of the final assessment, has much to offer. There is some scope for innovation, and the opportunity to examine a theme in some depth. The difficulties over originality of work and criteria of assessment remain, but they are not insuperable, and many C.S.E. boards have incorporated such a project, or even several pieces of course work drawn over a period, into their examination.

The whole point of an examination is to judge the work of an individual against an objective standard, determined by a comparison of the individual's work with that of his contemporaries on a common paper and with that of similar candidates on similar papers in the past. The more diverse the material, the less reliable the examination becomes, but we must not refuse to consider alternatives simply because there are initial difficulties. One board at A level, for example, offers an optional project paper which insists on an extensive bibliography, including journals and documentary sources, together with indications, where appropriate, by the candidate of methods used and places visited; and the narrowing down of the subject matter to research relevant to a particularly defined question. These requirements provide quite a searching test of the candidate's abilities to show enterprise in acquiring information, in synthesising it, and in keeping to the point. These are important features of historical training and the project method at this level provides an acceptable means to the end of historical excellence, in addition to the more conventional methods of teaching and examining.

## Setting a paper

Papers can be set only by close reference to a suitable syllabus. Perhaps, like a constitution, a teaching syllabus ought to be short and vague; but an examination syllabus should be a detailed list of topics; if no such list is generally available, you must prepare your own, so far as possible in a strictly chronological order. You should tell your candidates what topics you propose to examine; they have a right to know. Now set a question on every topic you have listed. When you have done this, a winnowing process is possible. You may find that there is considerable overlap between questions; in this case, some can be combined or, with luck, deleted. Ask yourself, 'What can I legitimately expect the candidate to know about this?' and then set a question designed to elicit this knowledge as a basis. You should aim at substantial coverage of the whole syllabus.

Setting examination papers by rehashing old ones is unsatisfactory and time-wasting. You will not achieve a proper balance; and if the question was as good as you could make it in its original form, any change can only be for the worse. For this reason, to attempt to spot (or eliminate) questions in public examinations by a study of past papers is futile – the examiner does not set from papers, he sets from a syllabus; every paper is new. Pupils love to look at past examination papers, of course. They should not be encouraged to do so; but they should be familiarised with the format of the examination paper – which should not be changed without fair notice – and they should be told that questions will be arranged to follow a chronological sequence[2] (possibly within a topical arrangement, such as British history, European history).

One should try to make questions as clear as possible. If clarity conflicts with grammatical precision, grammatical precision must go; if you wish to offer a triple choice, 'Either . . . or . . . or' is ungrammatical but clear. Try to get the subject of the question as near the beginning as possible; 'Explain the amount, nature and quality of the support and opposition aroused in Scotland and England in the first half of the eighteenth century by the Jacobite movement' is as bad a question as anyone could set. ('The Jacobite

---

[2] No sequence is possible in objective tests.

movement aroused both support and opposition . . . Explain this.') If you intend to ask a question about one topic, or figure, do not ask a question about something else. This may seem obvious, but consider the following example: 'Disraeli compared the opposition Front Bench to a range of exhausted volcanoes. Why did he say this?'

In general, however, if the grammar is not right, or if the expression is ungainly, the question is not clear. There are various useful locutions – a study of the examples given in this chapter will provide some of them. As you are setting questions, a really felicitous expression or elegant turn of phrase will from time to time flash across your mind, and you will be tempted to enshrine it for posterity in your paper. Beware; you will probably have left the candidate with nothing to write about. On the other hand, one should try to avoid jargon; the habit of examiners in using the word 'discuss' as if it were a verb of complete predication is both ungrammatical and impolite.

Given clarity of meaning(s), there is nothing wrong with ambiguity – 'What were the most important discoveries of the Renaissance?' The average candidate will answer the question in the single sense in which he has understood it; the good candidate will point out the ambiguity and define the sense in which he intends to answer. As we shall see later on, this will in no way disadvantage him. Another important aid to clarity is brevity; in general, the shorter the question, the better.

## Marking a paper

Marking examination papers is apparently regarded by many as one of the more painful of the many mortifications attached to the practice of teaching. It need not be painful at all; it can be interesting, even stimulating. The following dissertation is intended for the novice.

You must, of course, know what you are looking for, and you must not waste your time in agonised reappraisal; you must, in short, have confidence in yourself. Have courage; you do know what you are looking for, and you are quite right. One of the things that impressed in the course of some experience of examining the work of examiners at various levels for various authorities has been the consensus of opinion about the indefinable quantity of information, opinion or what-have-you which is worth a mark; examiners all over the country will give the same mark to the same essay. This is not to say that the same script will get the same grade from every examining authority; the pass mark may differ; as we shall see, it is based not only on the belief of examiners but on the holy writ of statistics and the accepted practice of the authority.

The first and golden rule is always to mark positively; never take marks off for anything. The candidate starts with zero and can gain the maximum. When he says something which you think is worth a mark, give him the mark – it is usually convenient to indicate this by a tick in the margin. At the end of the answer, add up the ticks. You can usually carry the total in your head, but it is as well to check; you will be surprised how often you are wrong (usually under) by a mark or so. If you have given more than the maximum, give the maximum, unless you feel that the essay is of such outstanding quality that the maximum does not do it justice; in this case give more than the maximum. The candidate will not do all the work as well as this; he will not score more than 100% on the paper. Bear in mind that there is no point in having marks that you do not use. Every time that the candidate does all that you can reasonably expect from a pupil of his age, he should get full marks; and this ought to occur fairly frequently. It follows from the injunction to mark positively that there is an infinite number of ways in which the candidate can gain full marks. In the same way, of course, you should use low marks. Your aim in a large group of several hundred is to obtain a spread of 100% over the whole batch you are examining. If, at the end of the exercise, you have a range of 80% you are doing well; a range of 50% (say between 20% and 70%) gives some cause for concern; and a range of 33% means that something is wrong – with the paper or the marking or both – *not* with the candidates. With smaller, and more selective, groups, the mark range will obviously be more restricted.

Another principle which is sometimes a help is always to interpret to the advantage of the candidate – to place the best possible construction on his work. One must not, however, strain common sense; a mental paraphrase of what the candidate has said, particularly if he has been taught by someone else, is helpful; one needs to keep a flexible mind. Furthermore, and this is important, the examiner in history is not primarily examining in English; if the candidate has communicated his meaning to you, it really does not matter if he has metathesised the second e and the o in emperor. However, some teachers would regard 'Gladeston' as an historical error. Ungainly expression is not incompatible with sound historiography; we can all think of examples from the works of those university historians who never use a word of one syllable when a word of four syllables will do, but whose ideas are nevertheless really seminal. If you feel, on moral grounds, that you really must reward presentation – and this is an entirely justifiable view – then the mark for presentation should be positive and separate, shown at the top of the script as, say 47 + 12, the first mark for historical excellence, the second for presentation. Incidentally, this technique will have a more compelling effect on your candidates than undisclosed deductions for mis-spelt and untidy work.

Once you have acquired sufficient experience to be able to discern the merit of the work more rapidly, you may prefer to mark in grades. Five, from A to E, can be carried in your mind without difficulty. By grading in this way, you do assess the merit of the essay as a whole; though the system of individual marks is undeniably safer for beginners. By the use of symbols such as + and −, + + and − −, grades can be subdivided to any desired extent, and of course, transnumerated, if you desire a total for the script. This method is advantageous if you have to mark out of an unusual maximum; if, after a lifetime of marking out of twenty, you are suddenly required to mark out of forty-five, the use of grades not only facilitates your work but makes it much more accurate.

## Public examinations

It would seem logical to start by surveying the market, then to offer a few respectful suggestions on how candidates may best be prepared, and to conclude by a discussion of what happens to the scripts submitted. But, with acknowledgements, 'we must beware of being guided by mere logic', and it is proposed to reverse the order.

### Setting

Question papers for public examinations go through a long process of scrutiny and revision before they see the light of day. The first draft is invariably submitted to a reviser or moderator and thereafter sometimes to a fairly large committee of fellow-examiners, school and university teachers, representatives of professional bodies; it receives trenchant, sometimes bitter, criticism, and the luckless author has to sit there, take it on the chin, make the alterations demanded, and sometimes go away and try again. Whether, after so many have had a hand in the gestation, the resultant birth is more or less monstrous is a debatable point; on the whole the revision by committee is probably worth it, if only because it does involve more practising teachers directly in

## MATRICULATION EXAMINATION.

*November 5, 1838.*

[Three hours only allowed for this Exercise.]

### ENGLISH HISTORY.

1. Describe the leading features of the Anglo-Saxon institutions. What changes appear to have taken place in the composition of the Wittenagemote? Was the general tendency of the Anglo-Saxon Institutions just before the Conquest toward a more or less popular form of government?

2. Mention the leading provisions of Magna Charta. What were the grievances which it was designed to remove? What classes of persons derived immediate benefit from it? How did it ultimately operate upon the whole community?

3. State the title under which the House of York claimed the Throne against Henry VI.; and those of Henry VII., Mary Queen of Scots, and Lady Jane Gray.

4. What was the effect of the Wars of the Roses on the Royal prerogative? What were the actual limits of the Royal authority under the most nearly absolute of the English Sovereigns?

5. Give an account of the Courts of Star Chamber and High Commission, describing their origin, the manner in which they were composed, the sphere of their jurisdiction, and the purposes to which they were applied.

6. Mention the leading facts in the history of the negotiation for the Spanish match under James I., and point out in what manner the issue tended to weaken the power of the Crown.

7. What were the engines and resources used by Charles I. to carry on the government without Parliaments? Relate the events which led to the calling of the Long Parliament.

8. Explain the historical allusions contained in the following passage:

> Did not our Worthies of the House,
> Before they broke the peace, break vows?
> For, having freed us first from both
> Th' Allegiance and Supremacy oath,
> Did they not then compel the nation
> To take and break the Protestation?
> To swear and after to recant
> The Solemn League and Covenant?
> To take th' Engagement, and disclaim it,
> Enforc'd by those who first did frame it?

State, as precisely as you can, the epochs here referred to, and the nature of the Protestation, the Solemn League and Covenant, and the Engagement.

9. Mention the parties engaged in the battles of Evesham, Tewksbury, and Naseby, their dates, and the results with which they were attended.

10. What was the nature of the Constitution established by the Instrument of Government? How did it differ from that which was created by the Humble Petition and Advice?

11. Describe the state of parties immediately before the Restoration, with the names, and some notice of the characters of the leaders. What share had Monk in bringing about the Restoration?

12. Give an account of the Cabal and its Members, and of their counsels, and explain in what way they affected the state of England and of Europe.

FIG. 24. *The first London Matriculation history paper, 1838*

examining. It is perhaps as well to say here that despite the claims of partisans of the Certificate of Secondary Education, that it is uniquely teacher-controlled, teachers are far more and bureaucrats far less in control of most of the General Certificate of Education Boards.

After the paper has been modified to meet the criticisms of its revisers, there follows a lengthy process of proof-reading and inspection, designed to ensure as far as possible that the paper contains no misprints or errors of fact. Of course, some mistakes are made; no human institutions are perfect, and good examining authorities are human.

## *Marking*

The various examining authorities have procedures for marking which, although generically similar, do vary considerably in detail. The account which follows is therefore to an extent fictional, but does give a general idea of what a typical authority might do.

As soon as the chief examiner has seen a fair sample of scripts from the candidates (usually on the day after the examination) he selects half-a-dozen or so for photostatic reproduction. These he evaluates, but does not mark. He notes down his tentative mark for each script. Obviously, one tries to secure a representative selection, both in coverage of the question-paper and in merit. When the photostats are ready he holds a meeting for all his assistant examiners.

Here he will first go in great detail through the mark-scheme which he has already prepared and circulated; he will discuss every question, and amend his scheme in the light of the experience which he and his assistants have gained from the scripts they have so far read. He will then turn to the photostats, choose one or two, and read them aloud to the examiners, indicating where, why and to what extent he has given marks. The object, of course, is to arrive at a consensus. This process takes a considerable time, and after it is completed some boards terminate the meeting, and examiners disperse to mark the other photostats and to harmonise their marks by correspondence; but other boards, more heroic, dourly press on.

The assistant examiners sit in the meeting and mark the rest of the photostats, while the chief examiner tries to catch his breath. Once individual marks for all the photostats are available, they can be compared one with another, and individual examiners can be called on to explain and justify the marks they have given. This method is perhaps brutal, but is undeniably extremely effective.

When the chief examiner is satisfied that a consensus is achieved – and this may be late at night – the meeting disbands.

Usually, one has about three or four weeks to mark about 450 scripts, though some authorities are able to allow longer. One does, of course, get faster as the work proceeds; ultimately, a rate of about six scripts to the hour is usually possible. In the course of the marking the chief examiner will be supplied with samples of the work of each of his assistants. In the first instance, he will see about 5% of the scripts marked by each examiner; sometimes, like Oliver Twist, he feels it to be his duty to ask, however reluctantly, for more. He will then furnish a report to the authority on the work of each assistant, where necessary recommending a correction factor. Correction is necessary in about 40% of cases, but the adjustment required very rarely exceeds 1 or 2% – the examiner is usually severe or lenient to this extent all the way up the scale. Very occasionally indeed (about once every ten years) one does find an examiner who is wildly inconsistent, in spite of all the checks. Then there is no other course for the chief examiner but to re-mark the lot. This he will do.

At this point – and not before – the chief examiner is invited to suggest a pass mark, usually based in the first instance on his opinion of the standard of the candidates' work having regard to the difficulty of the paper in the light of his experience; in fact, what is sometimes described by women as intuition and by men as an enlightened guess. When this has been done, another committee meeting is held, at which the authority's official will reveal what statistical evidence they have (as distribution curves, standard deviations, comparative pass rates) to support or contra-indicate the proposed mark. Usually, of course, it is necessary to fix several grade marks. In this case, one can sometimes facilitate the procedure by fixing two reference points, and determining the other grades by reference to them.

At this point the chief examiner, joined, if necessary, by his assistant chief examiners, undertakes a prolonged review of scripts bordering upon pass or critical grade marks. What this fine phrase means is that they re-mark the scripts in question; this is an arduous and difficult exercise which can and frequently does go on for weeks rather than days. Even when it is all over, and the results published, all reputable boards have an appeal procedure, which will involve still further re-marking of some scripts.

### Preparing for public examinations

The foregoing brief and incomplete survey is offered without apology, partly because many practising teachers seem to have little idea of the trouble which reputable examining authorities take over their work, and partly as an unashamed tribute to the qualities of those examiners, mostly practising teachers, who carry out these responsible duties. On the other hand, the following suggestions as to methods of preparing candidates for examinations are made with considerable diffidence, and indeed a sense of presumption; they are intended mainly for the novice. It is of course indisputably bad educational practice to spend much time preparing for an examination; it is also self-defeating. The following course should not occupy more than six weeks – say the first weeks of the summer term in which the (public) examination is to be held.

First, have regard to the abilities of your candidates, and to the time at their disposal. You cannot make a silk purse out of a sow's ear. If your candidates are not particularly 'academic' or are in other employment during the day, you must make things as easy for them as possible; so study the syllabus in conjunction with the rubric and discover the irreducible minimum of topics which they must know if they are to have a reasonable chance of finding the required number of questions to answer. It is better to know a little thoroughly than a lot vaguely. If your candidates know two topics really well, they may, if they are lucky with their questions (and the examiner *must* provide coverage of the whole syllabus) score nearly half marks; if they know twenty topics vaguely, they may still attempt only the same number of questions and they will be lucky if they score twenty per cent.

Now make sure that your candidates do know the facts about the topics you have selected. Take one topic at a time, and concentrate upon it. Short point tests (one-word answers) can be used. With any luck, your sixth formers will be so incensed by your reversion to a method they consider only suitable for the babies of the fifth, that they will make it a point of honour to score full marks. Alternatively, demand more or less lengthy oral answers: 'Alice, give me the names of all the territories inherited by Charles V'; 'Now, Dodgson, tell me the origin of each of them, and the ancestor he inherited it from'.

Now examine past question-papers, pick a representative selection of questions on the topic you are dealing with, and make your candidates copy them down. Make sure their copies are accurate, word for word. Now ask if there is anybody who does not clearly understand the questions. Repeat this question. Amplify it - 'Are there any words in any of these questions which you do not understand?' You will get no reply. Now turn to any member of the class and ask what is meant by the word 'Empire' in the first question. There will be a long pause. Start all over again, and continue the process until you are sure that your class really do pay careful attention to the words of every question, and that they have adequate though not necessarily identical working definitions of any historical terms (as 'statesman' for instance) with which they are likely to come into contact. Get them to ring or underline the operative words in the question, and to define them. Point out that if they are answering the question the words of the question will constantly recur in the answer.

When you are sure they have grasped all this, take a question and ask for an answer in one short sentence: 'What were the permanent results of the policies of Charles V?' – 'Habsburg control in Italy, and Imperial weakness in Germany'. Of course, it does not matter whether you agree with the answer; the examiner will accept anything that is not deliberately perverse. This is the conclusion of the essay; the candidate puts it down first; he then proceeds to deal with each topic in turn. 'Habsburg control in Italy was secured by (a) favourable political geography, (b) military success, (c) . . .'. Each paragraph starts with a topic sentence – if necessary as simple as 'Another reason why Charles was able to establish permanent Habsburg control . . . was . . .'. and the rest of the paragraph is devoted to factual justification of the topic sentence. The method is pedestrian, ungainly, and soul-destroying; it will result in pedestrian, ungainly, inartistic and uninspiring essays; but they will be answers to the questions set, they will be to the point, and they will avoid factual irrelevance. They will pass. If you are fortunate enough to have intelligent and literate candidates of course, this is unnecessary.

The last weeks before the examination may be spent in the practice of timed essays, written in class, as nearly under examination conditions as may be, without reference to authority. Until the student can liberate himself from notes and textbooks, he will find it difficult to liberate himself from a chronological sequence.

In the last fortnight before the examinations, your candidates will want to 'revise', as they call it, by which they mean that they want to look through their notes, and read bits of their textbooks. Let them. It will not do them much good, but if you try to keep them writing essays, they will be frustrated to the point of desperation. Try to make sure that they are revising what you have told them to learn, but, so far as possible, leave them alone. The trouble is that they will start to think 'Suppose I get a question on . . . I don't know anything about it . . . I'd better just look . . .' and, like Macbeth after the murder of Duncan, they will uselessly dissipate their efforts in an attempt to provide for every conceivable and inconceivable eventuality. History is a subject which offers more scope than many for such a waste of time. But you must be as tactful as you possibly can. Nothing is more irritating than to have told your students what topics to revise, to see them all come up, pat, one, two, three, four, in the question paper, to ask your pet student, 'Well, what did you think of it?' and to get the answer, 'I don't know, I revised all the wrong subjects . . .'.

It may be added that teachers often find it comforting to candidates to give them a detailed breakdown of preparation, per- haps in the form of a duplicated sheet. As well as the advice on revision, it might include a practical warning that they will feel at first on entry to the examination that they know nothing, but that on consideration the meaning of the questions will become clearer. They should wait for a few minutes before writing: (a) to read the instructions carefully; (b) to choose their questions care-   . fully and then (c) to prepare points on the first question to be answered. It is important to get the timing of each question right, and to be aware that points will occur to them as they are writing. They should also know how to compile their last question in the event of a serious shortage of time – i.e. the plan, and the one paragraph precis of the essay they should have written had time allowed; *not* the fragment of a full essay left unfinished. The advantage of this kind of practical guidance beforehand is that it calms the nerves and enables the candidates to retrieve what they do know.

One other point of especial importance to able candidates may be made; it also serves to restate the living qualities of even examination history. Much of the revision work should be divergent rather than convergent. Ideally, one does not want to drill them into producing the stock answer, and of necessity much of their course work will have produced rather ossified impressions, e.g. the only way to see the 1820s is as the decade of 'Liberal Toryism'. Revision ought to be geared as much as possible to jolting them out of set patterns of thought, and to seeing things in new perspectives, so that they enter the examination with open minds. This we believe to be one of the high qualities of an historical training.

## A comparative survey

While there is a large number of authorities in Britain setting ex- aminations in history, the teacher will find in effect that only very exceptionally does his choice for his candidates extend to more than two of them; he can enter candidates for the examinations either of the local Certificate of Secondary Education authority, or of the General Certificate of Education authority favoured by the school in which he is teaching. In effect this restriction does not matter; the syllabuses are much of a muchness though examining techniques differ – and in any case most Boards will accept individual syllabuses; the Boards do what they can to ensure that approximately equal demands are made on the candidates; and all these examinations are controlled and conducted in much the same way, though pass standards certainly vary from board to board and a change has something to commend it, especially as timetables are often standardised. A lot of nonsense has been talked about the C.S.E. being a uniquely teacher-controlled examination. In fact, both C.S.E. and G.C.E. are controlled in precisely the same way – by various committees consisting largely of practising teachers and headmasters, with some representatives from universities and other centres of further education, which employ other practising teachers to set and mark their examination papers. There is of course a bureaucracy, and here there is a good deal of individual difference. But many of the administrators in examining authorities were once practising teachers and know what the problems are.

C.S.E. Boards tend, with some notable exceptions, to offer a limited number of syllabuses for their centrally set and marked examinations (Mode 1). These are (usually) a period of British history, from about 1760 to about 1939; British social and economic history, over the same period (roughly); and world history from about 1919 to the present day. Syllabuses offered by G.C.E. Boards are normally far more numerous, more varied, more extensive or more limited, more general or more specialised; at Ordinary level the same Board will frequently offer syllabuses covering the whole range of British and European history from the Norman Conquest onwards. Other Boards offer a single paper, containing such a large number of questions that candidates can select any significant period for study, or if they choose, can study selected topics over a long period. This is not the whole of the story. All the Boards, C.S.E. and G.C.E. alike, are willing to set special papers on special syllabuses drafted by the school and approved by the Board, marked and moderated by the Board's examiners; this, in C.S.E. parlance, is called Mode 2. For this service, they will of course make you pay extra, and they will usually require about two years' notice. G.C.E. and C.S.E. Boards offer still another method, Mode 3; they will give a certificate on the results of examinations, and frequently course work too, set and marked inside the school, though they will require to approve the syllabus and moderate the results. This procedure, of course, involves the teacher in much more work, since it is a do-it-yourself examination; however, it has advantages in that you can test your candidates on what you yourself believe is really important.

A C.S.E. Mode 3 examination provides a school or group of schools with the opportunity of having a nationally recognised certificate based on a syllabus and examination which have been specifically designed to suit the needs of pupils concerned. Although the C.S.E. Boards differ slightly in the ways in which Mode 3 examinations are submitted, the following procedure is fairly typical. A history teacher wishing to have a Mode 3 approved should submit a copy of the aims and content of the syllabus to the Board, together with a full question paper and a mark scheme. The Boards advise teachers to be specific in formulating aims and objectives and to state clearly what the examination is intended to measure.

The mark scheme should contain two parts – the school assessment, which will be based on course work done during the five terms preceding the examination, will be outlined; the regional assessment, usually a written paper, should not only indicate precisely what types of question are to be set, but also how long each test will last; the mark scheme should show what proportion of marks are allocated to each question.

The syllabus should be a fairly detailed statement of the content upon which the examination is to be based. Most boards request that Mode 3 syllabuses should be submitted 21 months before the first examination is scheduled to take place. The history panel will be responsible for scrutinising the Mode 3 proposal. In particular it will check whether the title of the syllabus – which will ultimately appear on the certificate – is an accurate description, whether the scheme of examination can be moderated and whether the syllabus is suitable for the award of a full range of grades.

It is clear that the number of Mode 3 syllabuses is increasing, although it is not possible to give exact figures. Most of the fifteen C.S.E. Regional Examining Boards examine Mode 3 history syllabuses; for example, in 1972, the West Yorkshire and Lindsey Regional Examining Board had over 120 syllabuses in history while nearly 2,500 candidates were entered for Mode 3 history examinations run by the East Anglian Board. As would be expected there is a great variety of C.S.E. Mode 3 history syllabuses and each one is unique. The following are a few examples:

The history of Yorkshire
Britain in the Modern World

Medieval Church History and Architecture
Local History and Archaeology
The History of Building
Social and Economic History of Britain 1750–1950
The history of medicine and nursing

There seems to be no clear pattern in the relationship between the number of Mode 3 syllabuses submitted to the Boards and the number and range of Mode 1 syllabuses available. Moreover, it is difficult to ascertain the attitudes of individual Boards to Mode 3. It is not always clear how far the Boards actively assist this form of examination or encourage history teachers to accept Mode 1.

The increasing popularity of Mode 3 suggests that it commends itself to many history teachers. The most significant advantage is that the programme is geared to the needs and abilities of pupils in a particular school and area. The content of the syllabus can be chosen to suit the interests of the pupils and enthusiasms of the staff of the history department. Varied approaches and methods are encouraged. It is clear that, freed from the pressure to cover the traditional examination syllabus which is often so long, teachers and pupils can develop alternative and fresh methods of study. Fieldwork, the use of audio-visual aids and the exploitation of primary sources are frequent features of these courses. In short, the examination need not influence the methods of study. Furthermore, the various course work assessment procedures can be organised to give the various aptitudes and abilities of each student a chance to be displayed over an extended period. For example, most schools have experimented with the project or special study. Other history departments have included essays, periodic work on unseen and seen primary sources, current affairs diaries, fieldwork reports, models and an oral examination as part of the school assessment.

The regional assessment, which usually takes the form of a written examination, has also resulted in new techniques of assessment. However, it may be that lack of time, and isolation amongst some history teachers, have presented serious obstacles to innovation in this area. For example, there are few history teachers with the available resources to produce objective-type questions themselves. Nevertheless, some important developments have taken place in Mode 3 examinations, in particular the use of primary sources – pictorial and statistical as well as documentary. However, the most significant feature of the Mode 3 examination is that it is set by the history department of the school with the abilities of the pupils in mind. The written papers are marked by the teachers and then externally moderated by the Board. The final grade for each pupil is based on the course work, the order of merit for which is drawn up by the school and sent to the Regional Board's offices before the end of the Easter term, and the examination. In this way a pupil is not assessed entirely on a single two- or two-and-a-half-hour examination.

The C.S.E. Mode 3 undoubtedly places a tremendous responsibility on the teacher. Initially the scheme has to be submitted to the Board; each year the examination paper has to be set, meticulous records of marks for the course work have to be kept; standards not only between sets, but between present and past history groups, have to be maintained; the scripts have to be marked and two sets of grades (schools and regional assessment) sent to the Board. Partly as a consequence of these demands, history teachers in some areas have grouped together to prepare and submit a common Mode 3 syllabus and, subsequently, to give each other mutual support in the teaching, examining and moderating of this syllabus.

Most Boards, C.S.E. and G.C.E. alike, tend to offer some questions which require short (even one word) answers, some which require answers of paragraph length and some which require essays; and all of them have been doing this since their inception. The greatest changes in recent years have resulted from the introduction of course work and from the application of computers and the introduction of objective tests; but no Board has so far gone over completely to these methods. C.S.E. Boards do tend to include more questions based on source material or statistical tables demanding short answers and fewer essay questions in their papers. This increases the length of the paper, and many Boards have been forced to the expedient of allowing the candidate a quarter of an hour to read the paper before he starts to write. The total duration of the examination should not exceed two and a half hours; for a pupil of sixteen, this is quite enough. Objective tests, in particular, are a considerable nervous strain.

Some authorities, particularly C.S.E. Boards, require an estimate from the school of the abilities and attainment of each candidate. Some even make this estimate an integral part of the examination, counting for as much as 50% of the marks. In this case, what we have, in effect, are two examinations: one (the written paper) assessing the candidate's response to a formal test on a particular date; the other assessing his abilities, industry and response over the last two years (or whatever period is demanded). These are two very different things, and this must be clearly understood; there is no point in trying to forecast the candidate's examination mark. This procedure will, of course, penalise the idle intelligent.

There have recently been several attempts to introduce further examinations for pupils in their first year in the sixth form. Many of the arguments in their favour – so far as history is concerned – have been bad ones. To the pupil, the gap between what is demanded of him at sixteen and what is demanded at eighteen is not only enormous but qualitative. He has to learn to think in what to him is a new and painful manner; and this is something which he cannot do – unless he is exceptionally developed – in less than two years. Thus it is difficult to see what qualities a Certificate of Extended Education examination in history could test, which are not already tested by C.S.E. or O level.

What has been said about syllabuses at O level applies also to Advanced level examinations. Many Boards offer a great variety of syllabuses, some requiring reference to source material, edited and printed, some more general in character. Here again, it is possible for the teacher to devise his own syllabus if he wishes to do so, though most Boards will insist that it should include some foreign history.

While some questions requiring short answers do appear on the papers (on documents, for instance), in most cases the answer which is demanded is an essay. Most papers are of three hours' duration, and demand answers to four questions. It is difficult to lay down rules; but most candidates will not be able to answer satisfactorily in fewer than about 500 words; they should be warned of this and given practice in writing essays of this length in 45 minutes.

For the intelligent candidate, the examination for university entrance or scholarship is the most enjoyable he is ever likely to take, since these papers are designed to measure potential, and are therefore really unrestrictive. The candidate's enthusiasm may well be moderated by a sense of what may hang upon the results; but he should be encouraged, when answering, at any rate to have a go, and not to err upon the side of caution. Most universities still value ideas, however outlandish. Most of the questions in these papers in effect consist of a proposition which the candidate is invited to prove or disprove by reference to whatever historical illustrations he is in a position to select. Many universities require all candidates to attempt a general paper, and, for reasons obvious to historians, it may well fall to them to prepare candidates for this. It is therefore perhaps permissible to conclude with an example taken from such a paper – a stroke of sheer genius, and the model of a good question.

> 'A primrose by the river's brim
> A simple primrose was to him
> And it was nothing more.'
> What ought it to have been?

# History for the slow learner

The increase in the number of comprehensive schools has meant that more and more teachers are faced, perhaps for the first time and late in their career, with a class of pupils which is identified by, and which often stoically accepts, the label of 'the less able', or which is of mixed ability, depending on the philosophy of the school.[1] The sensitive and the wise will share with the newly-trained the hesitancy that comes from inexperience, and many have felt, as they did during their first term, that history and the specialist historian have no place in the education of such pupils. Though an understandable reaction, this is not true, and is to surrender too easily. In any case, it misses the point. To say that he should not be there is of no help to the history teacher faced with a class of thirty or more pupils.

The initial problem for the history teacher is to establish as precisely as he can why the individuals in the form have been classified as less able. The label itself is not a complete answer. Initially, these pupils tend to identify themselves by their poor achievement in classwork and in tests, and then, except in mixed-ability situations, have that identity confirmed by banding or streaming: a decision which, experience suggests, soon acts as a self-fulfilling prophecy. Though the pupils share this common classification, within the form various sub-groups can usually be distinguished:

(a)   the intelligent but idle,

(b)   those of low intelligence but who are well-motivated when they can understand what is required; usually from secure homes; this group includes those often known as 'late developers' or 'slow starters',

(c)   those of below average intelligence who are resistant to the school; frequently they come from homes with social problems.

The percentage which each group will form in the class will vary, but the history teacher must recognise that the class is homogeneous in name and achievement only. His approach will have to be

[1] *The Report on Mixed Ability Teaching* (A.M.A.) deals with the matter in greater detail.

flexible, and the class lesson will have a less regular role than it might with more able pupils of similar age.

The precise nature of the problem with which the history teacher has to deal is influenced largely by the school organisation. Thus, he may have a single class of 30 or more less able pupils, though many schools manage to keep groups of streamed slow learners down to twenty pupils, or he may have three or four of them in a mixed-ability set. As a general rule, small classes of the less able will probably be preferable, at least as an introduction to teaching these pupils. But there can be no absolute definition of the most successful teaching situation, since so much will depend on the resources which are available, and on the sympathies of the teacher. Some highly experienced teachers advise, 'They [the less able] must be separated in small classes'; whilst others, equally experienced but now teaching forms of mixed ability, assert 'We have noticed that in general the motivation of the less able pupils is higher and that there is a significant development of the "late developer". Some pupils enter with the "less able" tag, but shake it off.' Not all our correspondents agree with this view, however. In a mixed ability situation the teacher is forced to deal with pupils on an individual, or small group, basis. This will help the child whose achievement is generally low for, unlike a class of more intelligent children, a class of the less able is far more a class of individuals, less patient and less willing to submerge their individualism into a group. In a streamed class it is still possible to do individual and group work, of course, but the history teacher will have perhaps 30 pupils all of whom are prone to fuss and need constant help with the simplest tasks, whereas in a mixed-ability form there are a large number of pupils able to follow written instructions and work on their own, and perhaps only three or four of the less able. In this situation, of course, the teacher has to ensure that his time is not dominated by the few at the expense of the majority.

A further administrative factor which influences the teaching of these groups, and which annually poses a problem for the head of department, is that of deciding how the department's teaching load should be distributed. Mixed-ability organisation obviates the need for decisions between classes of the same age, but where such decisions have to be made it is a mistake to concentrate the ablest teaching exclusively in examination and potential examination forms.

It should be recognised, however, that the able teacher of academic pupils may, perhaps even for that reason, be the reverse of able in teaching slow learners. The criterion in allocating staff should be making the best use of teaching resources, and this is not necessarily achieved by an equality of periods with the less able pupils among the members of the department.

The good teacher of the less able, like his counterpart with more able pupils, is born rather than made, but the historian who makes a special effort to treat these pupils as individuals and shows that he is interested in them by exchanging a few words of conversation at break or on passing in the corridor, will have fewer problems in the classroom, for they will be more likely to be interested in him and in his subject. Those who find themselves teaching completely across the ability range will have considerable mental gymnastics to perform, and will find that the amount of time needed for preparation for low ability forms is as great, though the preparation is of a different kind, as for a sixth form – a fact which should be recognised by school officialdom by the grant of a lighter teaching load, though this is unusual.

The objectives of the history teacher with a class of slow learners will, in general terms, be the same as those for more able forms. If there is a difference it must be that the teacher with the less able must be more aware of his immediate objectives: he must set out to gain and hold the pupils' interest, and then to build up the confidence that comes from success and which creates a further desire to succeed. He will, of course, try to do this with all his classes but if he forgets with the less able his failure will be the more noticeable, for they will not be patient with him. If he achieves these immediate objectives, others become feasible, even if at a relatively unsophisticated level: to extend the pupil's ability to make judgements, to understand the relationship between cause and effect, to communicate in writing, orally, visually and dramatically, to extend his imagination by opening up a new and fascinating dimension – time.[2]

In establishing suitable courses, two most important criteria must be borne in mind: there must be adequate materials of the right level available, and, if possible, the subjects should have an immediate interest or significance for the pupils. Some historians are able to transmit their enthusiasm for their subject, to conjure up interest in an unlikely topic, but most teachers would be wiser to choose their topics on other considerations besides their own interests. Some history teachers, experienced with these pupils, advise allowing them to follow their own interests, though administratively the provision of adequate materials for unknown topics is difficult to say the least; others advise local history as a starting-point; still more turn to an integrated approach, but, useful and

[2] See Chapter 1.

successful though that can be, a mere change of name will not solve any problems and it can be argued that the integrated concept is too grand for immature minds.[3] It is argued by some teachers that, at least superficially, the content of courses for the less able should appear to be the same as for their more intelligent peers, which it will be if classes are organised on a mixed-ability basis. A common curriculum and the same teachers helps avoid the sense of rejection which aggravates the problem of the less able.

With older pupils of 14 to 16 the contemporary relevance, or significance, of the material studied is essential. One course, which can provide the basis for further experiment, taught successfully, dealt with a series of topics from the last 150 years which were taken up to the present. These included:

| | |
|---|---|
| Public health | The emancipation of women |
| At work | People at war |
| Leisure | Leaders of the people |

The variety which exists in the content of the courses which have been successfully taught demonstrates, however, that more important than the content is the method which is employed.

When considering which teaching method to employ with the less able, the history teacher should bear in mind three essentials: the need for explanations, worksheets and resources which will enable the pupil to understand and work at the concrete operation level of thought;[4] secondly, the need for variety of technique and for flexibility within a lesson; and finally, the need for careful, detailed preparation.

Adequate preparation is, of course, essential at all levels of ability, but with the less able that preparation must include what the teacher intends to say in order to ensure that the class will understand the vocabulary of the tasks and the material. It must also include preparation of the materials in the classroom if the lesson is to begin smoothly; this means that supplies of pens, pencils, rulers, rubbers, crayons, scissors, cardboard, plain and ruled paper must be immediately to hand. Even the most imaginative lesson presentation can fall flat if, when the class is asked to draw or write, ten minutes of chaos results because a dozen people have not brought a pen or a pencil. Similarly, the problem of books left at home is best avoided by the use of books or of files which the teacher keeps. The historian will generally find files preferable to books, for then work can be pinned to a board for display, taken down and clipped in the appropriate place in the file. As the files

3 See Chapter 11.
4 For a discussion of this, see Chapter 1, p. 2.

are stored in the class's history room there is no danger of damage in transit.

Flexibility and variety are essential, both within a single lesson and in a series of lessons covering a topic. The teacher would do well always to bear in mind the limited ability to concentrate of most of these pupils. Successful lessons often have a strong visual content: filmstrips are usually too long but can be cut up into slides and made available for the pupil to use with a viewer. Some filmstrips need a story-telling approach and are best dealt with in sections by the teacher; historical films too, are very useful, especially if the class has been forewarned to find the answers to a few simple questions during the film. A valuable role can also be played by radio and television broadcasts – so long as they are carefully selected – as pegs on which to hang a variety of activities. The important thing is to make the stimulus material so alive as to enable the pupil to be an active participant in the learning process rather than the passive recipient of information.[5] A tape-recorder enables a group of pupils to conduct interviews; these may be imaginary, in which case they will obviously have to do the research to find out the appropriate questions and answers and will need careful guidance to the sources available; or, having started a study, they might be able to conduct an interview with a contemporary of the event, such as a battle, a visit to a doctor before the National Health Service, or the Great Depression. Such interviews have been found to be a useful counter to the belief that history is concerned only with great people, and they can give a pupil a rare sense of importance when he can interview his own parents or grandparents and present his findings to the class. Old family albums can also be a valuable source of interest and information, but in any work involving families of the pupils great care has to be taken not to give the impression of injudicious enquiry.

Fieldwork can form a useful starting-point for a topic, and a fortunate few may be able to participate in an excavation; for most schools, a visit to a site or a museum is quite practicable, but must be prepared in such a way as to give the pupils tasks to do so that they are not merely passive observers. Drama in the classroom automatically presumes pupil involvement, and can be an effective way of explaining a difficult concept or of presenting the results of an exploration of a topic. Experience with drama, however, varies, and its success depends on the age and sophistication of the pupils,

[5] A discussion of the use of source materials which involve active participation will be found in Chapter 6. It may be stressed here that local source materials allow of *re-creation* which is intellectually easier and more appealing than an analytical approach.

their experience in using drama (if they have taken part in it since the first year, they are more willing to do so in the fourth), and (most important) the confidence, experience and sympathy of the teacher in handling this method. Here particularly, but also in all practical work, adequate preparation is essential; no practical activity can be an easy alternative for the teacher.

All these devices will, of course, be employed by the history teacher with more able children. The difference is that with the less academic pupils they will tend to form the natural order of things, and the class lesson and written work will therefore have a smaller role to play. The class lesson does have its part: it will introduce a topic, when its function will be to stimulate and to intrigue; it will be needed to explain administrative details for group work, projects, etc.; during the course of work on a topic it will be the occasion to explain any general problems or points of interest that have arisen; it will be used for story-telling; at the end of individual or group work it will draw all the strands together. In all this, however, the teacher must be careful not to get carried away by his own voice. He will be unusually gifted if he can hold the attention of the class by his own voice for longer than 15 or 20 minutes.

It is an enlightening experience to ask one's pupils which teaching method they find most effective. This question, explained fully and then asked of one class of less able pupils who had experienced a variety of approaches, indicated that they thought copied notes and oral explanation most successful. Perhaps it should not be surprising. Less able pupils prefer copying because it is easier than expressing their own thoughts, and it can be done accurately to give an impression of a competent and successful piece of work. The value of such teaching depends largely on the quality of the oral explanation which accompanies the notes. The teacher must prepare his oral work no less thoroughly than his plans for written work, and must ensure that he explains the concepts he uses in terms that can be understood at a concrete level of operation, if possible in terms of the child's own experience.[6] Thus, instead of talking about the vote he would be wiser to hold an election in the classroom. No concept can be taken for granted; even the most basic like worship, monarchy, vote, democracy, need very careful explanation for full understanding, as they often do even for more able pupils. Yet even if he accompanies his notes with a very good explanation, it will, generally, be better for the pupil to find out

6 See J. Coltham, *The Development of Thinking and Learning of History* (Historical Association, 1971), and P. H. J. H. Gosden and D. W. Sylvester, *History for the Average Child* (Blackwell, 1968).

for himself. The historian with the less able will, if he has prepared well, find that he has fewer problems if he removes himself as quickly as is practicable from the lesson in which he deals with the class as a group, and begins work on an individual basis.

Individual, or small group, work will probably necessitate work cards, or assignment sheets. Instructions can, of course, be written on a blackboard or overhead projector, but if so it should be done before the beginning of a lesson as the class will need the teacher's complete attention as soon as it arrives. A mass of written instruction is quite daunting, and work-cards should include maps, diagrams and pictures where appropriate. Assignments are essential for a mixed-ability class. Those for the less able may be separate from the others, or there may be a common work-sheet with an initial section which even the slowest child can do, and then a further section of alternative things to do which provides for work at different levels. In a mixed-ability situation work speed will, of course, vary greatly. This can present administrative problems, for when the teacher wishes to introduce a new topic the less able pupils will be far behind. In such a situation the only, albeit partial, solution is to require less work of the slow learner (though detailed instruction on work-cards should not make it appear so), and to give all pupils a realistic completion date for their tasks when they begin them.

It has already been suggested that the historian should look further than written work for the presentation of material by the pupil, and he would be wise to consider alternative forms such as charts, maps, diagrams, strip-cartoons, sketches, models, 'radio' programmes, etc. Written work does not come easily to the less able and is frequently associated with failure. Of course, these pupils especially have to be encouraged to develop their ability to communicate, but unless he is very careful the history teacher eager to develop written competence in his pupils will simply turn them against the subject, and that will mean he will achieve nothing. Written work, therefore, is best used like most medicine: regularly, but in small doses. Wherever possible it should be camouflaged. Thus it can be in the form of a script for a play or radio programme, or an interview to be tape-recorded; it can be a diary, or a ship's log; it can be in the creation of a 'newspaper'. At such times we are all teachers of English, but if we are wise we will find only a few mistakes and seek to reward any achievement, however small. However, all pupils, of whatever ability, should have exercises in continuous prose.

Elsewhere in the book the desirability of speedy marking,

preferably in front of the pupil is emphasised.[7] With less able pupils this is essential. Errors, though not all, should be pointed out almost as soon as they occur as the teacher moves round the class at work. If this can be done, the end result will be a piece of work which the pupil will feel is good and can be marked accordingly. Success will go on to breed success.

There are those who argue that examinations have no place in the education of the less able who appear to have appallingly defective memories. Yet these pupils include experts on the record of certain footballers, or on their favourite pop singer. It is surprising what the well-motivated child can learn. There are also those who argue that, for social reasons, these pupils should be treated as other groups and therefore they too should have annual examinations. If the examination itself, and the marks gained, are kept in perspective, there is little harm to be done. If the principles, laid out elsewhere, of testing what the pupil can reasonably be expected to know, and of marking generously, are followed, and if too much emphasis on written work can be avoided, then the result can be a success and a boost to confidence.[8] The need to encourage success might well lead the history teacher here to permit a narrower spread of marks than would be acceptable with more able pupils.

It is clear that examinations for this group cannot be of the one and a half hour, four essay question variety, to be completed sitting in the school hall. It would not be unreasonable to include in the test questions which involve book-using, drawing (though beware of the assumption that less able pupils are all very good drawers), oral examining, even model-making or tape-recording. The assessment of the year's work will be an important part too, especially for older pupils who can benefit from the incentive that a Mode 3 C.S.E. course can provide. All this is time and resource consuming, but it will have to be so if it is to be just to the pupils. It will bear saying again that teaching the less able demands at least as much time and patience as teaching older or more able pupils, perhaps more. The history teacher must accept this, as he must accept that, having tried his utmost in teaching these pupils, he will still be aware of a large degree of failure. As one correspondent wrote: '. . . usually about 70% of classes have been keenly interested and wanted "to get on", or "do more homework". I rarely ask for more.'

7 See Chapter 7.
8 See Chapter 8.

# The sixth form

**10**

Much that has been written and assumed in the past about the place and nature of history in the sixth form is now increasingly brought into question. This questioning has largely been prompted by changes in the composition of sixth forms. More students are staying on in the sixth form but, in proportion, fewer intend to go on to universities; for some of them the academic demands of Advanced level are too exacting. This change in the nature of the sixth form has led to criticism of traditional courses and methods but tradition has its defenders too.

There is [writes A. E. Dyson] a real danger that academic success and aptitude may be penalised, implicitly, or even explicitly, as sixth form restructuring develops. There are educationists who hanker after equality of attainment, and regard the development and proclamation of particular merits as offensive. One hears the suggestion that since certain academic courses are 'irrelevant' to many new sixth-formers, the general syllabus should be rethought. Under the pressure of such reorganisation, traditional subjects might be dropped, and this process can be rationalised as a virtue . . . In the face of such developments, one has to say that the basic commitment of the sixth-form must be to 'subjects' – which is to say that it must be to the achievements in arts, sciences and wisdom of the human race . . . Any teacher who has himself been enriched by his subject, and celebrates it, will know that it is the most important thing he has to pass on . . .[1]

From a spate of writing on this theme, two articles by Mary Price[2] and Martin Roberts[3] respectively are of particular value in showing the need to keep syllabuses and teaching methods under constant review. Linked with the doubts about the traditional syllabus is the view of those who believe that history and sociology must become one. The debates will continue. They are relevant for the teacher of history, if his practice is to be rooted in principle, but he

[1] A. E. Dyson, 'The Sixth-form: Some Current Problems' in *The Basic Unity of Education* (published on behalf of the National Council for Educational Standards by the Critical Quarterly Society, 1972).

[2] Mary Price, 'History in Danger' in *History*, LIII No. 179 (October 1968) (Historical Association).

[3] Martin Roberts, 'Contemporary Problems of Sixth-form History' in *History*, LIV No. 182 (October 1969) (Historical Association).

has, in addition, to face the everyday practical problems of teaching in the sixth form and it is with these that this chapter is primarily concerned.

## The nature of sixth-form work

The sixth form gives to the history teacher the fullest opportunity of practising the historian's craft. For many teachers, it is this work which most completely satisfies them. One of the reasons for this is that, at its best, it provides an individual confrontation with maturing minds. The sensitive, patient and tactful teacher will have the opportunity of guiding students from their immediate post-O level inexperience through the skills and experiences he has himself enjoyed to the fuller maturity of the near undergraduate. His job is to pose questions rather than provide answers; to encourage individual work rather than to teach a class; and to share with his pupils his own love of his subject.

It is however not always quite like this – although teachers should always bear the ideal in mind. There are many more sixth formers studying history now than ever before and, while there seems to be more success now in keeping set sizes down (the average seems to be about 12–15) more could yet be done, for, in general, a set of more than 12 is rarely satisfactory. Moreover, present-day sets vary a great deal in aim and ability. This has led some schools to stream their sixth-form sets by ability but this is more usually rejected as impracticable or undesirable. With sets of mixed ability, therefore, the range is greater than ever: some will be scholarly in their inclinations, and intend perhaps to read history at a university; while others may have chosen history not because they necessarily want to do it, but because it is the least unsatisfactory of the options open to them as a third Advanced level subject. This is a challenge to the skill and patience of the teacher, for clearly the commitment to the subject will be equally diverse; he will need a flexibility of approach and method greater than in the past. Most schools still impose some kind of academic test on entry to an Advanced level course and this is surely wise; not all pupils can hope to cope successfully with advanced work in history. Most schools now seem to ensure that the individual sixth-form historian is taught by at least two different teachers to give him, it is to be hoped, a variety of experience: this should be the aim wherever possible.

It is to be hoped, too, that strenuous efforts will be made to ensure that the quality and qualification of the sixth-form teacher will be the highest possible. The qualities of a good history teacher are discussed elsewhere (see pp. 5–11), and these apply above all to the teacher in the sixth form. The old idea that only the most senior teacher is fit to teach the sixth has almost gone, and about time too – age is not the appropriate criterion. In fact the young graduate will often have more success with the academic Advanced level sets than he will lower down the school where teaching experience is even more valuable. It remains true, however, that a man who knows what he teaches and loves what he knows will be in less danger of teaching something other than history, ignorant of the nature of his own subject. It is doubly important therefore for the good sixth-form teacher that he should keep himself up to date, attend conferences, read the academic journals, and follow developments and controversies which affect his work; even, where possible, that he should write books, lecture to outside groups, and publish articles; in short, he should aim to become a specialist. It is not always possible, however, to persuade pupils, parents, even headmasters, governors and local authorities of the importance of the subject; without their cooperation the ideal will not be attainable. Nevertheless, every effort must be made to create as nearly the right circumstances as possible. A practicable and reasonable compromise is nearly always possible.

Given that these difficulties exist, it is still possible for the existing A level courses to provide a suitable curriculum for many of our sixth formers. Clearly not all of these will benefit in the same way. Their aim is, after all, not the same: some will hope to go on to read history at a university; others will read another subject and for them history is more of a means to an end; some will not go to a university at all but into other forms of higher education, or into the professions or business. Nevertheless, it is to be hoped that all will gain a deeper understanding of the complexities of human life and problems, of people and their diversity and unity and of themselves. Many will join that large population among adults who read history for fun. It is in the sixth form that one can expect discussion to be more frequent and better informed; that one can expect a livelier interest in the arts and in politics and their relation to history, and a more mature understanding of adult motive. As the sixth former, spurred on by the individual attention of his teacher, gains mastery of his subject, he will grow in confidence as well as in knowledge and skills. Gradually a genuine spirit of enquiry will develop so that the imaginative recreation of the past and a growing ability to make his own judgements will promote in each pupil some individuality of style. He will gain from the sixth form at its best some insight into true scholarship, into the meaning of intellectual integrity, and a sense of perspective in a rapidly changing world.

## The content and nature of the course

The content of a history course in the sixth form poses problems rather different from those met with in other subjects. In mathematics, for example, it is necessary to build on what has been learnt before; the nature of the subject itself in this case determines the order in which things are taught. In history this is not so: while there are many advantages in studying the subject chronologically in the lower school (and this question is discussed elsewhere, see pp. 21–2), it is not necessary for any pupil beginning the sixth-form course to have had any particular background of factual knowledge. It is of course advisable that they should have some preparation in such skills as reading critically, note-making, essay-writing and so on, which they will develop in the sixth. History is a subject where the more advanced the work the more mature and deeper the interpretation; it is not so much, therefore, the period of study that is vital, as the manner in which it is studied. This is not to deny the importance of factual knowledge; there has been a healthy reaction in our generation against 'kings and things', against dates, and the memorising of facts: it is possible that this reaction has gone too far. A reasonable familiarity with dates and facts provides a kind of 'mental scaffolding' and may need to be learnt, but usually, in advanced work, these will be acquired fairly painlessly in the course of reading and increasing familiarity with the work. The complex nature of a historical 'fact' does need explaining to sixth formers. The teacher should insist that each is part of a complex web of knowledge and often varies in significance from historian to historian. The sixth former has to learn to use the 'facts' as evidence to support his interpretations, and to assess what weight each will bear.

Another important task of the sixth-form teacher is to encourage the accurate use of language: although not strictly true, it is worth making this point dramatically by stating categorically that the English language possesses no synonyms; there is only one word available to express exactly the thought intended, and it is the pupil's job to find it. Careful and accurate reasoning depends on accuracy in the use of language: many of our pupils will also be studying English and this is a help in some ways, for language is capable of delicate nuances which these pupils are likely to understand better than others. We should also make sure that the pupils recognise, first, that a word may change its meaning over a period (this is especially important when using documentary sources) and that it is its meaning in its own period which is relevant; and, second, that there are 'jargon' words in history as in other studies; we should warn them, therefore, against a too ready assumption that they fully understand these short-hand terms. All this will contribute to the growth of a mature understanding and, incidentally, underlines the necessity of individual attention by the teacher.

It is probably not true that all history is equally worth studying, but the choice is ultimately one for the head of department to make in the light of all the circumstances at his school; it may be of some interest that, from the necessarily small sample of those schools which replied to the committee's questionnaire, 7% of the outline papers studied were primarily medieval; 55% were primarily 16th–18th centuries; 36% were primarily modern; and 2% primarily economic and social. About 50% entered pupils also for a special subject paper and a small proportion for the Cambridge Project. There are four factors which the head of department will probably want to consider: first, the advantages of a course which covers a reasonable period of time; most boards offer outline papers and the committee feels that selection for study of a period of about two hundred years is probably about right. Examining boards normally set two outline papers, one in British and one in European or world history; there are probably advantages in studying the same period in each, so that there is some 'carry over' from the work done in the one to the other, and also to demonstrate the continuity of British History with European, but opinions differ about this. A special subject is often optional and sometimes compulsory: its advantage is that it gives the opportunity for study in depth and perhaps for use of documents; but some correspondents feel that it is too difficult for the weaker pupil; others, that a frequent change of special subject imposes undue strains on the sixth-form library budget. Those teachers who enter pupils for the Cambridge Board's optional Project find that it poses fewer problems over the use of books and some are enthusiastic about it as a method of encouraging historical skills. It may well be something which other Boards will follow in the future: briefly, it involves a pupil in selecting a theme for private study, persuading the examiners of its value and practicability, researching and reading and then presenting a manuscript of 5000 words, fully referenced; he will then be interviewed upon it, bringing with him notes he has made in preparing it. Full details can be obtained from the Cambridge Board.

Secondly, the head of department will want to consider the advantage of studying at Advanced level a period different from that studied at Ordinary level. There are distinct advantages in studying a period other than that studied immediately prior to entry to the sixth form: for one thing it offers a fresh start to be made, with all the attendant psychological advantages this has – on the analogy of the fresh start of a new exercise book in the lower school. For another it ensures that all start equal in ignorance; and more important, it emphasises the difference between the sixth form and the lower school – a difference which we should try to maintain, if our aim is to uphold standards in the sixth. On the other hand, there are those who believe that a familiarity with at least the outline of the work is a positive help, especially to the less able. On balance the arguments seem to favour the choosing of a different period for advanced work, and perhaps one as far removed as possible from it.

Thirdly, the period should be one which has been sufficiently written on by professional historians writing in English, for there to be a number of points of view and controversies, so that the sixth formers are given an opportunity to follow controversies and historical problems, and in their own way to take part in them. This is important, for it is stimulating to sixth forms, but in practice it is doubtful if any choice likely to be offered by an examination board is short of debate. Fourthly, some have felt, and they have a point, that a further consideration should be the familiarity, at least of the best students, with languages other than English. A whole new perspective is gained in some periods by the ability to read comfortably in, for example, French or medieval Latin: it is possible to exaggerate the difficulties likely to be incurred by an absence of this ability, but, for those who possess it there is no reason why it should not be encouraged and put to use in the choice of a period for the best set.

Another aspect of Advanced level work which requires separate attention is the Special paper. This paper should be taken only by those of high ability in the subject since it provides a searching test of historical understanding well beyond the capacity of the mediocre candidate. There is no doubt that preparation for this paper requires special provision in the time-table – though one period a week is sufficient – and teaching of very high calibre. In some subjects the Special paper differs so little from the main content of the Advanced level paper that separate teaching is not required; this is certainly not so in history. The questions asked are much less concerned with the accumulation of knowledge about individual regions, ministries, and episodes than Advanced level papers are, and are much more concerned with matters of large-scale significance, such as the influence of the various '-isms' in history: absolutism, mercantilism, nationalism, liberalism, Romanticism, and so on; with the development of the arts and of civilisations; with the nature of history and the problems of historical study. It is not surprising that the view was advanced at a conference of teachers at Cambridge that performance in the Special paper was a better guide than Advanced level results to a student's capacity for higher education.

Preparation for this paper provides admirable training, therefore, for those who will be taking Open Scholarship examinations; in schools where candidates are entered in their fourth term for these scholarships this is a strong argument for starting study of the history Special paper in the lower sixth. The paper is also valuable for those students who, while not intending to enter for an Open Scholarship examination in history, have broad intellectual interests in all their subjects. Examining boards vary in the number of Special papers which students are allowed to take; on this point, therefore, the regulations need to be consulted.

To conclude, every head of department should, at some time, look at the syllabuses of the different boards, and think critically about the period his own sixth are studying, but should not be in too much of a hurry to change. More important is to try to ensure that all the advanced pupils are studying in the right way: that all are getting some insight into the difficulties and pleasures of historical study; that all are learning to think for themselves, and to analyse and expound historical problems.

## Methods

In one sense, there are as many methods as there are teachers and, in an ideal world, this could be a very short section indeed: if it works go on with it. However, some practical guidance, with examples of successful methods used by other teachers, is probably helpful. In many ways teaching in the sixth form need not be so very different from teaching in the lower school, which should after all, at least in part, be a preparation for the sixth; just as the sixth in its turn should be, at least in part, a preparation for university work. The kind of work expected of the sixth has already been looked at: how, in practice, to achieve it is the corollary of this. On their first entry to the sixth, we are dealing with students who have just left the fifth form. They will inevitably need more guidance than would be desirable for second-year sixth formers; it is worth remembering therefore that we are dealing with a two-year course, and our methods and expectations must be tailored to the developing maturity and experience of the students. This is a weaning process, normally: gradually dependence on the teacher and the textbook must be withdrawn, and at a rate which suits the individual students. There is much to be said for an introductory course, perhaps of two or three weeks, when the nature and purpose of history can be discussed. This can be accompanied by exercises in the nature of historical reasoning. These can come from the teacher's own experience, or by the use of selected passages for comment taken from the work of practising historians – so long as their length and complexity is not too great. There are books, like the admirable *Lines of Thought*,[4] which contain suitable exercises. If carried on too long, however, this will be frustrating, for the students, naturally enough, want to get down to the historical work itself. Another factor to consider is that the history student in the sixth is also studying other subjects, which will make demands on his time and mental energy. The committee has found that the great majority of the schools with which it has corresponded allow between six and nine 40-minute periods for A level history per week; with time limited in this way, it is necessary to use it effectively. This does not mean a total reliance on the lecture, for this is deadening; nor does it mean 'letting them loose in the library', for this will, on its own, almost certainly involve a huge waste of time. It means careful planning, flexibility, a variety of methods and a sense of purpose on the part of the teacher.

Certain specific skills have to be taught; some will have had a good grounding in these before they reach the sixth; others will not. The most important are effective reading, essay-writing, and note-making. All involve the student working a great deal on his own and trouble should be taken to make sure that time is allowed for this in class, as well as in 'private study' periods and at home: incidentally, the term 'free period' should be avoided, because it gives some sixth formers quite a wrong impression of what they should be doing in it. The advantage of making class time available is that it enables the teacher to keep an eye on what the pupils are doing. Lower sixth formers work better if supervised; they need guidance and frequently have questions which can then be answered as soon as they arise.

Reading is the heart and soul of sixth-form work. Its effectiveness depends on two principal factors: first, an adequate stock of library books, preferably readily available to the students, either in the sixth-form room, if there is one, or in a history library. There is some controversy as to whether there should be a separate history library, or whether it should form part of the general school library: on the whole, librarians tend to prefer the latter, but what is essential is that the books should be available and reasonably secure. A high proportion of the annual 'capitation' should be

[4] R. W. Young, *Lines of Thought* (Oxford University Press, rev. ed. 1965).

made available for the history library, unless the library fund is administered separately. Books are rising rapidly in price and it is important to keep pointing this out to whoever will listen. Some schools seem still to have derisory library allowances. The other factor in encouraging effective reading is, of course, clear guidance from the teacher: it is worth 'spoon feeding' lower sixth formers, at least at first, not only with *short* reading lists but also page references since there is seldom any need to read a book from cover to cover. Specific advice can be given about what to expect from a particular book – its bias, its omissions and its value. The aim will be to help students ultimately to do this for themselves. Guidance should therefore be given about how to find books – some help with the Dewey Decimal Classification is invaluable, as is the use of the library catalogues – and how to use the introduction, contents page and index, once the book has been found, to estimate its value. It is incidentally a useful technique, if used sparingly, to set as a piece of written work a review of a particular book. Pupils should, perhaps, be encouraged right from the start to add a bibliography to their essays – with comments on the books used.

Closely connected with the art of reading is the craft of note-making. There are three kinds of notes in general, and all need teaching. First, the making of notes in class from a lecture, or a tape or a discussion. It is important to explain that not everything which is said is worth noting: at first, headings – either duplicated, or on the blackboard or on the overhead projector – will help the pupil to see what is vital and what, for example, is intended as a more or less trivial aside for the sake of amusement. He will have to learn to use abbreviations and to remember later what they stood for: practice will make perfect. The teacher should make sure he is not going too fast, and it is important that he should be close enough to the pupils to watch their speed: when difficulties occur – lack of understanding, or an unfamiliar name – he will be able to stop and elucidate; when sets are a reasonable size, and the atmosphere is sufficiently informal, this should be easy enough. Questions should be encouraged. Second, and more important, is the making of notes from books. This again has to be learnt, for the tendency of the inexperienced is to make too many notes and, hence, not to see the wood for the trees. If the emphasis is placed on the reading rather than the notes which come out of it, much needless waste of time and energy can be avoided. Pupils should be encouraged always to write at the head of these notes the source; they should keep their notes in loose-leaf folders, so that they can add to their existing stock notes from other sources on the same topic. It has been found helpful to encourage them to read pieces of increasing length, before setting pen to paper: perhaps a paragraph or two, then a page or two, then a whole section or chapter: this will help them to get the perspective right, especially if they do not look back over what they have read before making the note – except for the occasional name or date which may have slipped out with the less essential matter. There is a third kind of note, namely the occasional setting of a chapter 'to be noted': this really constitutes the making of a precis of it. It is dull work and should only be used when there is no alternative. It is sometimes essential, however, and the need for grinding tedious work will have to be both accepted and expected by sixth formers occasionally. It is most likely to be of value when a book is (i) seminal, (ii) irreplaceable and (iii) in short supply – usually when only one copy of it exists in the library. Some teachers do this themselves and duplicate the result but this is probably service above and beyond the call of duty. The technique is not unlike that of the precis in English and will be familiar to most of the pupils. It must be stressed however that this is a last resort.

Essay-writing is dealt with elsewhere in this chapter (see pp. 189–91) and elsewhere in the book (see pp. 116–22) but it is convenient to regard it as one of the most useful techniques to learn and one of the hardest to learn to do well.

It has already been suggested that the aim of the teacher should be a variety of methods suitable to the topic under discussion and to the ability of the students. To try something new is usually stimulating even when it fails; that teachers are much more ready to experiment than they used to be is an encouraging development. If the purpose of the teacher is clear, at least to him, and the basic skills are being acquired, then his role becomes more obvious. It is at once to be a guide and to be something more than this. He plays a role – even if a declining one as the pupils progress through to A-level standard – as the *teacher*, the source of much of the factual information the pupils acquire. There are any number of ways in which this can be efficiently done; some of the more common, or the more interesting, follow.

The traditional sixth-form lecture, or lesson or seminar, or whatever it is called, in which the teacher spends at least most of the period talking, is probably both over-used and under-rated. Its value in the sixth form lies in giving a context for the work about to be done: providing background, raising specific problems and difficulties in the work, pointing out differences between historians, elucidating controversial questions, predigesting new work in journals and so on which students cannot usually be expected to do on their own, dealing with matter inadequately dealt with in their books, and, above all, giving life and excitement to a particular topic. Some of these objects can be achieved through other means, but often less economically. It is vital, however, that it should not be used to do the job the students should be doing on their own in their own reading: there is no point in simply giving a narrative of events. Quite often, as the students develop self-confidence, there will break out spontaneous discussion, and this is to be encouraged, even when the topic the teacher has set himself to cover will not be finished in that period.

Discussion is a much harder technique for the teacher to use effectively. Too often it becomes simply a 'pooling of ignorance'. When therefore it does not arise spontaneously from a lesson, or from the handing back of essays, it needs careful preparation. There are several ways in which this can be done: first, to root the discussion in documents which are in front of them during the discussion: this may mean duplicating them, if no adequate number of printed documents is available; if these are coupled with specific questions and reading done beforehand, the result is frequently a satisfactory exchange of views. Another method is to get each student, guided by a work sheet common to all, to prepare an answer to a particular problem and to talk about it after a suitable period of private reading: some teachers have found this a useful technique.[5] Discussions can also be provoked by taped discussions, such as the Sussex or the Audio Learning tapes, if the students have sufficient preparation. It is also possible to contrive situations where discussion is basic, such as mock trials of, for instance, King John or Robespierre; if handled well, this can involve, not only the prosecutor, defence counsel and judge, but the rest of the class as jury; or, as a variation, a press conference given by, for example, Thomas Cromwell, to a hostile press corps. This is not a technique which everyone will warm to; it needs careful preparation by all those taking part, and it needs to be used sparingly. Most discussions, except those which occur spontaneously, can be made more valuable by taping them, or by appointing a 'rapporteur' to provide a summary of points made and conclusions reached. Experiment in this field for the teacher of imagination is certainly worthwhile; 'team-teaching' involving two masters is another commonly used way of provoking disagreement. The variations are endless; but it must be stressed that a 'discussion' should never be a fall-back for the teacher who has nothing prepared.

Reference has already been made to the duplicating of material, if only in passing. It is however increasingly easy to use duplication,

[5] J. B. Thomas, 'Group Teaching in Advanced Level History' in *Teaching History*, ii No. 5 (May 1971) (Historical Association).

for many schools now have a spirit duplicator or a stencil machine. Many will have a copier of some kind as well (see p. 70). What use to make of this tool is harder to define. The duplicating of notes or model answers seems to have little to recommend it. More productive uses exist. Duplicating can be used to provide an outline of a lecture with headings and references, as a guide, especially, for the lower sixth. It is possible to provide each student with his own copy of a document to which constant reference has to be made: for example, the Constitutions of Clarendon, or the Heads of the Proposals or the United States Constitution. Work sheets and assignment sheets on a specific topic are frequently useful, and some would say indispensable. These may include key dates, the principal topics and key questions, relevant books and/or references, and, to help to pin the work down, a selection of essay questions which may, or may not, be drawn from previous A-level papers. Sometimes, it is possible to use short and contradictory quotations from historians, to encourage critical reading, and frequently, discussion. Some examples are given on pp. 200–4. Some teachers also duplicate specific advice on note-making or advice on revision and the taking of examinations. A spirit duplicator or a copier is useful for maps: ideally, every sixth form historian should have his own historical atlas, but it is quite useful to have a sketch map duplicated in colours on a spirit duplicator, or a map from a book photo-copied. As long as the machinery is seen as a tool, rather than as a master, its use is broadly to be encouraged in so far as it furthers the end of helping students to work effectively on their own.

Inevitably, in the course of what has already been said, some reference has been made to audio-visual aids. There are those teaching in the sixth form who are very suspicious of audio-visual aids in advanced work. They argue that to 'sugar the pill' is to lower standards of rigour but, while it is necessary to insist on the primacy of reading and the essay as the principal marks of sixth-form education, they are wrong. Properly used, these aids can bring a new life even to the work of the brightest pupils; with the less able, they are a god-send, helping, as they may well do in the right hands, the stimulation of a historical imagination, and the bringing of the past to life. There is discussion elsewhere on the nature of the 'hard-ware' now available, and much of the discussion of its use is relevant to the sixth form (see Chapter 3). The same need exists as with the lower forms for careful preparation, and for intelligent follow-up work. Some of these aids are much more useful to the sixth form teacher than others: there are, for example, few films which are useful at this level. Probably the most commonly used aids are tape-recordings, slides, film strips, and overhead transparencies. There are now available a number of commercially-produced tapes of discussions by leading historians, of which the Sussex Tapes, although of variable quality, are the most commonly used. At a lower academic level, there are tapes linked with film strips, produced by Educational Audio-Visual Ltd among others, which some have found useful, though they would appeal primarily to the less able sixth former. It is also possible to tape from the radio some of the lectures being given for the Open University, and these will increasingly be of value as these courses develop; other talks from the radio (or if video-tape is available, from television) are also useful. Some teachers also use tapes of gramophone records of music of a period to help to convey an image: medieval plainchant, or eighteenth-century music, are obvious examples. Slides are, generally, much more useful than film strip and are more commonly used; in some cases, teachers (or indeed students) with a flair for photography produce their own; some are commercially bought; and some are made, easily enough, from film strips. Their most obvious uses are for art, architecture, and archaeology, for documents including, for instance, cartoons or press reports from old newspapers. The overhead projector is at least as useful in the sixth form as it is elsewhere in the school; its principal advantages over the blackboard are its ability to present a complex prepared map or diagram, the use of overlays, and the ability to get a document before the class readily. It has no disadvantages compared with the blackboard but cost. The field of audio-visual aids is growing all the time and it is worth consulting the catalogues from time to time to see what might be useful. But they are an *aid*, and should be used with discretion as part of a total strategy, where they will be really useful, and not simply because they are available.

## Facilities

To make the most effective use of the aids available, and to create an atmosphere in which discussion is encouraged, and further, to encourage the skills of the young historian, the proper surroundings must be provided. There are teachers who succeed remarkably well in a teaching situation which the committee would regard as far from ideal; nevertheless, an ideal does exist, and certain features make the ideal more nearly attainable. They include proper provision of books, a suitable room and furniture, a suitably sized set, possession of, or easy access to, appropriate equipment, and the right curricular balance.

The provision of adequate and suitable books has already been touched upon, but perhaps a word or two about their provenance will not be out of place here. Whether the books are to be housed in the history room or in an easily accessible, though separate, library, they must clearly be the right books. The regular buying in ones and twos of new books by reputable historians should be a substantial call on the funds available. The scientists spend relatively large sums on their laboratories: the library is the historian's equivalent. Small sets of the most useful secondary sources should also be available. On the whole there is probably not much to be said for the handing out at the beginning of the course to each student a copy of a textbook: the implication is that this is the book on which he will rely primarily for his material. It is much better that he should have, for example, G. R. Elton's *England under the Tudors*, available as part of a small set, alongside other books on specialised aspects of the period; the Nelson outline *History of England* in 8 volumes, or the indispensable *Oxford History of England*, are other examples of this 'genre' which are good but not to be used as textbooks in the lower school sense. Every effort should be made to persuade the students to read as widely as they are able in the more specialist studies such as biographies, books which result from specialised research in a particular topic, and where possible, documents. A typical reading list on, for instance, 'King John and Magna Carta' might be:

General or Special studies:
F. Barlow, *The Feudal Kingdom of England* (Longmans)
G. W. S. Barrow, *Feudal Britain* (Arnold)
A. L. Poole, *From Domesday to Magna Carta* (O.U.P.)
S. Painter, *The Reign of King John* (Johns Hopkins Press)
W. L. Warren, *King John* (Eyre & Spottiswoode)
J. C. Holt, *The Northerners* (O.U.P.)
J. C. Holt, *Magna Carta* (O.U.P.)
W. S. McKechnie, *Magna Carta* (Glasgow) – old but seminal
J. C. Holt, *King John* (Historical Association Pamphlet G.53)
J. C. Dickenson, *The Great Charter* (Historical Association Pamphlet G.31)

Documentary:
N. Downs (ed.), *Basic Documents in Medieval History* (Anvil: Van Nostrand)
J. A. P. Jones, *King John and Magna Carta* (Longmans: Seminar Studies in History)

On Reformation Europe, as another example: P. J. Helm, *History of Europe, or* V. H. H. Green, *Renaissance and Reformation*, would serve as general books. Other reading might well include: A. G. Dickens, *Reformation and Society in Sixteenth-Century Europe*; G. R. Elton, *Reformation Europe*; R. H. Bainton, *The Reformation of the Sixteenth Century*; P. Hughes, *A Short History of the Reformation*; K. Brandi, *Charles V*; H. Trevor-Roper, *Religion, Reformation and Social Change*. It will not always be possible to have immediately available (for financial reasons, usually) sufficient copies of enough books: it should not be forgotten that quite often the public libraries provide a useful ancillary source; so does the Historical Association's library, for books may be borrowed for a useful period in quite large numbers by schools which are corporate members; it is also often possible to persuade students to buy paper-backed books, when these will be especially useful. There is a lot to be said for students beginning to build up a library of their own as soon as possible. There are book-sellers, such as Books for Students, who will arrange a paper-back exhibition at schools over one or two days for sale to the students, and this, if properly prepared, can result in the purchase of quite a number of useful books. It is our experience, however, that the firms need preliminary guidance about the kind of books to include which are appropriate for the level of the students at the school: of course, where a suitable local bookshop exists, a private arrangement can often be made with them.

The physical surroundings for sixth-form teaching are also important: the ideal would probably be a suite of two or more rooms used exclusively by the history sixth. They should not be too large or too small: if we are aiming at a set of not more than 12–15, it is necessary that there should be sufficient room for various arrangements of furniture, but not for a large room in which the set gets easily lost. Some groups may be as small as 2 or 3 – third-year Open Scholarship students, for example – and anyway it is a good idea for the history staff to have somewhere to meet together, to store textbooks, or for the head of department to use as a study; a small room adjacent to the main teaching rooms is therefore an asset. If this room is lockable then expensive equipment can be securely stored there: it is a nuisance to store this in a room which is also being used, probably, as a form room. The main advantage of a room that is being used, at least mainly, as a history sixth room is that it can be arranged to suit the needs of these sets. The walls can be decorated – preferably by the students – with suitable posters, drawings, newspaper-cuttings or whatever. The furniture can be suitable for the kind of teaching expected in the sixth: some sixth-form history rooms still rely heavily on tables or even desks, but flexibility is hard to achieve in these circumstances: tables are often too heavy to move around. It is convenient for a sixth-form room to have the tables arranged together, for example, with the chairs round them, for seminars, but this is not a suitable arrangement for showing slides, or, even, for effective use of the overhead projectors; desks have little or nothing to be said for them at this level. The best solution is to have light armchairs which have a removable desk-top which can be swung across for note-making; these will have to be used in conjunction with adequate locker space for the storage of books. A teacher's desk is not essential – even if it is convenient for storing things – and may get in the way of the immediate contact which encourages discussion. Some sixth-form rooms also have carpeting and curtains, which may improve morale, or may become simply messy through misuse. Blackout is necessary, if slides are to be shown. Much of the problem of fitting out a history room for the most effective use of teaching aids is discussed elsewhere (see Chapter 3).

There are two further points which may conveniently be discussed here. First, it should be the duty of the sixth-form history teacher, and, probably, of the head of the department, to make it clear to intending sixth-form historians that not all students who take Advanced level history in the sixth form are necessarily going to do well. The heavy load of reading, for example, and the special need for a particular kind of analytical skill make it likely that some students who might do well in another A level subject, requiring other talents, should not attempt history at this level. The Ordinary level history grade is not always a good guide to possible success at A level: the English literature grade may prove a better criterion. Other subjects have made it clear that a special talent is required: Greek or mathematics are recognised not to be for everyone at Advanced level. Historians have not always been sure enough of what qualities they are looking for in the candidate for A-level work; this still requires thought and discussion. It is however not fair to allow a student to start the course who has no reasonable chance of completing it successfully, when more apt alternatives exist. Secondly, it should be part of the responsibility of the head of history to try to achieve a reasonable balance in the subjects studied at A level (usually in consultation with the other heads of departments and the Headmaster): so that, for instance, it is not possible for a student (unless the circumstances are exceptional) to do so narrow a programme as history with economic history and economics – as it was in one school; or on the other hand, so unconnected a group as history, Greek and chemistry, which may have something to be said for its breadth but less for its educational value, since each requires at least one appropriate supporting subject for its full development. Appropriate combinations exist and, apart from watching closely the amount of reading and written work the combination requires, no absolute rule can be laid down: however, it seems to the committee that economics, geography, English, Latin, a modern language, perhaps mathematics, music or art, or the history of art, all provide suitable combining subjects with history, and that, where possible, steps should be taken to make sure that none of these is impossible to combine with history.

## Written work

History is primarily a written subject and it is examined at Advanced level appropriately by means of the essay. Much of the work of the sixth-form teacher will therefore be in the training of students in the particular skills associated with this means of communication. Written work is fully discussed elsewhere (see pp. 114–35) and much of what appears there is very relevant to the work of the sixth form. A recent book which should be in the hands of all sixth-formers preparing for A level history is N. H. Brasher's *The Young Historian* (O.U.P., 1970), for this admirably states the problems and suggests solutions. The several kinds of essay regularly in use in sixth forms include those which form a part of the fortnightly assignment, with a title given in advance and written at home with reference books available; the essay may be an account of the work of an individual: 'Discuss the part played by Frederick II in the decline of the Empire in the thirteenth century'; or it may be more directly 'analytical' – this fashionable word may be misleading, and should perhaps be re-considered by history teachers: see J. H. Hexter, *The History Primer* (Allen Green, 1971) – 'Account for the failure of the restored monarchy in France 1814–1830'; in other words, the narrative and the explication are mixed in different proportions in different questions. There are ways in which this last kind of essay can be very useful: it provides a training in organising material, in helping the inexperienced to break away from the more factual essay of the fifth form, and in expression. The teacher can help by giving guidance in planning essays, by giving various possible approaches, by giving skeleton essays, by discussing the topic before the essay is written, by showing the need to paragraph properly, and by showing the importance of giving supporting evidence for statements made. It is useful at first to require the students to present with the essay an outline, so that both they and the teacher can see at a glance the structure of the essay: this is by no means always self-evident! On the other hand, it should be the task of the sixth-form teacher to train the students to write shorter essays, increasingly in class, as they master the art of being relevant. This can also be done in several ways: a common practice is to give the set a topic and then on a pre-arranged day to set them a specific question, or choice of questions, to write in 45 minutes. This is good practice in the upper sixth, especially, for the kind of answers which the examination will require; but, more than that, it puts a premium on relevance and organisation, which are valuable in themselves. The writer is learning to take a point of view and to persuade: a good history essay is rather like a good judicial 'summing-up' – it recounts the arguments on both, or all, sides and gives reasons for rejecting or minimising some, and then comes to a conclusion. This method will probably gradually replace the long essay altogether as the end of the second year approaches and revision work begins: a set revising a topic should expect an essay on that topic at least once in the course of revision.

Written work is not however necessarily confined to the essay. There is room also for the project in the sixth form – a continuous special study which gives students a chance to get away from the limits of the syllabus. It helps to encourage that special interest in a specific aspect of the work – social history, or military history, or ecclesiastical history, or local history, for example – which adds to the enjoyment of the work and often to the commitment to it; it can give the opportunity for some kind of original work: if the facilities for local history are particularly good, the county archives will often provide a good opportunity for this kind of work; so will, perhaps, the records of the school itself. Some schools are able to support a historical journal of quite a high standard, consisting primarily of work produced in this way.

Marking essays is likely to be one of the most important, if least popular, aspects of the work of the sixth-form master. There are several points here. Some masters like to use a numerical scale, others use a system of A, B, C, etc. There is some danger of confusion with predicted A level grades but this can be overcome by clear explanation of the system used. There is not all that much to choose between the two systems, though the very inexactness of the letter-scale is its biggest advantage: there is less likelihood of students comparing too closely their mark in one essay with its predecessors or with each other in an unreasonable way; it also makes it easier to encourage those who need it, and to mark down those who have become over-confident. More important is the comment written on the paper: attention should be drawn to inaccuracies of grammar, or spelling, or to inelegancies of style, but the principal aim will obviously be to draw attention to the points made well, and to those made badly, to misunderstandings and to omissions, to inaccuracies which materially affect the argument. All this can be best underlined by the individual return of essays and this is a practice which should be adopted wherever circumstances allow: if not with each student every time, then by a kind of rota-system, so that each student can spend at least ten minutes regularly discussing his work with the teacher. It is important here that the student should be comfortably seated by the teacher's side so that both can look at the essay together. Further, it is important, if this is to be really useful, that the essays should be returned with the minimum possible delay: there is nothing more frustrating to both teacher and pupil than discussing an essay so old that the pupil has forgotten what he did mean by a particularly obscure passage, or reference. Nevertheless, this is a most useful experience for both teacher and pupil and every effort should be made to ensure that it forms a regular part of the teaching work.

## History in the open-access sixth form

Though much that has been said earlier in this chapter applies to all pupils studying history above the age of 16, the growth of open-access sixth forms, both in all-through secondary schools and in sixth form colleges, poses certain special problems and challenges. In such institutions, the history teacher will be called upon to teach not only the able, traditional sixth former, but also pupils who are very different, both in ability and in the nature and duration of their courses. History is chosen by many of the less able because their deficiencies do not show as quickly, or as obviously, as in, say, mathematics or French.

Such pupils choose to continue their full-time education beyond the age of sixteen for a variety of reasons. Some may be simply work-shy, or unable to secure employment; most have a genuine desire to further their general educational qualification – a desire that is sometimes realistic, sometimes not. This desire is often born of the demands of the employment market for higher qualifications. In this, as in other respects, we live in an inflationary age, and many careers previously open to the pupil with four or five O-level passes are now demanding some A-level qualification.

At the lowest level of ability are those pupils who enter the sixth with very poor C.S.E. qualifications, and who are perhaps looking for a chance to improve their grades. It is undesirable and educationally dishonest to provide repeat C.S.E. courses. In any case, most such students are hoping that a new start in a new environment may enable them to reach an O-level standard, and it is therefore probably better to start them on a 2-year O-level course, the first year of which can act as a foundation year, when one is developing the same technical proficiency as in the first term of the one-year course (see below). If progress is satisfactory, they can then be moved into a one-year course for their second year.

The 2-year O-level demand may eventually be met by the proposed Certificate of Extended Education, which should be capable of being shaped to the particular needs of these pupils rather more satisfactorily than the existing alternatives. However, this is likely to be the case only if C.E.E. stresses the acquisition of practical skills; there are some disturbing signs that its architects are designing courses which depend upon a degree of abstract conceptualisation which most of these pupils are incapable of developing. It is dangerous nonsense to suppose that such pupils can usefully pursue courses such as 'The nature of modern society' or 'Social ethics', when they are so deficient in basic skills such as reading and writing to the level required for a good C.S.E. grade. To build upon a basis of semi-literacy, necessarily superficial acquaintance with material which has to be appreciated at an advanced level to serve any useful purpose is bad educational practice.

A large number of open-access sixth-form pupils will be studying O-level history. Most of them will be doing so because they have already failed it at the first attempt, or have not been thought capable of taking it earlier. Those who are repeating it pose an awkward problem in the sixth form college, since they come from a number of secondary schools, which follow a variety of different O-level syllabuses. No sixth-form college can cater for the multiplicity of syllabuses needed by such pupils, and it is therefore necessary to determine which of them are reasonably capable of repeating the examination after one term's work with occasional supervision, and which need a full year's course. The latter will then have to accept the college's own syllabus. In this, as in many matters, close liaison with the secondary 'feeder' schools is essential, and the sixth-form college historian should try to establish close and regular contact with his secondary school colleagues.

Sixth-form O-level pupils are older and often more generally mature than the traditional O-level candidate, and their weaknesses stem as much from particular technical difficulties as from general academic inadequacy. For these reasons, very attractive syllabuses are the Cambridge Board's 'World affairs since 1919' and S.U.J.B.'s 'World affairs since 1945'. They are popular with these pupils, and capable of being taught in such a way as to allow for individual specialisation and individual tuition, provided that the class does not exceed about fifteen in number.

One way of approaching the work is to devote the first term to a rapid review of the whole syllabus, taking a topic a week and concentrating on the development of a general understanding of the main issues involved (perhaps reinforced by some guidance on evening television viewing), and on the cultivation of technical proficiency in reading, note-making, essay planning and paragraph-writing. By the end of such a term, the pupil should be capable of working effectively, and should have a sound general knowledge as a basis for his selection of topics on which to specialise, and as a backcloth against which to appreciate these topics in broad perspective. The second and third terms can then be spent working with small groups on their chosen topics, with much pupil-time devoted to work from assignment-sheets, and with much teacher-time spent on individual tuition.

The open-access A-level pupil, again, poses special problems. Many schools allow pupils to start an A-level course without imposing an academic qualification for entry, and there is much to be said for this. A pupil's previous record is no good guide to his ultimate A-level potential, and it would in any case be a denial of much that we preach elsewhere to argue that the only value of taking an A-level course consists in passing it. Much good can be done even for those who may well eventually fail – though they should be left in no doubt about the probable eventual result.

These pupils often have a sincere willingness accompanied by a total lack of awareness of the real nature of A-level work, and this is especially likely when they have come to a sixth-form college from schools which have no A-level work or experience. There is an inclination to regard A level as merely a natural extension of O level – substantially the same, only more of it. This lack of appreciation is often caused by having been previously exposed to a surfeit of what is loosely called 'project work', and the shock of formal written work, heavy reading loads and rigorous academic standards can often be great. Such pupils need to be brought face to face with the demands of the work early enough for a change of course to be effected if necessary, but not so precipitately as to alienate them or destroy their fragile confidence. To this end, a brief 'induction' course at the end of their fifth year can be valuable. Close liaison with tutors and with careers staff is necessary, to maintain a continual review of individual pupils, so that changes of course can be made as and when necessary. It is, however, important not to pre-judge pupils, who may often lack the necessary skills not because they are totally incapable of acquiring them, but because they have never previously encountered them.

The teacher of a traditional A-level set perhaps thinks in terms of a division between those who will achieve a good grade and those who will 'merely' pass; the open-access teacher needs to think in terms of a second division, between those who will probably fail and those who will achieve a modest grade of pass. His set will span a wider ability range, and streaming is undesirable, since it would prevent choice of options and would not bring the less able pupils into contact with good A-level work. It is one thing for the teacher to say what is needed; it is much better for the pupil to see it being produced by some of his peers. Nor need the latter feel – or be – penalised if the emphasis is on teaching different individuals differently, according to their varied needs and capacities. Smallish sets, up to a maximum of twelve in number, are therefore essential, and one needs to organise one's work in such a way as to be able to give a great deal of individual tuition. Furthermore, both pupils and teachers should have an ample allocation of free periods, so that the department can organise 'surgeries' for individual pupils. This ideal may be more capable of realisation in a sixth-form college than in an all-through secondary school.

In the early stages of the A-level course, it is necessary to concentrate upon basic skills, which one can more or less take for granted from the 'traditional' A-level pupil – vocabulary, how to read, how to make notes, how to plan essays, how to write them. Such work needs to be carefully structured, with plenty of detailed guidance, regular assignments of a limited nature carefully followed up, and the whole enterprise imbued with encouragement and constructive criticism. To this end, there is a need for more manuals of *The Young Historian*[6] type, but geared somewhat less ambitiously than that book.

The end of the first year of the course should be the occasion for a thorough review of the progress of individuals, with provision for some to drop back and re-take the first year, regarding their first effort at it, in retrospect, as an O–A 'bridge' year. Hopefully this would be necessary in only a few cases, and it is less likely if, in the first instance, one can recommend British Constitution as a preferable course for pupils seeking a one or two A level job qualification. A one-year course in O level British Constitution can lead to a one-year course in the same subject at A level, which may make more sense for such pupils from the point of view both of the inherent difficulties of the two subjects and of the nature of their content.

The history teacher in the open-access sixth form will probably find that he has a role to play in the provision of general, non-examined courses. This is likely to be a large sector, because open-access sixth form pupils often have a limited examination course timetable, resulting in the necessity to provide general courses,

6 See p. 189.

and also because the nature of many open-access institutions is such that they place much faith in 'general education', and the historian is often required to play a central part in it. Indeed, history is a useful educational base for general studies. This work can often be very exacting, and is not made any easier if the classes contain that recalcitrant element to which many non-examined courses are prone. The historian's contribution to joint-subject courses is discussed elsewhere in this book. If he teaches individual-subject courses, he should give careful thought to the selection of suitable historical themes, and might consider imparting a practical flavour to these activities, from which he could extend outwards once interest has been aroused. Two successful methods of this type are the simulation game based on current situations, such as those in China, the Middle East, Germany and Ulster; and brass-rubbing expeditions leading to associated work in such fields as craft, heraldry, local history and costume, depending upon individual interests. There is, for example, a C.S.E. syllabus on 'The historian at work'. One should be aware of the possible danger of repeating such common fifth-year courses as local studies and civics, and try wherever possible to determine what is most suitable, from one's range of options, for each new group that one receives. It is a good idea to discuss possible activities when one first meets a new group; it is a mistake to have a set course which is dispensed to all comers.

## Open Scholarship work

The third-year sixth, where it is available for the Open Scholarship candidate, has a value beyond doubt. However, many candidates for the Open Scholarships offered by Oxford, Cambridge, and a few other universities, now enter for them in their fourth term in the Sixth rather than in their seventh term, either because there is no third-year set, or for personal reasons. Some correspondents were opposed to the concept of attempting Open Scholarship examinations after only four terms in the sixth. The main objection was the lack of maturity of these candidates, which is likely to tell against them in the examination itself by comparison with post-Advanced-level candidates, in spite of the often iterated assertion that the examiners are looking for promise, in practice an elusive quality difficult to isolate from others which greater experience gives. Even when successful the four-term candidate is likely to be less mature than most of his contemporaries at university. Others, however, discount these arguments and believe, with some justice, that preparation of a candidate will at least strengthen his Advanced-level work, even if he does not gain an award or place in the Open Scholarship examination.

The number of those trying to secure history Scholarships will, almost invariably, be too small to justify their being taught as a separate set. For four-term candidates the best which can be hoped is that they will be given one Scholarship period a week in the lower and upper sixth. They will also be taking the history Special paper, whose value as a link with scholarship work has already been mentioned. The seventh-term candidate will already have benefited from these arrangements but for him, too, time in school for preparation for the examination is short. The 'third-year' sixth form is usually a misnomer, for the examinations for Oxford and Cambridge are taken in the seventh term of the sixth form and, for other universities, are completed by the end of January; most of the students will leave at the end of that month. Preparation should therefore be undertaken well before the beginning of the summer holiday and thus before the A-level results are known: if mistakes have been made they can usually be rectified easily enough; it is broadly true that the likely candidate will have an A or a B grade, but the experienced teacher at this level has a 'nose' for the scholar and will sometimes feel justified in entering students with lower grades than this. In one sense the whole of the sixth form is preparation for scholarship work: but a suitable reading plan should be in the hands of the intending candidate before the summer holiday. If the examination is to be taken in the fourth term then it is necessary to create time, either in the timetable, or after school, for this preparation: at least an hour a week is required. It is more than ever desirable at this stage for the pupil to have more than one master: it is not a 'perk' to be hogged by the senior history master.

The aim is not notably different from the aim for sixth-form work in general: to broaden interests, to encourage the ability for independent work and critical thought, to make use of the experience gained in historical method, interpretation of conflicting evidence, and the art of writing history. Preparation will provide an opportunity for both widening and deepening the knowledge and understanding of the candidate. The examinations are different in purpose from G.C.E. A levels: they are looking for potential more than achievement – less, how much he has been taught, more, how much can he be taught. A lively mind, a critical approach, a broad interest outside the narrowly academic in what is going on about him, even sometimes a certain arrogance; these are the qualities the university wants to see, and these characteristics provide the teacher with his own criteria for selecting the likely candidate.

The content of the course must lead to a strengthening of these qualities; its detail is less important than its purpose. It is worth stressing, however, that the examination will normally include a translation paper, and a facility in languages – two, where possible – should be nurtured: performance in this paper will help the college to distinguish between two, otherwise similarly qualified, candidates, in what is a highly competitive examination. Similarly, there will usually be some form of general paper in which a poor performance will penalise the candidate. Apart from these considerations there are other guiding principles. The work offered at Advanced level must be the basis for the outline papers; it will usually need strengthening: reading more widely in the period, especially the more recondite works, such as articles in the learned journals, or studying past historians such as Gibbon or Macaulay; relating more closely the developments in one part of the period with those in another, that is, sitting back and looking at the period as a whole, is another useful way of strengthening the work; it is sometimes also a good idea to extend the repertoire of the student either forward or backward; this will add interest and understanding, and at the same time, increase the range of questions which can be attempted. A student who has studied English and European history between 1500 and 1700, for example, will gain a great deal if he studies as well in this course the later Middle Ages, or the eighteenth century; it will add an extra perspective to the outline work. Another valuable way of making use of the work already done and strengthening it, is to take a theme which is important in it and compare it with examples of apparently similar expressions of it drawn from other periods: for example, the student of eighteenth-century Europe might care to study absolute monarchy in the period of its rise in the later Middle Ages or of its decline in the nineteenth or twentieth centuries; he could study revolutions in the eighteenth, nineteenth and twentieth centuries; the student of the European Middle Ages may usefully compare the Investiture Dispute with the later history of struggle between Church and State. The simple revision and rehashing of notes made for Advanced level is not only dull, it is rarely effective.

This is the right time to look at the nature of history: the young historian has both experience and commitment at this stage; there are many useful books which should be in the sixth-form library: Marc Bloch's *The Historian's Craft*, R. G. Collingwood's *The Idea of History*, and many others (see p. 199). It is a good plan for the teacher to look at particular themes: causation and the nature of explanation in history, for example, and to relate them not only to the philosophers of history but to the actual works of practising historians, especially those with which the student is already vaguely familiar. Not all pupils (nor all teachers, for that matter) will feel this is for them; but it is a very valuable exercise if done systematically. Reading review articles in leading journals will also help and give standards of judgement.

More generally, efforts should be made to encourage as wide reading as possible and not just history books, but great novels, newspapers, the literary and political weeklies, so that an interest can be encouraged, or sometimes the seed of an interest planted. A wide interest in at least some of the following would be expected from a scholarship candidate in history: in the arts, in music, in politics (both theoretical and day-to-day party politics), in general economic problems, and in advances in science or sociology and so on: it is important that the student should 'know what is going on'. This like so much else at this stage cannot be 'taught', but it can be encouraged and to some extent 'caught' from a lively teacher.

The methods adopted will be those appropriate to a small group of very able pupils. Formal teaching will not find a place at this level. The aim is to train them to ask awkward questions, and this is best done by a seminar, or tutorial approach. It is a good plan to have a pupil prepared either to read aloud an essay on a title on which all of them have written an essay, leading to discussion, criticism and constructive comment, or to have them in turn prepare a paper to be read and commented on; the pupil opens the discussion, draws attention to the main issues and is answered by the others; infrequent intervention by the teacher will be required to prevent the argument going too far adrift. It is, as always, a good plan to vary the format as much as possible, but discussion will always remain the basis of the work: a Socratic method, where the teacher asks probing questions and the pupils reply, comes naturally to some and has much to recommend it. It is also well worthwhile getting together as many as possible of the scholarship candidates from other disciplines and hearing their views on what is going on in their subjects: if a group of their teachers also come, a reasonably sized group of up to a dozen can cross-fertilise each other's ideas: it is, for example, interesting to discuss scientific method, inductive and deductive reasoning, and whether history is a 'science', with both the natural scientists and the social scientists. A little philosophy, especially in the theory of knowledge, lends itself well to this approach. Many have found it useful to arrange for longer sessions than the 45 minute period, from time to time: either in the lunch break, or better still, after school at a teacher's house. This may be easier to arrange in a boarding school, but is by no means impossible in many day schools. Essays will be frequent and their individual return both more easily arranged and more important than in the A-level sets: marking and commenting needs to be both oral and written and should be even more detailed, for part of the purpose of the course at this level is to encourage a really mature and exact style in historical writing.

It is worth remembering some dangers: if insensitively handled, students at this stage can easily fall into the trap of producing work of great (and tedious) length under the impression that weighty learning is to be preferred to liveliness, boldness in ideas, freshness in style, an eye for vivid detail and a critical approach to sources. Another warning: it is futile to try to make a silk purse from a sow's ear; each student, in each succeeding year, will have his own strengths and weaknesses. It does not follow that because something worked with one group, it will necessarily work with the next. In some years, even when the student has a reasonable chance of getting a place, the level of the work will not match that of previous candidates: the teacher must tailor the course to suit the students he has actually got. It is the candidate for whom the course is intended, not the teacher; although for many teachers this work produces some of the most satisfying moments in the week, this is not the main point. Still, the satisfaction is there, if the students are of the right calibre, and the work stimulates them. It is startling, sometimes, to observe the 'sea-change' which comes over the set as the few available weeks pass; a genuine bridge is being built between the sixth former and the undergraduate.

In this work, then, is to be seen the quintessence of all sixth-form teaching: the steady development over the years of a capacity for individual study, of the ability to argue persuasively and accurately both orally and in writing, of the ability to assess the weight to be given to historical facts; even more, of a burgeoning interest in the concerns of the wider world outside the school and of a balanced judgement and independence of mind which help to make a mature citizen.

### A select reading list on the nature and theory of history for third-year sixth-form students

G. Barraclough, *History in a Changing World* (Blackwell, 1956)
M. L. B. Bloch, *The Historian's Craft* (Manchester U.P., 1954)
H. Butterfield, *The Whig Interpretation of History* (Bell, 1931)
E. H. Carr, *What is History?* (Penguin, 1970)
R. G. Collingwood, *The Idea of History* (Oxford, 1973)
G. R. Elton, *The Practice of History* (Fontana, 1969)
P. L. Gardiner, *Theories of History* (Allen and Unwin, 1960)
P. Geyl, *Debates with Historians* (World Publications, 1958)

J. H. Hexter, *The History Primer* (Allen Green, 1971)
G. Kitson Clark, *The Critical Historian* (London, 1967)
K. Popper, *The Poverty of Historicism* (R.K.P., 1960)
G. R. Renier, *History: its purpose and method* (Allen and Unwin, 1950)
A. L. Rowse, *The Use of History* (E.U.P., 1970)
O. Spengler, *The Decline of the West* (Allen and Unwin, 1961)
A. Toynbee, *A Study of History* (Oxford, 1972)
H. R. Trevor-Roper, *Man and Events* (Harper, 1957)
W. H. Walsh, *An Introduction to the Philosophy of History* (Hutchinson, 1967)

## Examples of work-sheets, assignment-sheets and other duplicated material

(1) A duplicated sheet used with a large group of over 30 in a team-teaching situation, as a guide to a lecture of 50 minutes.

*Peel and the Conservative Party*

1. Introduction:
   – the ancestry of the party
   – the name of the 'Conservative Party'

'But we forget; Sir Robert Peel is not the leader of the Tory party . . . In a Parliamentary sense that great party has ceased to exist; but I will believe it still exists in the thought and sentiment and consecrated memory of the English nation . . . Even now it is not dead but sleepeth; . . . Toryism will yet arise from the tomb over which Bolingbroke shed his last tear, to bring back strength to the Crown, liberty to the subject and to announce that power has only one duty – to secure the social welfare of the People' (Disraeli, *Sybil* [1845]).

'We are now, as we always have been, decidedly and conscientiously attached to what is called the Tory, and which might with more propriety be called the Conservative Party' (*Quarterly Review* [January 1830]).

2. Conservatism 1815–41
   (i) Lord Liverpool's Governments 1815–27
       The Duke of Wellington's Government 1828–30
       – defeats of 1830–2
       – not a new party
       – changed political situation
       – new awareness of class
   (ii) Tory options in 1832
       (a) Party of the landed aristocrats

'For the sake of the landed interest itself Conservatism as a national party could not take its stand on landed Toryism alone' (Gash)

       (b) Alliance with emerging working class
       (c) Alliance with the middle class

'I believe such an aristocracy to be essential to the purposes of good government. The question only is – what in a certain state of public opinion, and in a certain position of society, is the most effectual way of maintaining the legitimate influence and authority of a territorial aristocracy . . . I said long ago that I thought agricultural prosperity was woven in with manufacturing prosperity; and depended more on it than on the Corn Laws . . .' (Peel in House of Commons on 4 May 1846).

**3.** Peel and his achievement 1832–46

    – brief outline of events 1832–46

'But if the spirit of the Reform Bill implies merely a careful review of institutions, civil and ecclesiastical, undertaken in a friendly temper, combining with firm maintenance of established rights, the correction of proved abuses and the redress of real grievances – in that case I can for myself and my colleagues undertake to act in such a spirit and with such intentions' (Peel in Tamworth Manifesto, 1834).

    – election of 1841
    – policies: (a) commercial measures
               (b) Bank Charter Act 1844
               (c) Ireland – Irish Colleges
                              – Devon Commission
                              – Maynooth grant
    – Repeal of the Corn Laws, 1846

**4.** The consequences of repeal

    – division of the party
    – the Peelite 'exile'
    – new Disraelian Conservative Party

'I keep horses in three counties and they tell me I shall save £1500 a year by free trade. I don't care for that. What I cannot bear is being sold' (Bentinck). (Then follows a breakdown of election returns 1841–57 to show the effects of the split.)

This sheet was used with another containing book references and so on; its purpose was to provide an outline of the lecture only: it also provides a guide to reading and note-making.

(2) A duplicated study guide on domestic affairs 1905–14.

*Key dates*

| | | |
|---|---|---|
| Dec. | 1905 | Balfour resigned; Campbell-Bannerman formed a caretaker Liberal ministry |
| Jan. | 1906 | General Election – Liberal landslide |
| | | Trade Disputes Act |
| | | Self-government granted to the Transvaal |
| | 1908 | Asquith succeeded Campbell-Bannerman; Lloyd George – Chancellor of the Exchequer |
| | | Old age pensions |
| | 1909 | Trade Boards Act |
| | | 'People's Budget' |
| Jan. | 1910 | General Election |
| May | 1910 | Death of King Edward VII |
| Dec. | 1910 | General Election |
| | 1911 | Parliament Act |
| | | National Insurance Act |

1913     Trade Union Act
          'Cat and Mouse' Act
Aug. 1914     Outbreak of the First World War

*Topics*

(a) *The General Election of 1906*

Why did the Conservatives lose? / Why did the Liberals win?

(b) *The formation of the government*

The government's lack of definite programme
Opposition tactics (Balfour and Lansdowne)

(c) *The government's achievements, 1906–9*

 (i) Imperial policy – the Boer Republics
 (ii) Trade Disputes Act
 (iii) Social welfare measures – school meals and medical services
 (iv) Small Holdings Act, 1907
 (v) Lloyd George's trade measures:
  (a) Merchant Shipping Act, 1906; (b) Patents Act, 1907; (c) Port of London Authority, 1908
 (vi) Haldane's army reforms
 (vii) Asquith at the Exchequer, 1906–8
 (viii) Cabinet changes of 1908: their significance
 (ix) Churchill at the Board of Trade:
  (a) Labour Exchanges, 1909; (b) Trade Board Act, 1909
 (x) Home Office and Local Government Board

(d) *Constitutional crisis over the House of Lords*

 (i) Historical background to the crisis: the House of Lords in the nineteenth century
 (ii) Attitude of the House of Lords to Liberal legislation 1906–9
 (iii) Lloyd George's 'People's Budget', 1909:
  (a) its terms; (b) reactions to it
 (iv) The Parliament of 1910
 (v) The Parliament Act of 1911 (see also separate handout on this topic)

(e) *'The Strange Death of Liberal England'*

 (i) The 'Dangerfield Thesis', 1936
 (ii) The government and labour relations:
  (a) Osborne Case, 1908–9; (b) National Insurance Act; (c) Home Office reforms after 1910; (d) T.U. militance: 'syndicalism'; (e) Trade Union Act, 1913
 (iii) The Suffragettes: 'Votes for Women'
 (iv) Ireland: the struggle for Home Rule
 (v) Trevor Wilson's analysis: 'The Downfall of the Liberal Party'

*References*

(A) *General*

Wood, pp. 412–29; Edwards, pp. 370–421; Ensor, pp. 384–526; Pelling, pp. 47–71; Seaman, pp. 25–59.

**(B)** *More detailed*

Colin Cross, *The Liberals in Power, 1905–14*
Donald Read, *Edwardian England*
John Wilson, *C-B. A Life of Sir Henry Campbell-Bannerman*
Roy Jenkins, *Asquith*
Randolph Churchill, *Winston Churchill Vol. II The Young Statesman, 1901–14*
Chapter on Lloyd George in John Derry, *The Radical Tradition*
Roy Jenkins, *Mr Balfour's Poodle*
G. Dangerfield, *The Strange Death of Liberal England*
Roger Fulford, *Votes for Women*
Henry Pelling, *A History of British Trade Unionism*, pp. 123–48
S. Nowell-Smith (ed.), *Edwardian England*
Trevor Wilson, *The Downfall of the Liberal Party, 1914–35*

**(C)** *Also* (general interest)

J. B. Priestley, *The Edwardians*
Philip Magnus, *Edward VII*
Harold Nicolson, *King George V*
Geoffrey Marcus, *Before the Lamps went out*
Lady Violet Bonham Carter, *Winston Churchill as I knew him*
Winston Churchill, *Great Contemporaries*
Kenneth Young, *Balfour*
Robert Blake, *The Unknown Prime Minister* (Bonar Law)

*Questions*

How do you account for the Liberal triumph in the 1906 Election?
'Balfour must share responsibility with Chamberlain for the 1906 Election defeat.' Comment on this statement.
Assess the importance of the social reforms of the Liberal Governments of 1905–14.
Describe and explain the growing violence of social and political movements in the period 1906–14.
Discuss the content and the consequences of the 'People's Budget' of 1909.
Why and with what consequences was the Parliament Act of 1911 passed?
Describe the policies and achievements of Lloyd George between 1905 and 1914.

This example is typical of many in use in sixth forms; it is perhaps the most familiar kind of study guides in use.

(3) The next one is designed for the less able sixth former and it is abridged: it contains, in full, 54 questions on Russia from 1917 to 1941; they are more detailed than A-level questions and are 'custom-built' for their purpose; this sheet is accompanied by another which gives the precise reference for its answer in up to eight books for each question; there are further general references to other more advanced books. In the question sheet, the *italicised* phrases are to form a note heading.

*History O and A-level question sheet – 1917, Lenin and Stalin*

  1. What form of government did the *Provisional Government* wish to set

up in Russia and what were the differences between *Prince Lvov* and *Kerensky's* views on the methods that should be used?

2. What were the *weaknesses of the Provisional Government's* position? (a) Why were they unable and unwilling to make *peace with Germany*? (b) What effects did the continuation of the war produce? (c) Why was there *famine* in Russia in 1917 and what was the result? (d) What was the revolutionary Soviet movement that spread through Russia in 1917 and challenged the Provisional Government and helped to isolate it from the people? (e) What changes did it promote in *the army*? (f) Why did the Provisional Government use force against *strikes*?

3. What *opposition* did the Provisional Government face by October 1917?

4. What crisis did the Provisional Government survive from the Bolsheviks in July?

5. Why did Kerensky call a *Pre-Parliament*, and why did it not support him?

6. Why was there a clash between Kerensky and *Kernilov*? Who assisted Kerensky to win?

and so on.

(4) The last example is of a fortnightly assignment and may or may not be duplicated. This is probably the best length for each 'unit' of study. It is designed for a set of very mixed ability. It is given here in outline for the format is clearly flexible.

*Subject*: Trade Unionism and the rise of the Labour Party to 1914.

*Reading*: textbook . . . with page references

*Keir Hardie* (Clarendon Biography)

Archive booklets on British Trade Unionism; Rise of the Labour Party; Liberals and the Welfare State.

*History Today* – articles specified

Historical Association pamphlet: *Edwardian England*

Library books (which are placed in classrooms so that appropriate books can be given out in class)

*Lessons*

1. General introduction – outline reading, a note framework as a guide, talk around the subject highlighting main features.

2 and 3. Specific discussion of passages set for prior reading, e.g. from the Archive booklets.

At about this time an essay title will be given, either for doing in class or at home.

4. Record: Kenneth Morgan talking about the rise of new unionism and Labour in S. Wales.

5. Sussex Tape – discussion of the general topic.

6. Discussion in class on general points which emerge from the essays here being returned: common weaknesses, errors of understanding or of essay technique.

7 and 8. Private study: note-making, reading, further work arising from weaknesses in essays, etc. The opportunity is taken to see individuals about their work.

There are more than 8 periods in a fortnight at this school and the remainder are used variously, and interposed between the lessons here outlined; it increased the opportunity to see individuals privately in tutorials to about 40% of the total time available for the unit.

# 11 History and interdisciplinary studies

The advocates of interdisciplinary, or integrated, studies often speak with the confidence of those who have found the way to salvation, and urge others to follow their lead. Their opponents, on the other hand, tend to view them with the disapproval of the orthodox for the heretic. All this is very confusing for the history teacher anxious to keep his subject in the forefront of educational practice. Should he support the call for formally integrated studies, and risk the purists' accusations of having 'sold out' his subject; should he retain his subject discipline with its traditional identity and risk what is currently in education the damaging accusation of being a reactionary; or should he, like a good historian, follow a *via media*?

The history teacher in this dilemma must first establish what integrated studies will mean in practice in his school. Too often that label is attached to a course which is less than integrated, and frequently less than a disciplined study. If three subjects are to be integrated how will the course be organised? Will one teacher be asked to teach three subjects, or will there be a team of three subject specialists? Is the course a device merely to make the timetable fit, perhaps meaning a reduction in the number of periods allocated to those subjects? Will adequate resources and facilities be provided? Most important, are the staff who will teach the course sympathetic to the approach, and aware of the heavy demands that will be made upon them? Who is to draw up the syllabus; will it be the responsibility of a coordinator or director of integrated studies? Does the historical content of the course make academic and pedagogic sense? What will the integrated course offer that the history teacher can not? We should be clear that integrated studies *per se* are not an amalgam of separate subject gobbets but one subject to which various disciplines contribute; and it is this which causes concern to many specialist teachers. It is not, moreover, a second-best solution for second-best pupils, a view widely held and one that often determines the provision of, and approach to, integrated studies.

Integration has been defined in the University of Keele Integrated Studies Project as

the exploration of a large area, theme, or problem which:
(a) requires the help of more than one subject discipline for its full understanding, and
(b) is best taught by the concerted action of a group of teachers.

The historian should establish that both elements implicit in this definition will be present in any scheme to which he lends his support: that the particular discipline of his subject will be retained, though *integral* to the course, not subsumed in it; and that the course will be taught by a team of specialists in the subjects which are to be integrated.

G. M. Trevelyan has observed that history is not a 'subject', but 'the house that contains all subjects', and the history teacher might well feel that he is capable of directing his pupils along several paths without formal integration. Even such a 'narrow' historical topic as a study of shipbuilding in the eighteenth century could involve political, economic, industrial and naval history, as well as a knowledge of timber, workmanship, accounts, hydrodynamics, electrolysis, marine biology and so on. The historian could argue that it is highly unlikely that any formally integrated course would include such a variety of subject specialists, but this is no argument for avoiding integrated studies altogether. If it is true that history is best taught by specialist teachers, so is it true of other subjects, and the history teacher would be foolish not to call upon their services if integrated studies can make them available.

If, having considered the arguments, the history teacher has any reservations he would be wrong to support the introduction of an integrated course. The best curriculum development always comes from the shop floor of education. If the teacher in the classroom suspects that a new approach will fail, then it will. The history teacher need not, however, dismiss integrated studies in the fear that the discipline of his subject will be inevitably lost. If he can keep a firm guiding hand on the framing of the syllabus, and an historian in the team of teachers responsible for the course, this need not be so. There are history teachers who claim that they have found their pupils more receptive to their discipline since the subject appeared not to be taught for its own sake but to make clear the answer to part of a larger problem.

For those who feel that they can safeguard their subject discipline, there are also administrative advantages to be gained from integrated studies that can be of benefit to the classroom teacher. Not least is the greater flexibility which the allocation of a larger number of periods a week permits. It is also, however, the prospect of administrative convenience which has great appeal to the school administrator, and the historian must take care that this convenience is not at the expense of his subject. There are instances of fewer periods being allocated to integrated studies than to the same subjects when taught separately. Conversely, there are some examples, though fewer in number and more often with slow learners, of more time being made available for integrated studies than for separate subjects.

A more immediately apparent advantage for the specialist considering an integrated course is the prospect of avoiding the duplication which occurs when subjects overlap, and the opportunity to employ allied subject disciplines in the service of history – the seductive prospect of demonstrating the unity of knowledge and of making obvious the fundamental importance of history. Yet the history teacher might well resist these siren arguments. As for the former, the unity of knowledge is too grand a concept for immature minds, and as for the latter, the historian can demonstrate the relevance of his subject without integrated studies. The history teacher is quite capable of answering all the critics of his subject as a separate discipline, but he should not dismiss integrated studies as an inevitably inferior device suitable only for the less able. The best integrated course is that which retains the skills and elements of its component disciplines, and it need not be easier nor less academic than the study of separate subjects. The best integrated teaching, like the best subject teaching, can stimulate and motivate, but there are no panaceas in teaching, and integrated studies will not, of itself, solve any teaching problem. The historian must resist the advocates of what is merely educationally fashionable and decide each case on its merits.

Links with other subjects need not, of course, be formal. As one correspondent wrote: 'We have occasional links with other subjects, and that is all that is needed.' Certainly the history teacher should circulate his syllabus, and should enquire of the other departments the content of their courses and in what ways there can be mutual interchange. Most will be found willing to cooperate in occasional, if not in more formal, schemes for inter-disciplinary teaching. Thus, when dealing with life in Tudor England the music department might cover the music of the period; the English department might study some of the literature or perhaps do some relevant drama work; the art department might dwell on the art of the period, or permit the use of an historical theme for the pupil's own art work; and the history department might cover its traditional ground. The possibilities for such cooperation are considerable: work on navigation can involve maths and geography; the craft department in one school has been enthusiastic in employing pupils' skills to make models of siege engines and cannon, and has played a major part in the study of industrial archaeology, not only sharing an academic interest but also providing practical skills to restore, for example, a water-wheel and a mill. These *ad hoc* arrangements are less pretentious than a formally integrated course, but they have no less value and are the least (and often the best) that we can do. Perhaps because of their novelty, they have greater impact on the pupil. Nor, with these occasional arrangements, often reached over a cup of tea in the staffroom, need integration ever appear forced, for they last only as long as they are useful. The cooperative study of two or three such topics a year can be a happy compromise between the proponents and opponents of integrated courses. This degree of integration which demonstrates the relationship between subjects may well be sufficient in the early years of secondary education as a step towards demonstrating the unity of knowledge – a task which has greater significance in sixth-form general studies.

In practice, integration is most common in the first years of secondary schooling, when pupils are 11 to 13, or 14. For the pupil fresh from primary or middle school, faced with a bewildering number of teachers, the introduction of an integrated course can mean that the pupil spends one third of his time at school with a single teacher. It is true that some pupils, especially in our largest schools, find the procession of subject specialists, for three or four lessons each a week, confusing. There is an alternative, however, that will satisfy both those who urge stability for the pupil, and the individual subject specialist. The child will not suffer if integrated studies are taught by a team of subject specialists, for he will still be able to spend a large part of his integrated studies time with one teacher, but specialist subject teachers will be available when they are needed. In practice, the experience of such teams is that pupils soon identify with 'their team', and feel that they have a particularly close relationship with not one but three teachers. Often variety of teachers is itself valuable. Personality conflicts can be oppressive for both teacher and pupils when they are together for fourteen lessons a week. Nor should it be forgotten that there are pupils who leave their primary schools happily anticipating a variety of teachers and subject specialisation.

The teaching of an integrated course need vary very little from the problem-orientated approach employed by many teachers of history as a specialist discipline and discussed elsewhere in the book. The teacher would be wise to take full advantage of the administrative flexibility permitted by the large number of periods available. If three subjects are to be integrated, then three forms, each under a different subject specialist, should be timetabled at the same time, preferably to include a complete morning or afternoon. This permits visits outside the school without inconvenience to colleagues or damage to other aspects of the pupil's education. It also permits a valuable start to a new topic with, say, an introduction and a film before break, and afterwards a lead lesson, for all three groups, and then a return to classrooms to begin the follow-up work. Even when there are no visits to be made or new topics to be started, the teacher can, with a little imagination, exploit this period of time and need not fear its length. With an integrated course there will be a variety of tasks for the pupil to do, exploiting different subject elements, and the length of time available makes it possible for groups to be involved in the preparation of drama work, tapes, models, etc. – all those things for which 35 or 40 minute lessons are too short.

Within the team, each specialist will take responsibility for aspects of the course that relate to his subject. He will give lead lessons, he will prepare assignments, he will advise on sources, and he will always be available for reference whenever the team are teaching. There is no reason why, during periods of individual work by the pupils, they should not be free to work in the room of the teacher who is the specialist in the part of the course that they are then studying, especially if the three rooms are adjacent. Pupils working on their own are soon spread out over an assignment, especially if it gives them a choice of activity, so there should be no problem of over-crowding in one room. The pupils should not feel that they have to move if they wish to have the security of working in one room with one teacher; for the others, the habit of visiting the history room and the use of the reference library will be good training for future years.

Administratively, the team should plan at least one term ahead, and should arrange a weekly meeting to review current progress. Ideally, this meeting should be timetabled – a small compensation for the time the team will spend in planning and preparation. Within the team, a coordinator is essential to ensure that the administration of the course works smoothly. A 'director', however, can be a danger, for the success of such schemes depends largely upon each teacher's involvement in decision-making.

As for the content of the course, that will depend largely on the interests of the teachers and the availability of resources. The historian will probably find it most rewarding to contribute to topics that will permit a detailed study, rather than broad, general themes. As is true of all history teaching, it is the personal detail that stimulates the imagination, that brings history alive – so important a factor with pupils of this age.[1] There are many ready-made courses on the market, and the historian embarking on an integrated scheme would be advised to examine them and learn from their style and content.

Some aspects he will reject, for they will not meet his requirements; similarly, he will study and reject some ideas adopted by other schools. It is unlikely that any course, other than one produced by the team in collaboration with the departments involved, will meet their particular requirements, and they will have to analyse those requirements before they start.

Primary schools have led the way with the integration of subjects, and the secondary school beginning such a course would be advised to approach contributory schools to ensure that there is no unnecessary duplication. Later, unless integrated courses are to be pursued to G.C.E. and C.S.E., equal consideration will have to be given to the process of de-integration. If pupils who have known only integrated courses have to choose separate subjects at the end of their third year they will have inadequate experience on which to base their decision. It may, therefore, be thought desirable to teach history as a separate subject in the third year.

For the fourth and fifth years, there are Boards that offer environmental studies syllabuses, and some schools have employed the Mode 3 syllabus to examine subjects taught by teams in an integrated setting.[2] For G.C.E. in one such school, separate assessments are made for each of the four disciplines that form part of the integrated course.

In history . . . the integrated course work is correlated with the work carried out on a chosen history project, and throughout the final year tests are provided under more formal examination conditions. These tests include at least one essay question of the sort to be found in any O-level paper, and an oral test. External moderators appointed by the Associated Examining Board ensure that standards are maintained. Similar arrangements are made for those who sit C.S.E.[3]

This form of teaching and examining is no easy option for teacher or pupil.

[1] See Appendix 2, pages 247–51: Assignment for an integrated studies course for the first year.

[2] Examining Boards offering environmental studies at G.C.E. O level in 1973 were the Associated Examining Board and the Oxford Delegacy of Local Examinations. No C.S.E. Board offered an Environmental Studies Mode 1 examination in 1973. The University of London School Examinations Council intends to implement the A level Environmental Studies Syllabus, published by N.F.E.R.

[3] P. W. R. Foot, article in *Resources in Education* (April 1972).

At this level especially there are dangers of which the history teacher must be well aware. He must ensure that the courses his pupils follow from 11 to 16 are balanced, and do not dwell exclusively on social and economic history, the recent past or the immediate locality. He must also appreciate that the potential A-level student is unlikely to have the background knowledge that a more formally ordered course can provide. Yet there are also advantages, not least the motivation which this approach can stimulate.

For less academic classes, especially since the school-leaving age has been raised to 16, the urge to provide something 'new' and 'relevant' has led many schools to introduce integrated courses, often under the name of environmental studies. That the historian has a role to play in educating these pupils is undeniable, and he may fulfil that role through an integrated course, but when such studies are limited to the immediate environment the wisdom of these courses is questionable. Frequently the biggest handicap of these pupils is their narrow experience and limited horizons. They lose the 'red-blooded' element of history. To compile a course completely around their locality does little to remedy this, and can provoke apathy – it is so familiar, or seems so, already. These obstacles can be avoided, for much depends on the teacher and the locality, but they should not be minimised. (For a fuller discussion of these points, see Chapters 12 and 13.) The less able child, moreover, is often completely unaware of the integrated nature of the course he is following, and more than one pupil has responded to a grand integrated scheme with the request, 'Please sir, can't we do proper history, like the others?'

The history teacher looking for an approach to these pupils may well be advised to retain his subject identity, based on the advice, confirmed by experience, contained in the Schools Council booklet *Humanities for the Young School Leaver*.[4] 'Intellectually, the early school-leavers have their limitations, but their imaginations can be roused if a starting-point can be found that they can see to be significant.' The teacher should employ 'the process of direct personal inquiry, of testing evidence, and of exercising judgement in the selection and interpretation of material, at however unsophisticated a level. This is learning in an active and not a passive sense.' In other words, these objectives are best achieved within the conventional subject classification; and a fuller discussion of history for the less able will be found in Chapter 9.

In the sixth form, the role of the historian in inter-disciplinary

[4] Schools Council, *Humanities for the Young School Leaver, An Approach through History* (Evans/Methuen Educational, 1969).

studies will probably be limited to what was called by Crowther 'minority time' and is now usually known as general studies. In most schools the sixth form retains its traditional subject divisions despite repeated accusations of over-specialisation. Lower down the school, the pressure for change has tended to come from the pupils who have been inclined to 'vote with their feet' when they were unable to see the relevance of courses presented for their education. They have presented disciplinary problems, and so a new way of engaging their attention has been sought. In the sixth form the situation is somewhat different, for the necessity of gaining A-level passes for further education has made our pupils willing accomplices in accepting traditional subject divisions which many enjoy and find give intellectual satisfaction. This may well change as the character of the sixth form alters. It has been shown how widely sixth formers already differ from each other, both in their qualifications on entering the sixth, and in their objectives on leaving it.[5] This divergence must affect the courses that are offered for the student, though the changes may take place within the framework of traditional subject divisions, or outside it. The criteria for drawing up a curriculum for the sixth former, as indeed for any other pupil, are that it should be balanced and relevant, some would argue, to contemporary society. If the school can think not in terms of rigid subject divisions but in terms of those elements which go to make up such a curriculum, such as attitudes and skills, it may in the future prove possible to offer a formally integrated curriculum, or a series of assignments for the non-examination student which range across a number of subjects and are designed to enable him to develop the understanding and skills he needs and which we would wish him to have; but we must beware of making education too concerned with social and vocational considerations.

For most teachers these developments are in the future, and the historian's present role in sixth-form inter-disciplinary studies will be in the context of general studies courses. In part such a role will be compensatory. He will seek to bring to non-historians the attitudes and perspectives of the history student. Many of his pupils will have learnt to respect evidence, to demand proof, to have a disciplined imagination, to reason, as students of science subjects. For them, the history teacher will seek to do more than add knowledge of a different kind: he will try to instil a sensitive imagination, an understanding of the uniqueness of history, of people, periods and values different from his own. Yet compensatory

[5] Schools Council Working Paper 45, *16–19 Growth and Response*, Chapter I, The Sixth Form Today (Evans/Methuen Educational, 1972).

education is at best a remedy. It would be better that the need should be avoided by a balanced diet of main subjects.

Potentially more important than the compensatory element in general studies is the opportunity to demonstrate to those mature enough to appreciate it the concept of the unity of knowledge. The sixth former already often has the vote; he will soon be in a complex world which will require him to make decisions based on the information he has gained from different specialists, and an integrated general studies course can help him appreciate the complexity of decision-making through role-playing or simulation games, and teach him to be wary of those who offer easy and immediate solutions.

The choice of content for such a course is a wide one, but it should be built around the staff and resources available. The lack of appropriate books or, as happens in many schools, inadequate library facilities, may prevent the immediate introduction of some courses. It is not advisable therefore to define the best kind of syllabus, for in this field experiment and flexibility (according to local needs) will continue to be the most useful tactics, but the historian might consider the following examples as a basis for further experiment: the study of a particular period such as the Renaissance, exploring its many facets in cooperation if possible with other departments; the scientist in society – 'What is science? How and why has it divided into its modern studies? How have individual scientists faced up to their moral responsibility?' – or a more limited study of one controversial topic such as the theory of evolution, its impact and its consequences, involving the historian working in collaboration with the religious education and science departments.[6]

It is essential that the historian approaches the task of teaching this course with a sense of the importance and significance it holds, for the importance which he attributes to it will be reflected by his pupils. They will be sorely tempted to treat a course without an external examination as a timetable filler, and nothing more. In his teaching, the historian should more often than not adopt the role of discussion leader and guide rather than that of instructor or lecturer, though he should not entirely eschew this role. His task is not always to provide answers but to teach his pupils to ask the right questions.

The core of the study itself must be *active* work by the students. As individuals or in groups they must investigate topics very carefully chosen by the teacher; there must be class discussion based on short papers or talks given by

---

6 See Appendix 3, Topics for General Studies in the Sixth Form.

individual members in turn; there must also be periodic short essays done by all members of the class on general questions – questions involving interpretation, not mere narrative relating to the topic as a whole.[7]

The teacher must restrain himself from too frequently giving a full exposition of his own knowledge. His main work will be adequate preparation so that he may lead discussion beyond the merely superficial without checking hesitant contributions by his weight of authoritative learning. He would do well to provide books ready to hand on a special shelf or in a nearby cupboard, offering actual page numbers of relevant passages as a spur to individual reading. He must insist on written work being done by the pupils and so mark their efforts that he sets and advances standards of understanding and of expression – for at this level the relation of the two is very close. To discussion and written work the historian can add the use of simulation techniques which give the student a greater sense of involvement and appreciation of the complexity of decision-making.[8] If he does all this the historian will ensure that the course provides both an opportunity for individual interest and a real intellectual challenge for all concerned.

The importance with which the course will be viewed by pupils will also depend in part on the time which is allocated to it. The administration of the school is beyond the responsibility of the history teacher, but his influence should be brought to bear to gain four or so periods a week for one term. This is preferable to two periods a week for a year, but should be regarded only as the minimum acceptable. Four periods a week for a term would justify the expenditure of money and energy on resource material, since the work could be repeated with a fresh group each term. A lot of this material will be in book form, but there should also be audiovisual materials, assignments, press-cuttings and perhaps ready-made materials such as the units of the General Studies Project of the Schools Council.[9]

What should emerge at the end of the course is the feeling that historical problems are complex (but not without hope of solution) and, if we only succeed in emphasising at this stage that the correct answers matter less than asking the right questions, that will be a

[7] C. P. Hill, *The Teaching of History to Non-Specialists in Sixth Forms* (H.A. pamphlet, 1962), pp. 18–19.

[8] An excellent article appeared in *The World and the School*, No. 14, (Atlantic Information Centre for Teachers, October 1968), pp. 53–69, entitled 'Simulated Conflicts and International Crisis Games – report on the Manex project.'

[9] Schools Council General Studies Project at York, published by Longman/Penguin Educational. See also Schools Council publications: *General Studies and Special Subjects* (1969); *Resource Centres* (1969).

useful lesson, provided that we also make it clear that neither sixth formers nor we ourselves are thereby absolved from making judgements, however incomplete, or finding answers, however partial. If the historian succeeds in this throughout the year he may well feel that there will be no need for a formal examination at the end of it. Ideally the absence of an examination should provide a glimpse of the principle of education for its own sake, a novel experience for our examination-orientated pupils. Yet we do not live in an ideal world, and it can be argued that an examination is necessary as an incentive for serious study. The danger, not peculiar to general studies, is that the examination will become a major objective and the course will lose its flexibility. If this can be avoided, and if it does act as an incentive, then the examination will at least have done no harm. It is not a necessity, and there will be many teachers who will feel that their assessment of their pupils throughout the year is a more valid evaluation of the student, the teacher and of the course itself. If it does nothing else, a consideration of integrated studies at all levels should force the historian to examine his own teaching closely.

# Local history

**12**

The term local history generally means the study of a limited area within the compass of a short journey, using materials to which the pupil has ready access. Although the development of transport and the rise in living standards have, in theory, enlarged the hinterlands of any locality, it is still in practice difficult for any group of school children to study an area which is not within a few miles of the school. If the nature of the topic is academic, and can be read, there is no reason why pupils in one region should not study the history of another. But as local history is of a practical nature it is better confined to the immediate locality. The spread of towns and the drift of many school sites from the city centre to the residential periphery has meant the removal of the schools from the old-established and often the most historically exciting parts of the town, so that even a study of one's own town entails a journey of a mile or two. During the next decade or so, the widening of local history into regional history in the schools may well be impracticable, and teacher and pupil will perforce need to continue to confine their attentions to the immediate locality. For that reason, if for no others, the term 'local history' will suffice. But in practice, 'local history' has two distinct shades of meaning. There are those who use *local* history as a part of national history; to others local history is a part of local studies, popularly known as environmental studies.

Despite support for local history as an essential part of the school curriculum since the early years of the present century, its adoption in schools has been slow. This is not surprising, as, until comparatively recently, local history was regarded as a second-rate study by most universities, to be left to the parson and the enthusiastic amateur. Since 1945, the attitude of universities has changed. Detailed research by specialists in order to deny or confirm accepted generalisations has led to local history becoming a respectable field of scholarship in most universities. This activity by the academic historians has led to a revival of local history in adult education. Groups such as the W.E.A., University Extra-Mural departments, field clubs, local history societies, and sub-aqua clubs have brought together enthusiasts who pursue a hobby under expert guidance. The number of adults engaged in industrial archaeology, which is usually some form of local economic history, is evidence of the present popularity of local history. In the colleges of education, many of the dissertations done by students are on local history topics. In many primary schools local history, usually as a part of environmental or integrated studies, plays an important part in the development of the pupils. In some secondary schools local history is emerging as part of the Mode 3 C.S.E. history courses, and in a very few, special local history syllabuses are being followed for G.C.E. Ordinary and Advanced level examinations. But generally, local history is still largely neglected in secondary schools. The correspondent who wrote that 'local history is best used as a springboard to national or international history and not as an end in itself' is typical of many teachers of history in secondary schools. In most, local history is relegated from the 'official' history syllabus to the history society.

The reasons for the comparative neglect of local history in secondary schools are understandable; mobility of staff, lack of time, lack of resources, lack of enthusiasm for the neighbourhood, the pressures of external examinations, the increasing demands for worldwide history, and the need to do something different from that which is done in the primary schools. But all those reasons are extenuating circumstances rather than real barriers. Pupils can be entered for special syllabuses in external examinations; the inclusion of local history in the curriculum, even at the expense of the Greeks or Akbar the Great, is defensible; resources can be mobilised; time can be found; enthusiasm may be developed. The real reason is perhaps an attitude of mind. Many teachers have exaggerated the dilemma of 'parish pump' versus wider horizons. 'The Reformation is a more worthwhile study than the railway lines of Crewe.' Thus teachers are willing for their pupils to spend a few hours studying local history, but only as a respite from 'real' history. Yet there may well be very compelling reasons why 'parish pump' should be studied rather than the broader themes. The present secondary school pupil can today widen his horizons through means other than school. Television, foreign holidays, and a mobile society have all led to the removal of some curtains of ignorance and mystery. Today's child is immeasurably more sophisticated than his father's generation, and he may have different needs. It is more likely that today's pupil is at school in a locality in which neither he nor his parents were born. A 'rootless society' can benefit from the study of local history. Further, in any secondary school course, part of the aim should be inculcation of historical method, and overriding concern for content or topic should be avoided. Secondary pupils need, at some time, to begin with their own experience: to attempt observation and investigation; to use 'boot as well as book': to evaluate evidence and deduce therefrom: to be made wary of national historical generalisations. Local history is one of the best, though still imperfect, vehicles for that purpose.

## Local history in the curriculum

Although local history as a discipline *per se* has no great hold in secondary schools, most use local history in two ways. First, as a part of environmental studies, together with the geography, ecology and sociology of the area. This can be of value, providing the historical studies are directed by an historian, and providing the course has a more genuine purpose than mere administrative convenience. One difficulty which arises in such courses is that of the time scale, which must by necessity carry through to the present day. Because of this, too many courses are centred on the post-1800 period. More could be done to attempt such courses at a time set well into the past, so that pupils could study the various aspects of their community in, say, 1600. Secondly, and more usually, local history is used as an illustration of national themes. The Peasants' Revolt is studied by children in London; Hadrian's Wall by Cumbrians and Northumbrians: Portsmouth Dockyard by children in that city. Or local agricultural enclosures, workhouses, castles, schools, newspapers, Chartists, Roundheads, are studied as illustrations of larger topics. As one correspondent wrote: 'We refer to local events or examples as they illustrate or play a part in the national scene'.

More could, and should, be done. There is much to be said for an enquiry into personal, family, street, school, or town history as at least half-a-term's work in the first year at the secondary school. New pupils in a new school can start such topics on the same starting line. Family trees, the meaning and origin of surnames, the birthplace and occupation of father, grandfather, and great-grandfather are all comparatively easy yet rewarding investigations within the capacity of the eleven- or twelve-year-olds. It also is a valuable means whereby the teacher can get to know his pupils. There are, however, hazards. Some parents may feel that some kind of investigation into their private affairs is taking place; or there may be some cupboard skeletons that are better left undisturbed. These dangers can be obviated by two simple expedients. First, a letter of explanation can be sent to the parents, setting out the aims of the project. Second, each pupil could be given a choice of family, or street, or school. Assuming that parents agree, an elementary investigation into family can lead a pupil into many interesting historical paths; migration, changes in occupation, variations in a way of life, size of family, educational opportunities. With good fortune, some parents may well feel drawn into the school community through such a project, and it may facilitate communication between themselves and their children. Where pupils are drawn from different racial backgrounds, such work may aid integration.

Whilst many teachers in secondary schools are willing to allow local history in the first year, few make it part of the curriculum during the later years. A case could be made for the study of local history by those pupils who will be taking history in the sixth form, instead of their taking a traditional G.C.E. O level course. Such pupils could acquire, or at least become conversant with, those skills such as the difference between primary and secondary sources, the dangers of biassed contemporaries, the evaluation of evidence, methods of dating, which are a necessary pre-sixth-form training for an A level course. The fifteen- or sixteen-year-old is more resourceful, more capable of independent enquiry, and is able to study documentary material. Yet, by-and-large, the eleven- or twelve-year-old is exposed to such excitement, and is then bereft of it until he is an adult.

Those who feel thwarted by the lack of historical interest in their own locality could consider a short-term exchange of older pupils between schools. In an age when our pupils are encouraged to indulge in ski-ing in Austria or cruising in the Mediterranean, often during term-time, few teachers are brave enough to consider two weeks' historical work in another part of England. If, say, a group of sixth formers from Stoke-on-Trent exchanged school and home with a group from Portsmouth, both would gain. In the south of England some pupils study the Industrial Revolution without seeing a steel rolling-mill, a coal mine, a pottery, or a textile mill. In the Midlands, some pupils study the Napoleonic Wars far removed from the sea and from Austerlitz. If exchange is difficult, there are now a number of study centres owned by L.E.A.s which are residential. The geographers have used such facilities for many years; historians could, and should, do so.

Finally, too many schools concentrate on ancient or medieval local history or on modern local history, usually on socio-economic themes. There are other rich topics to be explored: Tudor and Stuart times, local politics, newspapers, military and naval commanders, financial affairs, and philosophical disputes.

## Overcoming difficulties

Whilst it is true that local history is more easily done in some parts of Britain than in others, no teacher, wherever he is, should claim that his locality has 'no history'. The young graduate who has spent three or four years in one of the older universities and who finds himself in a new school in a new town may at first despair. But he should not. Gradually he will begin to 'feel at home' in his new environment and will grow curious about its past. The greatest obstacle will be in the mind rather than in reality. He may spend some sterile months comparing his new home adversely with his own 'home'; he may feel that he is a bird of passage, there for only a year or two. However short his stay, his teaching will be the richer for an understanding of the past of the region in which he finds himself. Indeed, the overriding need for his pupils would be that they should be made conscious of their heritage. The local historian does not need a three-dimensional building or artefacts. The past is still present, though invisible. Work could begin on a simple study of the site on which the school stands, using maps from the Ordnance Survey, relatively cheap and covering most parts of Britain from the early nineteenth century. Some interesting discoveries may be made which may engender enthusiasm among the students. The reasons for the establishment of the new town, its water supply, its communications, its parliamentary constituencies, all can be profitable studies. The concrete jungle is no real excuse for the neglect of local history.

Nor need the existence of a young, itinerant and non-indigenous staff preclude local historical studies. The newcomer may well need some two or three years before he can supervise his pupils with confidence – but there are short cuts. In answer to the question, 'Does the rapid movement of staff from one locality to another lead to problems in local history?', correspondents were mindful of the difficulties, but considered that they could be overcome. Some schools give newcomers a folder of duplicated material in order to assist integration. Somewhere in the locality there will be an interested and enthusiastic local historian; usually such people are very ready to help the newcomer. In most schools, there will be one teacher who knows the locality and something of its history. The apostolic succession should be passed on; those with the knowledge should transmit it to their replacements, preferably in writing. In some education authorities, there are curriculum development centres which are producing study-kits, thus preserving the knowledge and the expertise of experienced teachers.

Record offices, now comparatively plentiful compared with 25 years ago, will be more readily accessible to some than to others. Answers from correspondents suggest that, apart from those in the extreme west and east of England, most are within 20 miles of a record office. Those in the large urban centres are more fortunately placed. Where a record office is more than ten miles away, frequent visits by pupils may be difficult. In such cases it is now comparatively easy to obtain reprographic copies of material. Even where there is a record office on the doorstep, it is not always wise to use that office as a base for work by the pupils. Many documents will need to be edited or even translated by the teacher. The history teacher who intends to take local history seriously is advised to learn some elementary Latin and palaeography, or he will be forced into narrower fields of study. He should not have to rely upon the archivist to do his work for him. His pupils will benefit from the edited or translated transcript, for the synthetic may be of more value than the original. To satisfy the purist, the pupil can be given a photocopy of the original, as well as the edited version.

Visits to record offices, to buildings and the like are now easier than they were. Most headmasters and school administrators are aware of the value of their pupils' getting out and about, and some local education authorities will make a grant towards expenses. If the teacher is in a rigid and inflexible system, then he can show willing by arranging for such work to be done during week-ends, or summer evenings, or in the vacations. He will then have a strong case for the arrangement of future work during normal school hours. The time spent on such work can be minimised by making the pupils read what has already been written beforehand, and by other necessary preparation. A portable tape-recorder, on which to record the words of inscriptions, or visual descriptions of the sites visited, will save tedious outdoor note-making. A Polaroid camera has the same usefulness.

Project work in local history will inevitably mean that pupils will need to get in touch with experts such as museum curators and archivists. The promiscuous 'letting them loose' on such people can lead to a deadening of the goodwill of even those who possess considerable bonhomie. Whenever possible, the teacher should know something about the topic on which his pupils are working and he should ensure that his pupils have read any articles or other secondary material. He is advised to scrutinise all letters written by his pupils to experts before they are sent. That this is not done is evident from the daily mail of curators and archivists. They receive requests such as 'I am studying Nelson. Please send me a booklist', or 'I am writing a history of Manchester. What do you know about it?'. The experts should be asked specific questions whose answers cannot readily be found out either by the pupil or by the teacher. If a letter is written to a private individual, a stamped addressed envelope should be enclosed; it may well be that such a courtesy should be accorded also to those institutions which are financed by the taxpayer, for few have large typing pools. However, the chance for his pupils to meet an important personality, the name on the spine of a book, should be grasped. One cannot expect such

FIG. 25. *Ironbridge*

people to provide their services for nothing frequently. But, if such a confrontation can be arranged, with the prior permission of the expert, a question and answer session, or a short talk, could be put on tape, and used with the next generation of pupils.

One of the difficulties in project work in local history is the discovery of plagiarism. It does occasionally happen that a pupil is commended for a piece of work which is an almost direct transcription of some recondite article. The teacher can reduce the possibility by two means; by insisting on a reading-list and knowing the sources himself: and by the frequent setting of written work in class under his supervision so that the writing style of his pupils is easily identifiable.

Most local history topics should be identified with national or international trends. If not, there is a danger that his pupils will exaggerate the importance of their own locality. The pupil will need to be aware of the normality or uniqueness of his region; that monasteries were also dissolved in other areas; that there were Chartists in other parts of England; that enclosure was a general movement; that other towns have castles and medieval remains. There should be constant cross-reference from national to local, and from local to national. Studied in that way, local history is less open to the charge of parochialism.

## The practice of local history

Several correspondents have pointed to a lack of resources and materials as the main reason why they do not pursue local history; others found the lack of time to prepare suitable material the greatest obstacle. Certainly local history courses need a considerable amount of forward planning, probably some twelve months in advance. Some elementary equipment and resources can be got together for about £200. The teacher will need to buy books, pamphlets and other printed sources, together with maps, past and present. He can then begin to immerse himself in the history of the locality, and he can make sight-seeing expeditions in his own time. After this initial phase, he will have ideas on possible topics for his pupils to pursue, and he can acquire reprographed multiple copies of certain material. Then he can obtain a few items such as a portable tape-recorder, squared paper, files, a camera and film.

Theorists will assume ideal conditions: the practising teacher must consider reality. Let us assume that the teacher is in a school where team-teaching is impossible; in which he has a class of thirty or more pupils for two or three isolated periods each week; and no permanent base in which models or charts can be kept. By a judicious choice of topics, local history can still be done. He may even be able to take the class out-and-about by asking for one of the periods to be at the end of an afternoon. Faced with thirty pupils he would be unwise to launch them all on the same topic, or the joy of discovery will be lost. But if each individual is allocated a separate theme, the teacher will have the impossible task of supervising thirty different pieces of work. A practical compromise would be to find ten topics, and to let the class team up in groups of three. The pupils should have a controlled choice of their workmates, so that they will be compatible; but the teacher should contrive to achieve a balance of skills and interests in each team. It may be possible to divide the work of each team into three parts, to ensure that there are no freewheelers. If all the ten themes have some common ground, or some degree of overlap, so much the better. Each group can then be given a broad theme, with a duplicated reading list on which the location of the material is added. The teacher can indicate some possible general lines of enquiry, and pose certain questions that can be considered. Each team should then spend several periods reading round the subject, including consideration of the local theme as part of a national trend. Then the group may well develop some enthusiasms inside the set topic, and the area of enquiry can be narrowed down.

If the topic chosen is one of which some buildings or physical objects exist, it is essential that the pupils are taken to them. The old device of a questionnaire has something to commend it, but it may be that the mere noting down of the answers prevents a full awareness of their significance. The teachers can goad or prod or induce the discovery process. Immediately up the line from a certain main line railway station, there is a footbridge over the line, but the steps up and down are outside the station. The teacher can take his pupils there, and ask them why; with luck, they will realise that the site of the station has been moved further down the line. Itineraries of walking and looking are now so commonplace that they need not be detailed here. The method is so obvious and inexpensive yet some teachers are unwilling to use it. A study of the trails set out by the Forestry Commission may serve as useful guides.

Whatever the nature of the work done, some form of written record should be the end product. Those with higher literary ability can produce a reasoned essay with illustrations; some may be able to do some statistical work, or maps, or drawings, or even a talk on tape. All the variations of other methods of history can be used – models, debates, playforms. Moreover, all should share in the work of the others, either by reading their summaries, or by listening to talks. Though some would claim that local history is especially suitable for those of weak literary ability, because the record can be something other than the 'traditional' essay, this is debatable. Local history is still history, and requires the same skills as any other forms.

## Types of work

The types of work will vary considerably from area to area, and examples of local history which have been successfully carried out are to be found in Appendices 4–6. Others have been published in

R. Douch, *Local History and the Teacher* (Routledge and Kegan Paul, 1967), A. Jamieson, *Practical History Teaching* (Evans, 1971), and T. Corfe, *History in the Field* (Blond, 1970). But there are some common denominators which may serve as illustration.

Most schools are near a railway, and a study of local railways could take the following pattern: reading about the development of the national network, and the place of the local line in it; the need for the railway when it was built; construction; the building of a double track, or different gauge; the station, its architectural style compared with others in the region; level crossings, junctions, embankments, tunnels; the railway today; closures under the Beeching Plan.

Integrated studies can be carried out by a combined assault on a particular town; mathematicians can do practical trigonometry, artists draw whilst others interview passers-by. There are infinite variations. Those who live near the sea can combine maritime history with marine biology and ecology. Agrarian history can benefit from some of the elements of chemistry. Those who prefer political history can well use local poll books, which show voters' names, and how they voted in the first half of the nineteenth century. Such a study could well lead to an understanding of the political groupings of the time. From parish registers or from tax returns it is possible to analyse the occupations of the citizens; if records are available from the early eighteenth century or before, the population would be small enough for a worthwhile analysis to be made. Schools of older foundation will certainly have historical treasures of their own: prints of former buildings, registers, minutes of the governing body. Even the newest foundations will have something; there are names of houses or of founders to be followed up.

Did the locality provide ships or stores for the Armada? Which side was it on during the Civil War? What happened during the General Strike of 1926? What party do its M.P.s belong to today? All are important questions; not all can be answered without a considerable amount of work by the teacher. But they are worth trying.

# History outside the classroom 13

Historians have long realised that their subject should not be confined within the classroom; they know that it is about people in the past – their buildings and artefacts, their art and written documents, their costume and way of life. Ideally, therefore, the subject should be studied out of school to a far greater extent than it is, and this chapter tries to identify how this might be done, and what pitfalls lurk for the unwary. But there is more to it than that, and thus we can consider many other ways in which the historical experience can be conveyed beyond the basic classroom teaching situation.

'Outside the classroom' means the often hard and tedious business of getting pupils to sample a wide variety of historical experience both inside and outside school. This will often involve visits and excursions to sites, castles, churches, museums, the local cinema or theatre when a suitable 'historical' drama is being shown. More detailed work in museums, and longer school journeys at home and abroad, could feature. With greater stress on original material, especially in the sixth form, the County Record Office might need regular visitation; perhaps the archivists will bring original documents into school. Other groups might be encouraged to undertake personal or group work in the fields of industrial and 'pure' archaeology, though this presents special difficulties because of the skills involved. Nevertheless, the pupil learns by *doing* for himself and in the whole field outside, in the last resort, there is no substitute for this.

Junior forms, and pupils of lesser ability, might be encouraged to undertake local surveys, to do some local fieldwork (field study centres have been established in many areas) and, at a personal level, to prepare a family history by interviewing relatives and working on family documents and relics. Model-making is rewarding to some pupils and teachers, and tedious to others, but is a valid exercise at this level. One correspondent noted that it flourished in his school in cycles of a few years, then was utterly ignored. Many pupils, even the most able, can gain considerable knowledge and pleasure from mounting an exhibition, perhaps to commemorate an event, or arising out of a particular topic that has evoked interest. Some schools reported that they ran a pupil-produced newspaper, or an audio-visual show with slides and taped voices on, for example, 'Stuart London', using excerpts from Pepys' diary.

Another facet is the bringing into school of outside agencies. They may be speakers who come as part of university extension facilities, or as guests of a school history society. Or the sixth form might be invited to attend branch meetings of the Historical Association. Film shows in school (see Section 3, p. 240), and games such as *Wargames* or *Diplomacy*, can be very popular. At an advanced level, there might be a senior school paper-reading circle, as an intellectual exercise and encounter, and as a preparation for higher education.

It is unlikely that any one school can mount all these activities outside the classroom, although some correspondents noted a wide variety. Clearly, the individual does what works for him in his context. He knows that history outside is not a soft option for staff or pupils and that it may involve 'in-fighting' with one's colleagues and long journeys by motorway and inter-city rail. Every activity must, whatever its purpose, be inherently enjoyable or else the trouble taken in its organisation will seem time ill spent.

Since such an activity demands departure from the norm and consequently disruption and inconvenience to others, it is important to be clear as to its importance, if only to justify it to head-teachers. History outside is an essential part of history teaching today; it forms an immensely valuable tool which – with good organisation – can add a stimulating new dimension to a topic. To stand on/study/touch/see the past brings it alive with dramatic impact. It enables the experience that R. G. Collingwood talked about in his *Autobiography*,[1] the argument that the past is always in the present but at various removes, to take substance for every pupil. The relevance and eternal youth of history are there for all to see.

Moreover, to go outside the classroom is to stress the active and the practical. It is good for the prestige of the subject – a most important factor – that it is seen to be more than chalk and talk and notes, however important those matters are. Pupils can learn for themselves that historians, like detectives, explore and utilise evidence. The Schools Council Project[2] has tried to develop lines of enquiry in this particular direction. In these kinds of techniques can be found an introduction to possible leisure pursuits, especially

[1] R. G. Collingwood, *Autobiography* (Oxford University Press, 1939).
[2] *History, Geography and Social Science 8–13.*

in later life. This latter factor, together with the development of psychomotor skills, the social benefits to be gained from an increased awareness of landscape and environment, and the realisation of the value or uselessness of a piece of paper, clay, or glass or whatever, is by no means negligible in an age of increasing leisure resulting from shorter working hours. At the very least, it is a useful antidote to too much television.

It must be stressed, however, that such activities are not mere escapism from routine; yet they are not overwhelmingly good *per se*, and they do not confer 'elite' status on those who undertake them. They are a part of the history teacher's regular duties, or ought to be seen as such; and the more sceptical would argue that some cost-effective formula should be applied in terms of return expected for staff effort put in. Perhaps the result would be humbling and a stimulation to greater thought about what is done, and why.

## Visits

The most relevant practical questions are how and where to organise such activities, and what problems are likely to emerge. Section 2 (p. 239) includes a list of useful addresses of bodies connected with the usual places visited by schools. It should be noted that a school membership of the National Trust is a possibility, and that the Department of the Environment grants schools free entrance to most of the buildings under its care.

Good organisation and preparation including a notified prior visit by the teacher are essential. The activity – whatever it is – should be an integral part of the topic being studied, arising out of pupils' questions but being open-ended in form so that the activity can raise new issues as well as answering current questions. It is certainly worth altering the syllabus so that an eminently visitable place in the locality features as 'an integral part of the topic being studied'. Things under one's nose, and therefore part of the immediate environment, should not be neglected in favour of more glamorous attractions further away.

In general, pupils must know what they have to do, and groups should not exceed fifteen for ease and efficiency of working. (Most L.E.A.s work to the ratio of 1 staff to 20 pupils, but this is too many for effective supervision.) The developing use of duplicated questionnaires, assignments or work-cards has been an excellent innovation in selecting points of interest and importance, and in giving a clear purpose to the work. A problem or a set of problems to be solved concentrates the mind and leads naturally into the vital follow-up lessons. Tom Corfe's *History in the Field* and Alan Jamieson's *Practical History Teaching* offer excellent guidance in this particular matter, and in many other related topics on history outside.

From this general analysis we may turn to a specific activity. A typical assignment sheet for a school visit might read as follows:

*Roman Britain – First-year trip to Chester*

### 1. The Grosvenor Museum

Study carefully the two galleries with Roman exhibits: the stones, and the general gallery. Note the texts of the grave stones and temple pillars; look at the life-sized soldier in wax, the scale models of the garrison town as it was, and the other exhibits.

Then answer the following questions, using diagrams where appropriate.

1. Explain how the garrison worked – its feeding arrangements, buildings, accommodation.

2. From the evidence you have seen suggest some countries of origin of soldiers in the XX Legion. What can you learn from this?

3. Write about and draw in detail the kit of a legionary.

### 2. The City Walls

After the walk round the old medieval wall – and still with the plan of the Roman garrison in mind – answer the following questions.

1. In what ways is modern Chester different from medieval/Roman Chester?

2. What were the strengths of the Roman and medieval towns? What were the weaknesses?

3. Draw a plan showing the three main stages of Chester's development.

3. From your general reading and discussions what reasons can you suggest for the siting of a major garrison town at Chester? Why has it declined in importance?

As an incidental but important benefit, it is worth noting that a number of valuable psychomotor skills can be developed in this way: walking, observation, measurement, sketching, tape-recording, photography, 'archaeology', brass rubbing, use of maps in the field are among the skills that can accrue as well as the more obvious points about enquiring into evidence. Moreover, a wider interpretation of what constitutes historical evidence can be provided by looking at artefacts, buildings and landscape.

### Museums

Museums are worth a special mention because of the way many of them are developing in terms of liaison with schools. The forma-

FIG. 26. *The Grosvenor Museum: (a) Roman galleries (b) Roman soldier*

FIG. 27. Museum exhibits: (a) Original shipbuilder's drawings in Buckler's Hard Maritime Museum (b) Street scene in Castle Museum, York

tion of a 'Group for Educational Services in Museums' in the 1960s reflected a growing desire amongst museum officers to offer a worthwhile educational service to schools. The group has met regularly and has published a guide to *School Museum Services*, available from their secretary. Many museums will lend materials to schools, sometimes accompanied by a member of the curator's staff to offer expert explanation. They offer for sale slides, postcards and brochures which correspondents reported systematically purchasing for their schools.

There is also the organised visit to a museum, with enormous benefits. Pupils have access to information and experience which the school cannot match, especially if the museum itself is alert to its opportunities. For instance, at the Liverpool Museum, there is a lecture room where pupils are briefed on the purpose of the visit and are able to handle certain exhibits. Assignment sheets are available if required. Liverpool colleagues speak of a genuine 'follow-up' to such a visit on Saturdays and during school holidays.

One correspondent supplied a Mode 3 C.S.E. Syllabus in Local and Museum Studies whose object is to involve pupils in the work of the museum, and to equip them with the skills basic to the running of a museum. Candidates have to conduct effective field research into the area by means of a village survey, study the mechanics and development of one craft skill, and practise some archaeology and museum techniques such as conservation, cataloguing and so on. Much of the work inevitably takes place outside the classroom and is clearly a valid exercise in historical learning and skills of an examination kind.

With museums, of all places, it is most important that the pupils are properly briefed and carefully disciplined and this can only be achieved by *prior* consultation with the museum concerned.

## School societies

The school history society offers a wide variety of possibilities for taking the subject outside the classroom, even if that is the meeting place. The atmosphere will be different in most cases: less formal, possibly more creative, perhaps even more enthusiastically received. The society ought, however, to grow in response to demand since without voluntary support it will die, however much effort the teacher puts in.

This granted, then the society can explore almost at will the interests and enthusiasms of its members; and it can open their eyes to wider fields. It can be quite simple in format. For example, one correspondent wrote of a history club for years one to three, meeting in the dinner hour working on projects, giving talks and making models e.g. on 'Aircraft of World War Two'. Topics need not be too elevated or elaborate, but pupils often gain intense enjoyment. It has to be remembered, though, that model-making may only teach model-making, or fill the psychological needs of the modellers. In no period of history were houses or ships built of balsa wood or cornflake packets.

There is scope too for senior societies, involved in reading papers, arranging historical entertainments, inviting outside speakers. Such senior clubs need a clear *raison d'être*, should be pupil orientated, and preferably pupil run.

### Visiting lecturers

Hearing visiting lecturers is a common variant on classroom teaching and can be valuable both because it often makes possible co-operation with other departments, and also because it brings pupils into contact with recent research and acknowledged experts. The lecturers can be obtained from university extra-mural departments, the W.E.A., local authorities and so on; but they may just as easily be enthusiastic local amateurs, or history staff from neighbouring schools who can lead discussions and bring fresh insights. This latter facility may develop into a day's inter-school conference with its attendant benefits; often branches of the Historical Association sponsor such activities. There is, however, a case to be made against visiting speakers – a case that asks how good they are and what kind of function they are supposed to fulfil. If their matter is very erudite, can they put it over at a level that is meaningful and relevant to our pupils?

### Outside assistance

The Historical Association has much to commend it to all history teachers. A low annual subscription (with income tax relief) entitles members to receive the journal *History*, various pamphlets and a copy of the *Annual Bulletin of Historical Literature*. There is a lending library and access at reduced rates to 'Aids for Teachers', revision leaflets, bibliographies and so on. Membership also carries a reduction for *History Today* and *Teaching History* subscriptions, permits attendance at the annual vacation school at some university, and carries branch membership. The history teacher can meet his 'own kind' through this body, a vital experience for all of us.

There is also a growing interest in local history and industrial archaeology, much of it amongst informed amateurs so that there may well be local societies that commend themselves to teacher and pupil alike, and which offer invaluable sources of information. County Record Offices usually have photocopying facilities which ought to be utilised to the full.

There are in addition a number of professional journals offering the results of recent academic work, a study of which is part and parcel of the history teacher's preparation outside the classroom. These include *History, The English Historical Review, The Economic History Review, Past and Present,* and so on.

No one historian can master all the field, so that selection out of a richness of sources will have to be made by the discriminating teacher.

## Industrial archaeology

This has probably been the biggest growth sector in the past ten years, now with its own journal published by David and Charles. As well as being an absorbing adult hobby, as correspondents testified, it can have a dramatic and practical impact on school work. Unlike 'pure' archaeology, it does not usually demand digging, nor the special skills associated with that. Moreover there are few areas of the country where industrial archaeology cannot be practised. Farms have old ploughs to catalogue and draw or photograph, there are canals or railways or roads to be mapped, old buildings to explore and index before they are demolished.

The whole field of post-industrial development in town and country – much of it now under attack because it 'spoils' the environment – is wide open to the amateur to preserve, restore, or record if it must perish. Pupils can readily be let loose on this, usually take to it with a will and can acquire what skills they lack as they proceed. Certainly it is a subject in which *learning* constantly takes place. Even the old plough will conform to some standard design which needs to be discovered from the library – a priceless activity in itself.

## The pitfalls

It seems wise to end on a cautionary note. A visit or other such activity is not a 'day out'. One should therefore not be vague nor be over ambitious, but have a reasonable work load, a proper follow-up procedure, and clear objectives. What follows is a consensus of the ten 'golden rules' for successful activities outside the classroom.

Fig. 28. *Pupils look for a tramway*

FIG. 29. *Peak Forest Tramway*

1. Courtesy to colleagues who may be inconvenienced.
2. Clear consultation with the Head about compliance with L.E.A. rulings on supervision, insurance, and educational objectives.
3. Clear understanding of the legal position in accidents to pupils (A.M.A. suggests an indemnifying letter from parents), and in damage to the person or property of a third party.
4. Clear transport arrangements with the firm involved.
5. Arrangements for frequent stops, precautions against travel sickness, and adequate first aid equipment.
6. Precise financial arrangements, especially for those who cannot or will not pay.
7. The adoption of professional standards and common courtesies in any relationship with outside bodies.
8. Proper discipline, even if it is quite different from the classroom in its application. Breaking the party into small manageable groups each with a teacher is a great help in this respect.
9. Clear briefing of accompanying colleagues so that they know the over-all plan and their own personal responsibilities within it.
10. Proper consultation with, and advance notification of all relevant details to, parents.

Always we should remember that these activities are a testing time for the relationship between teacher and pupils. If a teacher has not managed to control his pupils by personal relationship in the school he should not embark on such an activity; in fact the more liberal the kind of activity, the more it calls for something more than enthusiasm from the teacher in charge. Humanity, personality, leadership and experience are needed. Ignorance, omissions or mistakes could well ruin an activity that was meant to be a stimulating experience. Yet despite these difficulties and frequent disappointments, and the quite disproportionate amount of time and energy history outside the classroom demands, we persevere because we believe in it; or we never touch it.

## 1.  Two practical visits

### (a)  *London for sixth form – one night in London*

1.  Write to M.P. to get a date for conducted tour of Parliament.
2.  Book one night's hotel accommodation for agreed number.
3.  Negotiate travel concessions, times, etc. for rail or coach.
4.  Work out further itinerary and make suitable booking arrangements, e.g. Stock Exchange, theatre visit, etc.
5.  Call meeting of interested pupils, explain steps so far and present itemised letter to take home.
6.  Accept deposits, have reserves, take in full money a week before.
7.  Call final meeting two days before for briefing. State line

taken on dress, smoking, behaviour, etc., and what sanctions are to be adopted. Introduce other members of staff and state varied responsibilities. Make a proper appeal to their sense of responsibility.

8. In London allow free time (but never in less than 'twos'), check the groups and expect a summary of what they have seen. Have regular meeting times if group work is prolonged. Try to relax and enjoy yourself.

9. Meet in good time for return home. There are always stragglers.

(b) *Some N. Wales castles for second forms – day trip by coach*

1. Obtain Head's and staff consent in principle.

2. Obtain free entrance passes from Department of the Environment to the selected castles, Conway and Rhuddlan.

3. Obtain quotations from several coach firms.

4. Letter to parents giving cost, date, times, meal arrangements, itinerary and purpose of visit.

5. Draw up assignment sheets from material in resources centre at school and arrange for the separate forms to be briefed by colour slides and diagrams on what they are going to see.

6. Pray for fine weather. (Have contingency plans for foul weather.)

7. Make all necessary arrangements for groups, first aid, travel sickness precautions, behaviour on the coaches and at the castles and so on.

8. Relax on the day since relaxed pupils will work better. Hand out the assignment sheets on the coaches and other material such as diagrams and brief historical notes.

9. At each stop introduce yourself to the keeper and explain what you are intending to do. Rapidly rebrief the pupils and set them to work. Staff mingle, guide the idle and answer impossible questions from all and sundry. Staff note that they too need a better brief.

10. For the sake of pupils, staff, drivers and waiting parents, keep to the schedule, and above all to the timetable.

11. Remember a proper tidying up procedure, thanks, etc.

12. Set the work to be done at home and in school as a follow-up.

## 2. Useful addresses

County Record Offices and their services: available from L.E.A.s.

W.E.A. (for speakers): Temple House, 9 Upper Berkeley Street, London W1.

Department of the Environment: Regional Offices (for free passes).

University Extension Departments (for speakers): available locally.

C.E.W.C. (for speakers): 93 Albert Embankment, London SE1.

Archaeological bodies: C.B.A., 10 Bolton Gardens, London SW5.

The Historical Association: 59A Kennington Park Road, London SE11.

The National Trust: 42 Queen Anne's Gate, London SW1H 9AS.

The Group for Educational Services in Museums: c/o City Museum, Queen's Road, Bristol 8.

Many organisations publish pamphlets about their work, the buildings, etc., under their care, and catalogues of colour slides, post-cards and the like, available for sale.

## 3.  Films

One school uses four of these films a year, two in each of the autumn and spring terms, on a four-year cycle: a World War II type to begin the year, to show that history can be unashamedly entertaining, and for prestige advertising within the school:

*Duel in the Sky* (Central Film Library)
*Mastery at Sea* (Central Film Library)
*Story of Stalingrad* (Central Film Library)
*The Battle of Britain* (Central Film Library)

The rest cover a wide range of periods:

*Roman Britain, Romans in Britain* (Educational Foundation for Visual Aids)
*The Roman World* (National Audio-Visual Aids Centre)
*Life in a Medieval Town* (Coronet Gateway)
*The Vikings, Bayeux Tapestry* (Films de Compas)
*The Renaissance, The Pilgrims, The Industrial Revolution* (Rank)
*Culloden* (Concord)
*Nine Centuries of Coal* (N.C.B. Film Library)
*What about the workers?* (Rank)
*Women on the March* (Central Film Library)
*The People's Charter, The Story of Money, The Story of the Post* (C.F.L.)
*Once upon a time, Detection in Archaeology, News Agency* (C.F.L.)
*Speed the Plough* (Petroleum Films Bureau)
*The Oxfam Story* (Concord)
*Giants of Steam, England of Elizabeth* (British Transport Film Library)

Running times, hire charges, and details of other films can be obtained by consulting the catalogues of the various bodies. There is a comprehensive list in *Handbook for History Teachers* (edited by Burston and Green).

## 4. Some useful publications

M. E. Bryant, *The Museum and the School* (H.A. Teaching of History Leaflet No. 6, 1961)

W. H. Burston and C. W. Green, *Handbook for History Teachers* (1971 ed., pp. 168–171)

Tom Corfe, *History in the Field* (1970)

Tom Hastie, *History After Four O'Clock* (H.A. Leaflet, 1971)

Alan Jamieson, *Practical History Teaching* (1971)

*Out and About* (Schools Council, 1972)

*Pterodactyls and Old Lace* (Schools Council, 1972)

*Ancient Monuments and Historic Buildings* (H.M.S.O.)

*Museums and Galleries* (Index publishers) (annually)

*Historic Houses, Castles and Gardens* (Index) (annually)

*National Trust Pocket Guide to Britain* (published periodically)

*Catalogue of Colour Slides* (Department of the Environment)

*Teaching History* (The Historical Association)

*Journal of Transport History*

*Industrial Archaeology*

*Maritime History* (David and Charles)

*The Mariner's Mirror* (Society for Nautical Research)

*Museums and Education* (H.M.S.O. Education Survey 12, 1971)

# Appendix 1: An example of the use which can be made of drama in teaching history

## A KINGDOM DISPUTED: 1066 AND ALL THAT

### A one-act teaching-playlet for class use

Minimum props: a table and three chairs in any open area, and a stick to represent Harold's standard

Cast: King Harold
His brothers – Gurth and Leofwine
A Herald
Alred, a thegn
Four Normans

Time: A double period: one period for allocation of cast and rehearsal, then fifteen minutes running time – plus time to clear up and discuss the play

Scene: Harold seated at table (centre stage) facing audience; on his left is Gurth (seated, head bowed, inert). On his right is Leofwine (seated, head bowed, inert). Standing to the side is Alred (head bowed, inert). A Herald enters and addresses the audience.

HERALD: We are at the court of King Harold of England in the year 1066. Harold has been elected king by the witan, the assembly of nobles, and he is now discussing his grave situation with his two brothers and with Alred, a thegn. (*The* HERALD *points towards each of them as he speaks.*) Edward the Confessor has only recently died, and there are still some feelings of jealousy amongst the Lords because Harold, now elevated so highly, was a lord like themselves till recently. See the worried frown the new king wears – but his worst troubles lie still before him. If he is the hero of our play, then it is a tragedy, for Harold, as we all know, will be dead before the year is out. If he is the villain then his defeat is our victory. But, in fact, history takes no sides – it merely watches and records. (HERALD *leaves the stage. As he departs, all lift their heads and make movements.*)

GURTH: Well, my Sovereign and brother, you are now king in this realm. The witan has elected you, and all your thegns will rejoice. We now have a strong man on the throne. Godwin, our father, would have been proud.

Beloved though King Edward was, nobody liked the way he showed favours to his Norman friends – least of all you, my Sovereign. He was too much of a Norman and more like a monk than a king.

HAROLD (*sadly after a sigh*): You speak as if all our troubles are past, my brother Gurth; but I fancy they have hardly begun.

LEOFWINE: Aye, my Sovereign, that may be so. Our brother Tostig, whom you persuaded our late King to dismiss from his earldom of Northumbria for his cruelty, has raided the south coast and is even now plotting with King Harald Hardrada of Norway to return with a Viking army and reclaim his earldom.

GURTH: And Hardrada to claim a kingdom. Did not Canute rule a great northern Empire three decades ago? I fancy Hardrada has a mind to do the same.

LEOFWINE: It is your brother Tostig, my Sovereign, who has stirred him up. Did ever a king have a more faithless relation?

GURTH: But he is not the end of our brother's troubles, dear Leofwine. Is not Duke William of Normandy at this moment assembling a fleet across the Channel and inviting every adventurer in Europe to join him? He claims our late King Edward the Confessor left him the throne in 1051, and that he should rightfully be King.

ALRED (*moving across the stage*): That claim is false. It was not in his power to give. No king can will his kingdom to another as if it were his private property. But Duke William also claims that the solemn promise you, my Sovereign, made to him to help him gain the kingship is binding.

HAROLD (*rising to his feet angrily*): Alred I must tell you that promise was extracted from me as the price of my freedom. It was obtained from me by trickery. How can such an oath be binding?

GURTH: By the fact that you did swear it upon the most solemn relics. Have you forgotten, my Sovereign?

HAROLD: No man accuses me of oath-breaking. That promise was a trick – I knew not what was in the casket upon which I made the oath.

GURTH: Nevertheless, my Lord, is not a promise a promise, however it is obtained?

HAROLD: Have done, I say. Remember I am your king and not to be rebuked as if I were a common subject. (*He steps towards* GURTH *raising his hand.* GURTH *falls to his knees in front of* HAROLD.)

GURTH: Forgive me, my Sovereign, I did not mean to offend you. But your enemies claim that it is because of your broken oath that they seek your downfall.

HAROLD: My conscience is clear. If the bastard William had been elected by the witan, then I would have helped him and been his loyal subject. But such was not the case. *I* was elected king, *not* William – I cannot go against such choice whatever promises were made long ago in different circumstances – and under duress. No sin is beyond pardon, so no oath can be beyond recall. Anyway, the throne was never in my power to give.

GURTH: My Sovereign, I am your brother, and also your faithful and loyal subject as we all are here. Our fortunes prosper only with your success. If William or Tostig wins here, our position will count for nothing and our lives will be in jeopardy. We are your loyal subjects, not your enemies.

HAROLD (*quietly*): Ah well, be not alarmed at my ill-humour, good Gurth. (GURTH *raises himself and sits himself in a chair.*) Your loyalty is beyond question and you have done fealty to me and are my man. It is no time for me to be angry with my *loyal* subjects when I am surrounded by so many who may be *disloyal*. Never before has a king of England had to face his kingdom disputed by two such terrible and hostile armadas, both poised to invade – and knowing not which will strike first.

LEOFWINE: I wish they would strike each other and leave us alone in peace.

HAROLD: There is no hope of that, good Leofwine, unless, God forbid, we are vanquished by both of them. Meanwhile, we must just sit and wait. The problem is, which will sail first?

LEOFWINE: The wind, my Sovereign, will determine that. If it blows from the south the Duke William will be upon us; but if it settles in the east then the Vikings can be expected.

HAROLD: Then it is in the hands of the gods. What do the soothsayers say?

GURTH: They say that it will blow from the south, my Sovereign.

HAROLD: Then we must wait here in the south; but I wonder for how long . . . (*A commotion offstage.*) Whatever is that commotion?

HERALD (*runs in*): My Sovereign, my Sovereign, news from the north! The Vikings have landed in the Humber – Hardrada, Tostig and a great host from three hundred long-ships.

HAROLD (*bitterly*): So much for soothsayers.

HERALD: The northern earls, Edwin and Morcar, have been defeated my Lord – they were overborne at the Battle of Fulford, and I am come from them to urge your support, my Sovereign.

HAROLD: This is bad news indeed, but at least our period of waiting is over. (*He turns to the Lords.*) Go Gurth, summon your men; Leofwine, let us have the Housecarles ready to mount within the hour. We have a long journey northwards ahead of us, but with God's help, we will put an end to the attacks of the Viking raven on our shores for ever. (*He leaves the stage followed by the lords and the herald.*)

(*The* HERALD *returns to the stage.*)

HERALD: And now, good audience, you must imagine King Harold and his Housecarles riding north. There they surprise Hardrada's army and, in a bloody fight, Saxon wins over Viking. Hardrada and Tostig are killed and the enemy is fled. (*Exit the* HERALD.)

(HAROLD *enters followed jubilantly by* GURTH *and* LEOFWINE.)

GURTH: Was not that the mightiest of victories, my Sovereign? Did you not see the Vikings fly?

HAROLD: We were lucky so few carried shields with them.

LEOFWINE: They felt safe, but we surprised and slew them. Our victory at Stamford Bridge will now be recorded in history. All Hardrada gets of England is seven feet for his own grave!

HAROLD: It was a great victory, but we must remember our other enemy. Duke William has landed already at Pevensey. We must now prepare ourselves for the long journey south again.

LEOFWINE: Our men are tired, my Sovereign. We have many wounded. To go against the Normans means another nine days' ride. We will fight at a disadvantage.

HAROLD: That may be so, but the longer we delay, the more difficult it will be to do to William what we achieved with Hardrada. We cannot expect to have the advantage of surprise this time. But if God's favour holds, we can prevail again. Come brothers. (*Exit* HAROLD *and brothers.*)

(*The* HERALD *enters.*)

HERALD: And now good audience, we are near Hastings, on high ground with an incline sloping down before us. We are in Harold's camp on Senlac Hill. Down the slope is William's army in massed array. It is 9 o'clock in the morning. (*Stage hands put tables and chairs on their sides to represent a wood palisade. The* HERALD *points to it.*)

HERALD: And this is a palisade in front of Harold's army. (*Exit* HERALD.)
(*Enter* HAROLD, GURTH *and* LEOFWINE.)
HAROLD: Now is the day of decision – it's my lucky day – my natal day, the 14th of October. Surely no man can be defeated on his birthday!
GURTH: But, my Sovereign, today is Duke William's birthday also. You cannot both win. And they do say that the comet which appeared in April was an evil omen.
HAROLD: A bad omen, you say. Well, enough of omens – this palisade is our best defence.
GURTH: See yonder, my Sovereign. (*He points off stage to the Norman army.*) The enemy cavalry advance. But I fancy our Housecarles will prove themselves the finest soldiers in Europe.
LEOFWINE: The finest *foot* soldiers you mean. They may ride to battle, but they fight on foot. These Normans have cavalry, but we have none.
HAROLD: They may have horsemen but I fancy they are no match for our two-handed battle-axes. They call William 'the Conqueror', but he will not find fighting Saxons as easy as he does fighting in France.
GURTH: But they have bowmen also, my Sovereign, large numbers, too. They must have 7,000 men in their army altogether, quite as many as we have.
HAROLD: We are safe from arrows behind this palisade . . . the enemy cavalry will not dislodge us here, providing we stay tight. Their arrows cannot penetrate our palisade and shields. We have the Housecarles and we have the fyrd of Wessex – we lack only our Northern army. Where *are* Morcar and Edwin? I ordered them to come speedily to our aid with their Northern levies, but they have not come. Are they slow, or is this treachery?
(*Enter* ALRED)
ALRED: My Lord, our fyrd, our levies from the West Country, have disobeyed your orders. They have quit their strong position on the hill-top and have chased fleeing Norman cavalry. I suspect a trick – for they are being cut to pieces by Norman cavalry who are setting upon them from all sides – and they, poor men, are in the open in disarray.
(FOUR NORMANS *appear, firing imaginary bows into the air.*)
HAROLD: Treachery followed by disobedience. It is not a good omen.
GURTH (*pointing to the* NORMANS): My Sovereign, look! The enemy plays yet another trick. Their arrows do not pierce our shield-wall but they fire them into the air and rain them down upon our heads. Look up there, my Sovereign – an iron cloud approaches.
HAROLD: I sense my end – the fates are against us – where are those arrows you say? (*He looks up, then smacks his eye with his hand and falls to the ground with a loud cry.*)
GURTH (*Seeing his king fall he rushes to him and holds his head*): My Lords, come quickly, the King is hit. King Harold is dying.
LEOFWINE: Oh God. The fortunes are against us. The King is dead – oh! Saxon England, what will befall you now? (*The* FOUR NORMANS *advance slowly but menacingly from the side of the stage.*)
ALRED: And here come the enemy, my lords. Hold fast – they are upon us.
(LEOFWINE *kills the* 1ST NORMAN *but is killed by the* 2ND NORMAN *who in turn is killed by* GURTH. *All die with loud cries and dramatic gestures.*)
GURTH: The King is dead, my brother Leofwine is fallen and they better us in the fight. But I will hold the standard; they shall not have it till I am spent. (GURTH *clasps the standard and stands defiant.* TWO OTHER NORMANS *tackle* GURTH *who holds the standard erect until he dies.* ALRED *meanwhile escapes to a corner of the stage, front.*)
ALRED (*turning to the audience*): What bravery to die, but I want to live. I

see that all is lost and the worst has come. Thank God the night is falling that I may escape beneath its cover. All our Housecarles are dead and William has won the day. There is no more to be gained so I will run away. (ALRED *slips across the stage past the two remaining* NORMANS, *then stops and turns again to the audience.*)

ALRED: Don't judge me harshly; I can fight no more, there is no other way. (*Exit*)

3RD AND 4TH NORMANS (*in unison. They survey the slaughter, then advance to front stage and address the audience*): Well, our bloody work is done. Now to booty and to fun. (NORMANS *exit laughing.*)

(HERALD *enters.*)

HERALD: And so, dear audience, the battle is over and Harold and his brothers are dead. The witan elects William king, and he is crowned in Westminster Abbey on Christmas Day. Now is Norman-French to be the spoken tongue of all who count in England. Now are Saxon landowners dispossessed and Norman knights take their lands. Now is a man blinded if he snares a bird in a royal forest. Now are stone castles built, the White Tower holds London in awe, and the Domesday Book reveals all. 1066 is the most memorable year in English history. But to the ordinary Englishman – a serf obediently tending his lord's land in his quiet English village – nothing much happened and scarcely anything was changed. (*Curtain.*)

## A quiz of twenty questions on the teaching playlet 1066 and All That

1. Who was King Harold's predecessor who died in 1066?
2. What was the name of the body of nobles which in Saxon England elected the King?
3. What was the name of Harold's brother who fled to Norway, but returned with the invading Vikings in 1066?
4. What factor determined whether the Vikings or the Normans invaded first?
5. In what estuary did the Vikings land in the north of England?
6. At what battle in 1066 were the two northern earls defeated?
7. What were the names of the two northern earls?
8. At what battle was the King of Norway killed?
9. What was the Norwegian King called?
10. What piece of military equipment is it alleged in the playlet that the Vikings lacked at the battle in which the Norwegian King was killed?
11. Where did William land on the south coast?
12. On what hill did Harold take up a strong position?
13. What was the date of Harold's and William's birthday – also the day on which the Battle of Hastings was fought?
14. What appeared in April 1066 and was taken as an evil omen?
15. The Housecarles rode to battle on horseback but fought on foot. What was their main weapon?
16. How many men (to the nearest thousand) were on the battlefield of Hastings *altogether*?
17. Harold may have died in a cavalry charge. But according to one interpretation of the Bayeux Tapestry, and also in the playlet, what killed him?
18. Who held Harold's standard aloft till he himself was killed?
19. In what church was William crowned King on Christmas Day, 1066?
20. What survey of England of 1086 gives a comprehensive picture of England's land ownership?

# Appendix 2:   Integrated humanities

## UNIT ONE – THE ORIGINS OF CIVILISATION

1. *The origin of the earth*   The biblical explanation is contrasted with the basic scientific explanations. These are considered briefly but it should include some treatment of volcanoes and igneous rocks.

2. *The shape of the earth*   The early theories (Hebrew, Homer and the Mappa Mundi) are of interest and contrast well with the more scientific modern views. Material should include eclipses, satellites and modern examples of circumnavigations (including space men).

3. *Latitude and longitude*   Simple explanation and description, but to concentrate on the methods of using an atlas, which will need continuous reinforcement.

4. *Day and night*   Introduced by the Phaeton myth with the geographical explanation.

5. *The seasons*   Contrast of the Persephone myth with the geographical explanation.

6. *The origin of life*   A progression from the earlier study of volcanic rocks to explain how erosion produces sedimentary rocks. This introduces fossils and an outline of the evolutionary process explains how life developed as far as prehistoric animals.

7. *The origin of man*   The Adam and Eve myth can be contrasted with the theory of evolution as far as man is concerned. The later evolution of man can be used as a case study of evolution. The development of Palaeolithic man shows how his initial dependence on hunting, fishing and gathering gradually changed as he developed the knowledge to cultivate. The Fertile Crescent study area includes Jericho which can be used to provide information on the development of farming.

8. *Abraham*   The link between prehistoric and historic man is made through Abraham and the study of literary and archaeological evidence. The archaeology of Ur introduces the methods of the archaeologist (compared with those of the detective) which should include the scientific methods of locating a dig and dating finds, illustrated with reference to stratigraphy, pottery, coins and inscriptions.

## UNIT TWO – EARLY CIVILISATIONS

1. *The Minoan civilisation*   The link with Ur is provided by the date, *c.* 1800–1400 BC. This, and the following civilisations, to be located on the

Mediterranean map by reference to the atlas. The Theseus story, ending with the Minotaur episode, leads to the archaeology of Knossos. The importance of the bull is stressed as a symbol of this civilisation.

2. *Mycenae*  Mycenae was overtaking Minos as a power centre before the destruction of Knossos, and consideration of the tidal wave theory should include a reference back to the earlier work on volcanoes. Mycenaean centres need locating on a map and pictures of the way of life and architecture can be gained by considering Schliemann's excavations.

3. *Troy*  The legends surrounding the origins of the Trojan War should receive brief treatment and the story of the War itself can be taken from *The Iliad* to explain the quarrel, the death of Patroclus, Achilles' new armour and the death of Hector. Information from Schliemann's excavations backs up the narrative. The wooden horse story leads on to the episodes of Cyclops and Ulysses' return, from *The Odyssey*.
A time chart, and the link of the ram, bull and lion symbols, is necessary here.

4. *Egypt*  A reconsideration of Abraham's nomadic life contrasts with the fertility of the banks of the Nile where settled agriculture was possible. The periodic flooding of the Nile explains the fertility and provides an opportunity to revise the earlier sedimentology work. The Egyptian civilisation and way of life can be explained with reference to such objects as the pyramids and such people as Tutankhamun. Within this background, the story of Joseph can be told which leads to Moses and the Exodus. Possible geographical explanations of the plagues and the crossing of the Red Sea can be considered.

5. *The arrival in the Promised Land*  The arrival is seen through the story of Rahab and the spies, and the biblical accounts of the crossing of the Jordan and the battle of Jericho, compared and contrasted with archaeological and geographical explanations. The settlement of the tribes illustrates again the contrast between a nomadic and a settled existence, although in this case it is the rainfall in Canaan that creates the more favourable environment. The tribes lived separately except in times of danger when they united under Judges: the example of Gideon, which also illustrates the temptation to worship Baals (considered to be more appropriate gods for the farmer than the god of the wilderness).

6. *The Kingdom of Israel*  The story of David is taken as an illustration of Israel's creation and of some of its problems: the struggle with the Philistines, David and Saul, the capture of Jerusalem.

## UNIT THREE – EMPIRE-BUILDING

1. *Greece*  A reference back to Mycenae serves as an introduction. The development of city states brings in the importance of relief, shown by examples of layer shading. The independence of city states for geographical reasons is well brought out in the Persian Wars: the invasion of Darius and the Battle of Marathon 490 BC, and the invasion of Xerxes and the Battles of Thermopylae and Salamis 480 BC.

2. *Athens*  The way of life in Athens in the fifth century BC to include: house life, education, theatre, the Olympic games, military and naval affairs, elementary politics and architecture. Some contrast with Sparta and consideration of the fall of Athens and Sparta.

3. *Alexander the Great* A brief consideration of Alexander's life from 356–323 BC to show his determination at empire-building. A selection of episodes fitted on to a time chart and a map of his route of conquest. A brief reference to the division of his empire on his death and its ultimate replacement by Rome.

4. *Foundation of Rome* Considered as a myth and as another example of the process of empire-building in the Mediterranean area. Brief review of the conquest of Palestine by Pompey 63 BC and the Jewish rebellion of 54 BC. Palestine as a Roman province; Herod the Great, Roman puppet king 37 BC; the rebuilding of the temple. Background information on the Jewish home, school, synagogue and farming methods.

5. *The life of Christ* Historical evidence for Christ. Significant episodes of his life and examples of his teaching lead to the events of the last week of his life, according to biblical narrative and as expressed in the Pontius Pilate play. A summary coverage of the basic beliefs of Christians.

## UNIT FOUR – ROMAN BRITAIN

1. *Caesar's invasions* The landings in 55 and 54 BC based on his own commentary, with details of the Britons' methods of chariot fighting. Considered as a continuation of Rome's empire-building.

2. *Britain as the Romans found it* British tribes and their way of life. Local artefacts to be used to prove the local existence of the Britons and identification of their sites on 2½ in. O.S. maps leads to discussion and practice of the method of using grid references. General distribution of the Britons to emphasise the importance of the chalk uplands in southern Britain and especially the use of the hill fort as the defensive means. 2½ in O.S. maps of Maiden Castle used for study of contours for showing relief.

3. *Romanisation of Britain* Studied as a process following consideration of the Claudian invasion of AD 43; Roman soldiers; construction and importance of Roman roads; identification of local roads, towns, camps, farms; construction of similar camps and towns throughout Britain involving placename work. The frontier zone resulting in the construction of Hadrian's Wall; method of construction and life of a soldier. Reasons for the Wall, involving discussion of relief and climate and including climatic graph construction.

4. *Life in Roman Britain* Introduction through local artefacts and sites to emphasise local occurrences. Details of the life style from Fishbourne including agricultural advancements. Town life considered through the examples of Silchester and Verulamium which leads on to a study of the early arrival of Christianity in Britain. The silting of Fishbourne can be used for a revision of sedimentation.

5. *The fall of Rome* Early Saxon invasions of Britain lead to the construction of the 'Saxon shore' forts. The destruction of Fishbourne leads to a brief consideration of these Saxon invasions as part of the overall fall of the Roman Empire.

## UNIT FIVE – MEDIEVAL BRITAIN

1. *Anglo-Saxon England* The reasons for the Saxon invasions, and their methods of attack as seen at Sutton Hoo. Penetration of the land (including

the local area) using rivers and Roman roads, to include exercises which will illustrate the process of village site selection. Settlement plans; life and customs; agricultural improvements. Reintroduction of Christianity by Augustine and others. The importance of the church (cf. Minster Church at Paxton). The development of a united kingdom from the Saxon kingdoms.

2. *The Norman Conquest* Narrative based on contemporary accounts, concentrating on Bayeux Tapestry. Reasons for invasion; methods of defence and attack; castle construction, using local examples. Limits on Norman control as shown by Hereward the Wake's resistance in the Fens.

3. *Feudal society and the village* Evidence from Domesday Book, using the example of Eynesbury. The fabric of the village, including church, manor houses (local moated examples) and peasants' houses. Agricultural economy; the open field system and its organisation, methods of farming and tools used. Life in the village; dress, social structure and crafts.

4. *Towns* The concept of a town; description of buildings. Development around a market place where trade is fostered by the church, using the example of St Neots Priory. Emphasis of this link between village, town and church. Street plans; health problems; trades; town life. The advantages of agglomeration; settlement hierarchies; market areas, to include the application of these ideas to East Anglia.

5. *The Church* Link with village and town, especially through the example of St Neots Priory. Details of monasteries and the way of life of monks and nuns. Details of St Neots Priory. Town churches contrasted with village churches using local examples; simple architectural details.

## UNIT SIX – ELIZABETHAN ENGLAND

1. *The Reformation* The events that led to the split between the Roman Catholic and the Protestant churches. The general discontent as a result of taxes, attitudes and the sale of indulgences. Luther's attack on the established church and the invention of printing which helped his ideas to be spread. Henry VIII's desire for a male heir to the English throne and his resultant need for divorce. Henry's break with Rome and his establishment as head of the English church; the Bible in English and the dissolution of the monasteries. The contrast of Edward's and Mary's reigns leading to a fear of Catholics and to the political consequences of the Reformation in Elizabeth I's reign; the stories of Mary Queen of Scots and the Armada.

2. *Elizabethan society* Based upon details of the life of Sir Henry Unton which leads to a study of topics that illustrate the nature of Elizabethan society; growing up, dress, amusements, fighting, food and drink, travel and trade, furnishings, country houses, London, the Court, royal palaces, merchants and craftsmen, Queen Elizabeth, actors and the theatre and Speke Hall. An essential feature of this section is that the results of the topic work should be collected together to produce a class book on Elizabethan society.

3. *The age of exploration* Brief treatment of the more important explorers and discoveries to establish the known world of *c.* 1450, which can be plotted in map form. The importance of trade with emphasis on the European/Asian spice route and the Arabs' interference with this trade. This leads to a study of the Arabs to include their religion and way of life. The study of Vasco da Gama's voyage to India seeking a new route for the spice traders;

the problems met on the voyage and his impressions of the Indian people that he met. Consideration of the Indian sub-continent to include Hinduism and Buddhism as religions, the Indian way of life and a basic geographic background of such factors as relief, climate, agriculture, population and some of the problems inherent in Indian society.

# Appendix 3: Topics for general studies in the sixth form

## A. PORTRAIT OF THE VICTORIAN AGE 1837–1901

*Groups.* Since most of the course is based on lectures followed by questioning, the groups are mixed but large (60–100) – at least in the preliminary stages.

### Aims of the course

1.  To use the study of a particular period in history 'in the round' to impress upon the sixth form the essential unity of all studies.
2.  To examine the assumptions of the Victorian age, to appraise its ideals and reassess its controversies with a view to shedding some light on matters which puzzle us today.

### Methods

1.  A syllabus covering three terms (of two consecutive forty-five minute periods a week) is given below.
2.  This will be covered by lectures in which generous use will be made of films, film strips, slides, gramophone records, etc.
3.  Each of the lectures will possess a measure of independence; each should be made enjoyable as a separate item; and yet there should be a communicable coherence stamped upon the whole series.
4.  As many outside lecturers as possible will be invited to take part, supplemented by various members of the school staff.
5.  Educational visits to places of historical interest, etc., will be an essential part of the course.
6.  Each pupil will be required during the course to make a special study of one aspect of the work of his own choice or a number can choose to take part in a group project. Each pupil can be encouraged to undertake a piece of work outside the world of his A level subjects. A list of suggestions is appended.
7.  Particular stress will be laid on the locality.

### Syllabus

1.  Introducing the Victorians.
2.  The material background:
    (*a*) Industrial society – iron, coal and steel.
    (*b*) Rural life.

3. The theory of progress:
    (*a*) Origin and development of the idea of progress.
    (*b*) 1851 and the visibility of progress.
4. Changes in the public taste:
    (*a*) Architecture.
    (*b*) Music
    (*c*) Literature.
    (*d*) Sport and pastimes.
    (*e*) Food and drink.
    (*f*) Dress.
5. Victorian religious belief and controversy:
    (*a*) The Nonconformist conscience.
    (*b*) The Tractarian movement: Church revival and reform.
    (*c*) The strands of unbelief – George Eliot, T. H. Huxley.
6. Man and nature:
    (*a*) Evolution and human progress.
    (*b*) Geology changes the outlook.
    (*c*) Archaeology links geology to nature.
    (*d*) Physical science and the beliefs of the Victorians.
    (*e*) Man and nature: some artists' views, e.g. Millais, Holman Hunt, Landseer.
7. The liberal idea:
    (*a*) Victorian democracy: (i) national; (ii) local.
    (*b*) The virtues of self-help.
    (*c*) The nineteenth-century Press.
    (*d*) Radicalism and nationalism.
    (*e*) The development of education.
    (*f*) Radical democracy: (i) emergence of a working-class movement; (ii) Fabian socialism.
    (*g*) The idea of empire.
8. Man's relation to woman:
    (*a*) The Victorian family.
    (*b*) The emancipation of women: its motives and achievements.

## Projects

*Individual work:*

1. Comprehensive essay on any topic, suitably illustrated, e.g. nineteenth-century dress, poet, artist, engineer, scientist.
2. Using the County Record Office for source-material for a study of e.g. education (school log books), a local industry, roads, Poor Law, Quarter Sessions, etc.
3. An anthology of ballads, folk songs – with notes on composers, etc.
4. Imaginary conversations, e.g. Ruskin and a modern art critic; Sidney Webb and Harold Wilson; T. H. Huxley and Ritchie Calder; Tennyson and John Betjeman.

*Suggested literary themes:*

| | |
|---|---|
| (*a*) *Drama:* | Landmarks in nineteenth-century drama. |
| | Changes in popular taste. |
| | Dramatic critics and criticism. |
| | Status of the actor. |
| | Costume, scenery, and changes in theatre interiors. |

(*b*) *Poetry:*  Landmarks in nineteenth-century poetry.
Tennyson and the Victorian mind.
Nature in poetry.

(*c*) *Novel:*  Social changes and the novel.
Landmarks in nineteenth-century fiction.
The political novel.

(*d*) *Miscellaneous:*  Newspapers and presentation. Essays.
Nineteenth-century oratory.
Changes in speech, vocabulary, spelling and hand-writing.

*Group projects:*

(*a*) A musical At Home.
(*b*) Performance of a Victorian melodrama.
(*c*) Programme of recorded music.
(*d*) Nineteenth-century news-sheet.
(*e*) Study of an election.
(*f*) Notes on interviews with people born in the reign of Queen Victoria.
(*g*) Models – buildings, furniture, engineering works, etc.

## B.  THE U.S.A. – YESTERDAY AND TODAY

1.   A syllabus covering three terms (of two lessons a week) is given below.
2.   This will be covered by lectures in which generous use will be made of film strips, slides, gramophone records, films, etc.
3.   As many outside lecturers as possible will be used (all of whom are experts in their own subjects), supplemented by various members of the school staff.
4.   It is hoped to follow this up with similar studies in the future of such important countries as the U.S.S.R. and China.

*Autumn term*

1.   The Land – the geographical setting.
2.   The people.
3.   The making of the country; (*a*) the colonial period; (*b*) the winning of independence.
4.   The American system of government.
5.   The American politicians.
6.   Westward expansion – the frontier tradition.
7.   The uprooted – the immigrant.
8.   The sectional conflict – the brothers' war.
9.   The American dilemma – the Negro problem.
10. I heard America sing! – folk music.

*Spring term*

11. The era of expansion and reform.
12. Workers: (*a*) in field; (*b*) in factory.
13. The business man and government.
14. American youth at school.
15. American technological triumph.
16. The American poet.
17. The American looks at the world.
18. American art and architecture.

19. The journalist and public opinion.
20. Some American composers – the music of Barber and Copland.
21. The American cinema.

*Summer term*

22. A great American president: F. D. Roosevelt.
23. The North American novelist: Mark Twain, Willa Cather, Hemingway, Faulkner.
24. The Anglo-American connection: (*a*) yesterday; (*b*) today.
25. The American trade unions.
26. The American 'musical': music of Gershwin, Rodgers and Hammerstein, Bernstein.

# Appendix 4: Local history
# Six examples of work that has been done

## 1.  THE SAXONS

The pupil is given a simplified 1 in. geological map of the local area. The aim is to plot local sites of ancient settlement, and the evidence for such where the precise site is unknown.

*Procedure*

1.  Colour the gravel area of the map yellow.
2.  Design a key to show settlements according to age – Neolithic, Iron Age, Roman or Saxon.
3.  Using the key plot the following evidence onto the map
    171605 – Roman burial ground
    165595 – Saxon huts
    184598 – Iron Age settlement
    186602 – Roman fortifications
    186602 – Saxon fortifications
    186601 – Roman pottery
    193595 – Roman practice fort
    183628 – Neolithic hut
    173613 – Iron Age hut
    19 63  – full of Neolithic and Saxon remains.
    179582 – Saxon houses
     179591 and 179595 – villas and pottery
     13 63  – 5 villas
    234714 – Roman villa and Saxon houses
4.  Transfer information from the map onto a table which plots period against the geology of the site.
5.  Work; to draw out the conclusions that the pre-Roman sites are on the gravels. The Roman sites occupy clay as well as gravel sites.
6.  What are the reasons for this distribution of evidence?

## 2.  SAXON SETTLEMENT

Below is a map of part of East Anglia as the Saxons might have found it. It contained marshland, woodland and some dry areas covered in scrub. The aim of the exercise is to settle the area with villages. Each tribe rows up the river looking for suitable land, and settles as soon as it can. To get enough food and water and building materials to survive they need to have several sorts of land, such as meadow or pasture for their animals and forest for timber. But first of all they must find land with light soil which is well drained so that they can cultivate it straight away. They will of course need a lot of land so that settlements will not be too close together. They will need to be about 1½ miles apart. The settlers enter from the east.

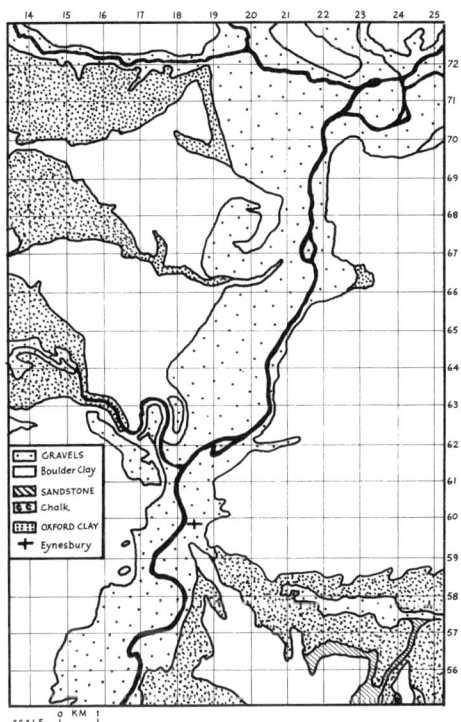

FIG. 30. *Simplified geological map of the Eynesbury/St Neots district.*

*Task*

1. Settle the first tribe to arrive and label their site A.
2. Settle later settlers labelling their sites B, C and so on.
3. Write down the six-figure reference of each village site.
4. In the case of one of the settlements write down in detail the advantages which the site offers.

## 3. THE SAXONS AT EYNESBURY AND ELTISLEY

Anglo-Saxon settlements were often built on a triangular pattern, a fence of wooden stakes and possibly a ditch enclosing the dwellings and grazing area. The enclosure would provide a refuge in time of danger, or at night. At other times cropping, grazing, etc., would be carried on outside the fenced area. The original form of the settlement is often reflected in the road and green shapes of today – both Eynesbury and Eltisley provide examples. Mapwork and deduction can be tested.

### Eltisley

1.    From the place name the pupils can deduce the race of the soldiers and the nature of the area in which they settled.

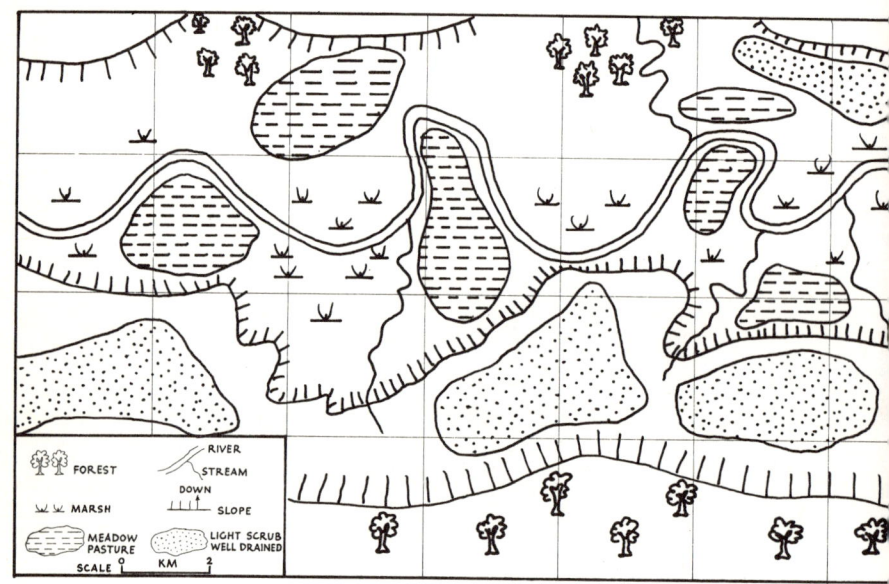

FIG. 31. *Saxon settlement plan*

2.    The line of the original fence can be guessed at by the pupils – essentially the buildings within the stockade would have faced inwards onto the green which came to be held in common and therefore preserved.
3.    Reasons for the roads entering at the points of the triangle can be suggested – probably the strongest points for defence. The continuity in road-building from trackway to tarmac can be mentioned.
4.    The buildings at 272597 are certainly an 'encroachment' onto the original green. Evidence on the ground points to the fact that the limits of the triangle were 269597, 272598, 273595.

### Eynesbury

An early site – Roman remains at 182596 indicative of this. Probably connected with crossing point for river – possibly at the end of Washbank road (182597).

Saxon settlement later occurred to the east – triangle of Luke Street, Berkley Street, Montague Street (184599, 184596, 188595).
Again (1) place name, (2) triangle, (3) almost total encroachment to be mentioned.

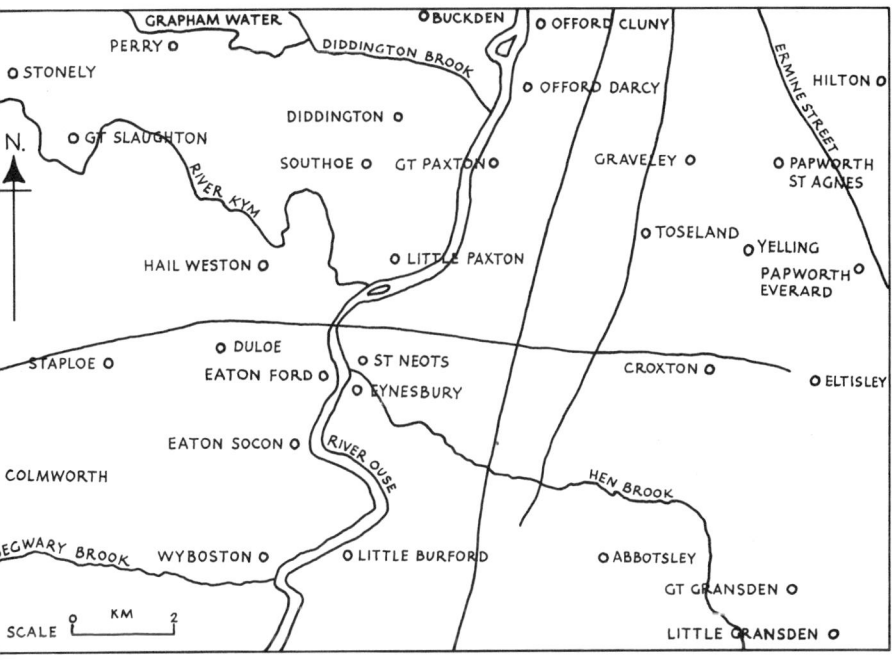

FIG. 32. *Map of settlement in the Eynesbury/St Neots district*

## 4. A SURVEY OF DATED BUILDINGS IN LEEK

It is possible to find out a great deal about the growth of a town, village or city by looking at the buildings and discovering when they were built. The dwellings with the earliest date on them in Leek are *almshouses at the corner of Compton and Broad Street.* Probably the next oldest are the cottages which belong to the Society of Friends on Overton Bank, and St Edward's Vicarage was built very shortly after these. *Haregate Hall* or *Greystones* in Stockwell Street were also built in the seventeenth century but there is no obvious date on them. Two other buildings which were built in the seventeenth century are *The Friends Meeting House,* Overton Bank, and the *Roebuck* in Derby Street. The only building which is older than these is the Church of St Edward the Confessor, and this church has been altered over the centuries.

These are just a few of the interesting buildings in Leek. You will be able to find many more as you go round the town. You will see that a good many buildings were put up in the nineteenth century (1800s) and you will find examples of building done in this century too. Buildings with dates will be recorded on a special sheet of paper. Try to be really accurate.

*The lamp post in the middle of Leek market place* was called the hub of Leek. Start looking for buildings with dates in this area; move on to Derby Street, Stockwell Street, Sheep Market, Stanley Street, St Edward Street, Overton Bank, Clerk Bank, Mill Street, West Street, Compton.

If you think that a building is of historical interest or of particular importance in the life of Leek, try to find out its date of building.

## 5.  WORK ON THE OLD MAPS OF LEEK

### 1.  Leek and district, 1747

   (a)  What is shown at Leek? What is the name of Leek's river?
   (b)  Are any other rivers shown?
   (c)  Where is the higher ground shown? How would this be shown on a map today?
   (d)  Is there any other abbey marked besides Dieula cres?
   (e)  What roads are shown into Leek? What villages do they pass through?
   (f)  Compare the map *Staffordshire Roads*, page 10. Are the roads the same? Is there any road missing that is marked on the road map?
   (g)  Where are the churches on this map?
   (h)  Is there anything missing from the map that you would find on a modern one?

### 2.  Leek in 1838

   (a)  What is the population of Leek at this time?
   (b)  When were fairs held in Leek?
   (c)  Look at streets and roads. Are any names different? Are there any toll-houses?
   (d)  Is there any kind of transport shown other than road transport?
   (e)  What industries and occupations are shown?
   (f)  Was there a bank? Where? What name?
   (g)  What churches were in Leek? Where?
   (h)  What chapels were there? Where?
   (i)  Was there a Post Office?
   (j)  What inns and hotels were there?

## 6.  A VISIT TO ST EDWARD'S PARISH CHURCH, LEEK

*Interior*

1.  Look at the monuments in the porch as you enter.
2.  Notice the shape of the church – can you recognise the *parlour, the nave, the chancel, the sanctuary and the transepts*?
3.  Did you know that *the altar is always at the east* end of the church, and *the font usually at the west end*?
4.  The chancel *was* divided from the nave by a carved screen, often surmounted by a *rood*, or cross. There may be a stairway in one of the side walls of the chancel by which the priest could climb to the top of the rood screen. (Screen removed by Puritans partly, perhaps.)
5.  Notice the *rounded Norman arch* on the inside of the west door in the Tower, and *the thickness of the parlour walls*.
6.  *Look for:* the *Rose Windows*; *a board* showing the names of Vicars of Leek since 1215 when the Abbey was founded, and Bishops of Lichfield from

664; *a grave slab* which might have marked the grave of a Sherwood Forester; and *the 'Now Thus' memorial.* (Do you know its story?) *A ducking stool* (for what was it used?); the font; *the Ashenhurst Monument* with the four wives and ten children.

7. *Look up at the ceiling.* Notice the beautiful Tudor roof over the nave. At a time when people cared little for the Church, the roof timbers were probably 'robbed' for building purposes.

The plain windows help to show up this beautiful roof. All stained glass would have made it very dark.

8. The galleries were introduced in the eighteenth century. The poor sat in the galleries generally, as the pews in the main body of the Church had to be rented.

9. Are there *any documents* on view? Or *any books* of special interest?

10. Notice the altar cloth and any other cloths with ecclesiastical embroidery. There was a quite well-known School of Embroidery in Leek. Further examples are in the Nicholson Institute.

11. There is a little window in the wall at the back of the gallery. There is a theory that this was the priest's look-out so that he could watch the Church and stop thieves from taking the treasures from the Church.

# Appendix 5: Local history worksheet: Eynesbury and St Neots

## THE SITE OF EYNESBURY

Try to imagine the land upon which Eynesbury and St Neots now stand without any buildings at all. Woodland stretches across the area and down to the banks of the River Ouse. We have returned in time to the days of the Ancient Britons.

Crossing the river is a problem to the few travellers that there are, as no bridges exist. To ford or cross the river, travellers choose the easiest and safest place – probably between Coneygeare and Eaton Socon. This now seems likely, for when the Romans settled in Britain they certainly built a camp at Coneygeare, probably to guard the trackway leading down to the river's edge which we know as Washbank Road.

When the Roman legions left Britain the crossing place was not forgotten. A village was soon to grow up on a site close to the old camp: a village laid out in a triangular shape fenced about with a palisade of wooden stakes for protection; the village we know as Eynesbury.

### Questions

1.  From what you know of how place names are formed, how do you think Eynesbury got its name?
2.  By examining the map below can you suggest where the original palisade of wooden stakes may have been?
3.  Draw a sketch map, based upon the map below [Fig. 33], of the site as it may have appeared in early Saxon times showing the river, the trackway to the ford, the remains of the Roman site and the stockaded village.

## THE GROWTH OF EYNESBURY

In Saxon times, Eynesbury must have grown into a large farming village, spreading outside the original palisade. Away across the fields and brook to the north of the village a priory was built in the tenth century, on the northern side of what is today St Neots Market Square. The land around the priory would have been open fields, however.

Following the Norman Conquest, the priory was refounded and rebuilt, but upon its old site. As time went by, some people built their homes close to the new priory. Many travellers must also have passed by, for in 1180 the monks built a wooden bridge (on the site of the present bridge) so that people travelling from Huntingdon, Kimbolton and Bedford in the west, and Godmanchester, Cambridge and Sandy in the east could cross the river easily.

Boats carrying corn must have passed along the river itself and the main road from London to York was not far away to the west.

**Question**

Make a sketch map to show the importance of the roads which converged on St Neots in Norman times. Locate on your map all the places mentioned in the last paragraph above.

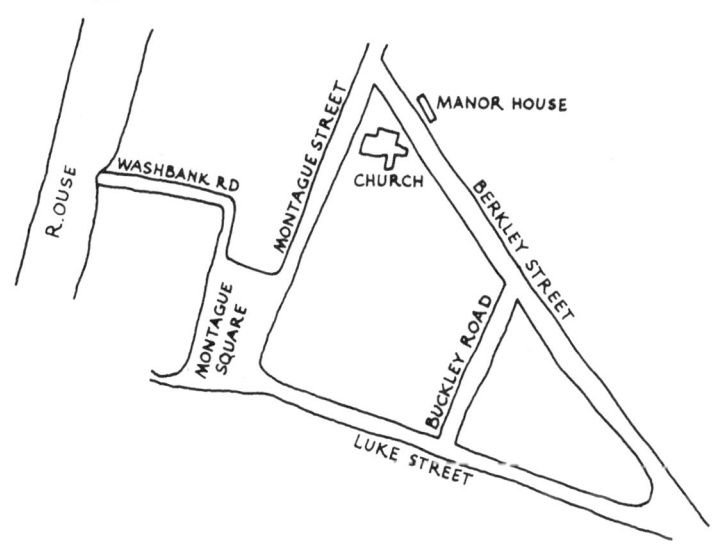

Fɪɢ. 33.

Probably many of the travellers stopped to rest at the priory, for churchmen were expected to entertain passers-by. Many of these travellers must have worshipped at the shrine in the priory where the sacred bones of St Neot were kept. Some pilgrims would have travelled especially to St Neot's priory to see these relics. King Henry III himself stopped there on a number of occasions.

## THE GROWTH OF ST NEOTS

The monks of the priory were fortunate in that King Henry I gave them the right to hold a market every Thursday and Henry II a fair lasting two days once every year. Naturally traders soon began to build their homes near the priory walls. In later years two further fairs were added. Indeed it did not take long for the area around the priory to become more important than the village of Eynesbury itself, and so during the reign of King Henry III (1216–72) the parishes were separated, and the town of St Neots officially came into existence. At this time St Neots was still really an agricultural village, however. Apart from a few goldsmiths who worked for the churchmen, all the village craftsmen made tools and implements for the local farmers. But the market was an important one and around it the town was to continue to grow.

**Question**

From the account above pick out the reasons why St Neots grew up where it did – there are several – and write a paragraph, in your own words, explaining the growth of the town.

While the market prospered, the days of the priory were numbered. Although important locally, the priory was far from being one of the great religious houses of England. At times the buildings were sadly in need of repair, and the commissioners' reports suggest that the behaviour of the monks was equally in need of reform. However, the priory lingered on until the reign of Henry VIII when it suffered a fate similar to most of its kind, being closed at the time of the King's quarrel with the Pope in Rome, and the buildings pulled down (1539). Little trace of the priory remained above ground. The old gateway on the west lingered longer than the main buildings, certain of the stones were used in constructing houses in the town (some have now found their way to the museum), but there seems to be no evidence for the theory that the stones were used in the building of the old town bridge. Indeed even the plan of the old buildings is difficult to discover as the area to the north of the market square has been built over. Archaeological excavation has revealed some of the plan, but doubt still remains as to the exact layout of the buildings. An approximate plan is given below.

**Question**

Make a copy of this plan [Fig. 34].

## ST NEOTS, THE MARKET AND TRADE

Although the priory had disappeared it left its mark upon the developing town of St Neots, as the map of the market square and priory site in 1757 shows.

**Questions**

Examine the 1757 map of the site and the table that accompanies it, carefully, and answer the following:

1.   Notice that the outline pattern of the roads is essentially the same as today. Make a list of these roads.
2.   Notice that the outlines of the tenements or buildings on the north side of the market square, south of the boundary line, are basically the same as the shop frontages of today. Who is shown to be the main owner of property in this area – the names are marked on the map?
3.   Are any of the old priory buildings shown on the map?

4. In the note on the bottom right hand corner of the map 'freeholders and copyholders' are referred to. Find out what these were.

5. Three inns are shown on the north side of the square. Make a note of these and say which remain. Can you suggest why three inns were needed? Remember the town was not as large as today.

6. The table relates to the map – there is a number key on the map to show which piece of property is which. The letters A.R.P. stand for measurements of size. Can you suggest what these measurements are? Having established what they are, can you work out the total size of the priory site?

7. We have seen that the priory site influenced the pattern of the market. Equally the fairs influenced the street pattern. Notice that High Street is wider than the adjoining roads for it was in this direction that the fairs would spill over from the market square.

I = Infirmary
D = Dormitory
R = Refectory
C = Cellarium
B = Buttery
K = Kitchen

FIG. 34.

It is easy to forget when thinking of the market today that markets such as St Neots depended principally upon trade in local agricultural produce, and that the land around the market towns was still farmed by many people.

**Questions**

Examine the map of the field divisions around St Neots. This map shows the strips of land owned by the Earl of Sandwich and the names of the people who farmed them. It is a compound map, in that several different areas of the locality are shown and no real effort has been made to draw the areas to scale.

Although some farmsteads obviously own their own land, this map of 1757 shows the patterns of the fields before their enclosure in 1771.

1. What do we mean when we speak of 'enclosure'? If you cannot remember, chapters 3 and 4 of *The Agrarian Revolution* will help you.
2. What do we mean when we speak of open field or strip farming, and what do the common baulks on our map look like and what were they for? (Chapter 2 of *The Agrarian Revolution*.)
3. Examine the St Neots map carefully. See if you can imagine where each set of strips shown was located in the local area. You can make a sketch map of the area to show their approximate location.
4. Make a list of the places shown on the map that bear the same names, or names that closely resemble them, today.

As you already know from your studies of local architecture, the buildings of the market square clearly show seventeenth-century styles. These were merchant houses and business premises, and reveal the prosperity of the town at this date. The waggon arches set into the buildings on the south side of the square tell of the business use of these premises, just as the arches leading into the inn yards show how the coaching trade made use of these hostelries.

An important factor making for added prosperity of the town at this time was the improvement of the River Ouse for navigation. In 1629 the river was made navigable from St Ives to within four miles of Bedford. The property on the south side of the market square became important for here were the wharves on Hen Brook giving a convenient access to the river trade.

To King's Lynn came the boats carrying Newcastle coal, Scandinavian wood, French, Spanish and Portuguese wines. To these goods that river barges would carry can be added the mainstays of internal trade: corn being taken to the flour mills, reeds for thatching and plastering being brought from the Fens, bricks, pipes and tiles from the claylands, lime for the fields.

Thus, from the seventeenth to the early twentieth century, the river became the main supply line for the town. The merchants of St Neots did not usually specialise in one commodity, but traded in bulk goods of many types as these nineteenth-century bill headings show:

1838               **J. B. SQUIRE & SON**

Opposite the Church
Corn, Seeds, Deals, Timber, Lath, Bricks, Tiles
Lime, Slates, Cement etc.

1856               **JAMES PAINE & SONS**

Corn, Coal, Deal, and Timber Merchants.
Ale and Porter Brewers.
Dealers in Malt, Hops, Flour, Meal, Pollard, Bran,
Bricks, Tiles, Lath, Lime, Poles, Staves, Tar,
Hair, Reed, Coke, Cement, Whiting, Salt, Grindstones,
Yorkshire stones, Firelumps, Tiles, Clay,
Clinkers, Pots, Linseed and Linseed Cake,
Grains, Rope, Dust etc., Stone Cills and
Sinks, Glass Tiles and Slates.

The importance of the river trade was only to give way after the First World War with the coming of motor transport.

**Questions**

1. From work you have already done this year, why do you think that river trade was so much more popular than trade by road?
2. Make a list of the types of goods being carried by the river barges.
3. Make a copy of the sketch map below that shows the relationship of the property on the south side of the market square to the wharves on Hen Brook and the industries connected with the river trade [Fig. 35].

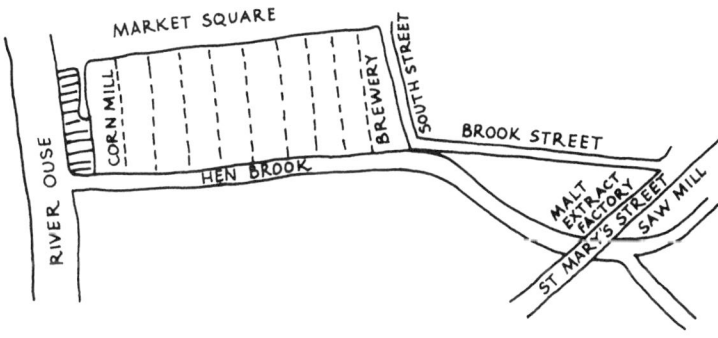

FIG. 35.

**Some additional tasks**

1. River navigation was not always a straightforward affair. Bitter arguments could arise about rights to use the river. Consult the report of an enquiry into the navigation of the River Ouse.
2. For an account of how one family's fortunes have been connected with the story of the river trade, see the pamphlet on the Diamond Jubilee of C. G. Tebbutt Ltd.
3. Examine the photocopy of the map of the area of St Neots which shows the number of public houses in St Neots in 1925. A key accompanies the numbers on the map. From your knowledge, how many of these public

houses exist today? Which have disappeared? Study one of the reports appealing for the closure of a public house and see what arguments were used to call for closure.

4.    Compose a list of industrial sites, past and present, that were probably related to the river trade.

5.    St Neots in 1893 – A Newspaper Study – consult the special worksheet.

6.    The Village Constables – consult the special worksheet.

# Appendix 6:  Local history worksheet

1. *The term local history.*  This should be interpreted as the study of one or several themes in the historical development of a limited geographical area. The following examples all fall within this definition: 'The School during the Civil War'; 'Regency Southampton'; 'St Mary's Church, Southampton during the sixteenth century'; 'Water supply in London in 1866'; 'The Pilgrim Fathers in Scrooby'.

2. *Choice of topic*  Students are advised to consider a subject with a limited time-span, such as a century or less. If the aspects of the subject are already wide, then the time-span should be severely limited. For example, 'Southampton during the eighteenth century' is too wide, but 'Southampton's water supply' in the same period might not be. Students are advised to narrow the topic as the work proceeds. The locality chosen need not be in Southampton or in Hampshire. There is, however, an advantage in choosing an area familiar to one student, within easy reach of home or school, or where a holiday is spent.

3. *Preliminary work*  Complete all reading and research before a word is written. Notes should be kept, either in loose-leaf files, or on index cards. Remember to note the source of the information at the time. Students should first consult secondary, i.e. printed published sources. Such works often contain a bibliography and primary sources. Students should also make themselves familiar with the national or wider history of the period. For example, Southampton newspapers in the 1820s contain evidence of several timber-merchants becoming bankrupt. Knowledge of the ending of timber import duties by the central government, and the consequent fall in timber prices, is essential for an interpretation of local economic conditions. There are valuable collections of books in the school, including the Select Library, and in the Reference Library at the Civic Centre.

4. *Visits to record offices and museums*  Students are advised to purchase *Handlist of Materials Available Locally for the Study of Local History* (published by the Historical Association, Southampton). The school history department has copies for sale. Archive material, such as maps, letters, documents, parish registers, wills, family papers, etc., are to be found in the Civic Centre, Southampton, and in the Record Office, Winchester. Other useful material can be studied in Southampton's four museums, or in Winchester, Salisbury, Christchurch, Portsmouth, or Buckler's Hard. Students who intend to search such material should write to the Archivist or Curator beforehand, suggesting a time and date of visit, and the area of study. Archivists and curators are always most helpful, but they should be asked specific questions and not worried with vague enquiries. As a principle, students should ask advice of the history teachers in school rather than 'outsiders'.

5. *Presentation of the entry*  The entry may be a series of maps, drawings, statistical material, essay or any form suitable to the topic. Whatever the

format, the entry should be in a file or enclosed in stiff covers. Where the entry is in essay form, the following should be observed:

(*a*) Title-page
(*b*) Table of contents, showing pages
(*c*) List of illustrations, maps, etc.
(*d*) Introduction, in about 200 words, stating the purpose, scope, means of investigation and conclusions (this should be written *last*)
(*e*) The main body of the work
(*f*) Appendices (if necessary)
(*g*) Glossary (if necessary)
(*h*) Bibliography. If this is large, it should be divided into primary, printed primary and secondary sources. Only books which have been of direct use should be cited, giving author (surname and initials, title of book with volume number (if any), edition, place and date of publication. For example:

> Walters, C., *History of Bishop's Waltham* (Winchester, 1844). 'F.T.S.', 'Whitsun Camp', in *Sotoniensis*, vol. LVII, no. 215 (Summer 1968), King Edward VI School, Southampton.

6. *Numbering the pages*  The first page of the main body of the work (5(*e*) above) should be page 1, and subsequent pages numbered consecutively in arabic numerals. (*a*) to (*d*) should be numbered in roman italics (e.g. i, iv).

7. *Handwriting or typing*  Write or type on one side of the paper only. Typing should be double-spaced, on quarto-sized paper.

8. *Length*  This must vary according to the subject, but students should avoid the common failing of prolixity. As a general rule, 10,000 words (40pp. as in 7 above) should be regarded as a maximum. But the piece of work should be original, and the findings might consist of only one or two pages. be indicated by a number in the text, or in a list at the end. Such sources should be shown thus:

1. R. Pococke, *Travels through England,* Vol. II, p. 114 (place and date of publication need not be shown if the work appears in the bibliography).

10. *Abbreviations*  If certain works or source references are cited frequently, it is permissible to use abbreviations, e.g. *V.C.H. for Victoria County History of Hampshire*, or C.R.O. for Southampton City Record Office. But a list of abbreviations should be shown after 5(*c*) above. The following abbreviations will be useful in footnote references:

ibid. (in the same place; when the source is the same as in the immediately preceding reference. But if a different page, add the page reference).
op. cit. or loc. cit. (in the work or place already cited). Example:
first time: Russell, *History of King Edward VI School, Southampton*, p. 115.
second time: Russell, op. cit., p. 245.
loc. cit. should be used for a collection of documents.
passim (references scattered through a book, and not on any particular page).
c. (chapter), cc. (chapters).
p. (page), pp. (pages).
sic (quoted correctly from the source, though it might appear to be wrong, e.g. 'acomodate (sic)').

seq. or f. (and the following page), seqq. or ff. (the following pages).
In most of the above, Latin abbreviations are used as they save time. Where
the English equivalent is as good, use the English, e.g.

'above' not '*supra*'
'below' not '*infra*'
'see' not '*vide*'.

# Select bibliography on the teaching of history

## 1. Bibliographies

Douch, R. *The Teaching of Geography, History and Related Local Studies* (University of Southampton, 2nd ed., 1957). A bibliography especially useful for works on special aspects of the subject, textbooks, bibliographies and lists, for articles in periodicals and for foreign works.

Fines, J. *The Teaching of History in the United Kingdom: A Select Bibliography* (Historical Association, 1969). An invaluable guide.

## 2. General works on the teaching of history

Happold, F. C. *The Approach to History* (Christophers, revised ed., 1950). Contains interesting examples of what can be achieved in individual imaginative work with junior and middle school pupils.

Education, Ministry of. *Teaching History* (H.M.S.O., 1952). A clear statement of the philosophy and ideals of history teaching, with some useful practical suggestions.

Hill, C. P. *Suggestions on the Teaching of History* (UNESCO, 1953). Summarises the views and suggestions of history teachers from thirty-two countries. A useful book dealing with general matters, syllabuses and method.

School Broadcasting Council for U.K. *History and School Broadcasting* (B.B.C., 1957). A valuable work, quite wide in its scope.

Dance, E. H. *History the Betrayer – A Study in Bias* (Hutchinson, 1960). A thought-provoking and lively if exaggerated attack on traditional attitudes.

Lyall, A., ed. *History Syllabuses and a World Perspective* (British Parliamentary Group for World Government, 1962, and Longmans, 2nd ed., 1967). A comparative survey of examination syllabuses in Britain and overseas.

Burston, W. H. *Principles of History Teaching* (Methuen, 1963). A study of the relationships between the practical problems of teaching history in school and theories about the nature of history as a subject.

Milliken, E. and E. K. *Handwork Method in the Teaching of History* (Wheaton, revised ed., 1963). A most valuable guide to model-making.

Carpenter, P. *History Teaching: the Era Approach* (Cambridge, 1964). A thorough examination of the 'patch' approach, with practical suggestions for syllabuses.

Lewis, E. M. *Teaching History in Secondary Schools* (Evans 1965). Especially useful for the principles of selection and the difficulties of an overcrowded syllabus. Contains book-lists and suggestions for their use with reference to particular topics.

Burston, W. H. and Thompson, D., eds. *Studies in the Nature and Teaching of History* (London, 1967). A stimulating series of articles in which the implications of research by philosophers, psychologists and sociologists for history teaching are discussed.

D.E.S. *Towards World History* (H.M.S.O., 1967). A general discussion with pertinent suggestions for syllabus construction.

Douch, R. *Local History and the Teacher* (Routledge and Kegan Paul, 1967). A useful introduction to local history.

Ferguson, S. *Projects in History* (Batsford, 1967). A most helpful and practical guide.

Krug, M. M. *History and the Social Sciences* (Ginn, 1967). A most readable analysis of theory and practice by an American educationalist.

Gosden, P. H. J. H. and Sylvester, D. W. *History for the Average Child* (Blackwell, 1968). Helpful advice on teaching pupils of average and below average ability.

D.E.S. *Archives and Education* (H.M.S.O., 1968). An informative survey.

Schools' Council. *The Certificate of Secondary Education: The Place of the Personal Topic – History* (H.M.S.O., 1968).

Booth, M. B. *History Betrayed?* (Longmans, 1969). A challenging study of various aspects of history teaching based on some interesting research techniques.

Fines, J., ed. *History* (Blond, 1969). An informative series of articles examining a variety of approaches and resources for particular periods of history.

Schools' Council *Humanities for the Young School Leaver: An Approach through History* (Evans/Methuen, 1969). A discussion of the contribution of history to the humanities with examples of schemes of work.

Elton, G. R. *The Practice of History* (Fontana, 1969). A provocative analysis of considerable interest to history teachers.

Brasher, N. H. *The Young Historian* (Oxford, 1970). A description of methods for improving the quality of written work of sixth form historians.

Ballard, M., ed. *New Movements in the Study and Teaching of History* (Temple Smith, 1970). A series of articles in which various recent developments are examined.

Corfe, T. *History in the Field* (Blond, 1970). A practical introduction to historical fieldwork.

Dance, E. H. *The Place of History in Secondary Teaching* (Harrap, 1970). A comparative study of history teaching in secondary schools in nineteen European countries.

Fairley, J. *Patch History and Creativity* (Longmans, 1970). A practical analysis of 'patch' history in the middle school.

D.E.S. *Museums in Education* (H.M.S.O., 1971). Practical guidance for the teacher.

Earle, A. and R. *How Shall I Teach History?* (Blackwell, 1971). An excitingly idiosyncratic look at history in the middle school.

Jamieson, A. *Practical History Teaching* (Evans, 1971). A useful guide for the development of practical approaches to history in the middle school.

Burston, W. H. and Green, C. W. *Handbook for History Teachers* (Methuen, 2nd ed., 1972). An invaluable reference work. There are articles on various aspects of history teaching and detailed lists of books and audio-visual aids.

Watts, D. G. *The Learning of History* (Routledge, 1972). A provocative study of thinking and learning in history, the nature of history as a discipline and its contribution to pupil development, together with suggestions for method.

Lamont, W., ed. *The Realities of Teaching History: Beginnings* (Chatto and Windus, 1972). Personal accounts of the experiences of young history teachers in the classroom.

## 3. Historical Association publications

*The Museum and the School.* Revised edition by M. E. Bryant (1961).

*Local History from Blue Books: Sessional Papers of the House of Commons,* by W. R. Powell (1962).

*The Teaching of History to Non-Specialists in Sixth Forms,* by C. P. Hill (1962).

*Notes on the Teaching of Far Eastern History,* by W. G. Beasley (1962).

*The Teaching of History in Secondary Schools,* by F. J. Dwyer (1964).

*Coins in the Classroom: An Introduction to Numismatics for Teachers,* by P. D. Whitting (1966).

*Russia – Notes on a Course for Secondary Schools.* Revised edition by P. D. Whitting (1966).

*Outline Course in Medieval Welsh History for the use of Teachers in Welsh Secondary Schools,* by A. J. Roderick (revised 1967).

*Teaching of Welsh History in Secondary Schools,* by A. H. Dodd (1967)

*An Introduction to Scottish History for Teachers,* by A. A. M. Duncan (1967).

*Notes on the Teaching of Empire and Commonwealth History,* by G. M. D. Howat (1967).

*Social Studies and the History Teacher,* by W. H. Burston (reprinted 1967).

*Sixth Form History Teaching,* by W. H. Burston (1967).

*The Use of Medieval Chronicles,* by John Taylor (1966).

*Archaeology for the Historian,* by D. P. Dymond (1967).

*County Records,* revised edition by F. G. Emmison and I. Gray (1967).

*A Junior History Booklist,* by M. Barton and K. Davies (1967).

*How to Read Local Archives 1550–1700,* by F. G. Emmison (1967).

*The USA – Notes on a Course for Secondary Schools,* revised edition by C. P. Hill and P. J. Harris (1967).

*The Teaching of African History,* by Z. Marsh and P. Collister (1968).

*Recent Historical Fiction for Secondary School Children (11–15 years),* by Kenneth Charlton (rewritten 1969).

*English Local History Handlist: A Short Bibliography and List of Sources,* 4th edition with place and subject indexes edited by F. G. Emmison (1969).

*Beginning Local History,* by L. W. Herne (revised 1970).

*The History Teacher and Other Disciplines,* by John Fines (1970).

*Historical Demography in Schools,* by Derek Turner (1970).

*Guide to Historical Periodicals in the English Language,* by J. L. Kirby (1970).

*The Historian's Contribution to Anglo-American Misunderstanding,* by R. A. Billington and others (1970).

*Medieval Local Records: A Reading Aid,* by K. C. Newton (1971).

*History After Four O'Clock,* by T. Hastie (1971).

*Studying Urban History in Schools,* by G. A. Chinnery (1971).

*The Development of Thinking and the Learning of History,* by Jeanette B. Coltham (1971).

*Educational Objectives for the Study of History,* by Jeanette B. Coltham and John Fines (1971).

*A Select List of Aids of Use in the Teaching of Recent History,* by G. R. Brooks (1971).

*History at the Universities,* by R. P. Blows (1971).

*Local Record Sources in Print and in Progress,* by J. Youngs (1972).

*The Use of Film in History Teaching*, by N. Pronay, B. R. Smith and T. Hastie (1972).

*Teaching History*, published by the Historical Association in May and November of each year, contains articles designed to give practical assistance to the class teacher, particularly of more junior forms.

# Index